Mel Tormé

MEL TORMÉ

A Chronicle of His Recordings, Books and Films

by
GEORGE HULME

McFarland & Company, Inc., Publishers
Jefferson, North Carolina, and London

> *The present work is a reprint of the library bound edition of*
> Mel Tormé: A Chronicle of His Recordings, Books and
> Films, *first published in 2000 by McFarland.*

LIBRARY OF CONGRESS CATALOGUING-IN-PUBLICATION DATA

Hulme, George, 1930–
Mel Tormé : a chronicle of his recordings, books and films / by
George Hulme.
p. cm.
Includes indexes.

ISBN 978-0-7864-3743-6
softcover : 50# alkaline paper ∞

1. Tormâ [sic], Mel, 1925–[1999]—Discography.   2. Tormâ [sic], Mel,
1925–[1999]—Film catalogs.   3. Tormâ [sic], Mel, 1925–[1999]—Chronology.
ML156.7.T65 H85   2008   016.78242164'092—dc21   00-37243

British Library cataloguing data are available

©2000 George Hulme. All rights reserved

*No part of this book may be reproduced or transmitted in any form
or by any means, electronic or mechanical, including photocopying
or recording, or by any information storage and retrieval system,
without permission in writing from the publisher.*

On the cover: Mel Tormé, 1940s (Photofest); background ©2008 Shutterstock

Manufactured in the United States of America

*McFarland & Company, Inc., Publishers
Box 611, Jefferson, North Carolina 28640
www.mcfarlandpub.com*

To Jean, my wife,
for her unfailing support and understanding

CONTENTS

Preface	1

PART 1: INTRODUCTION

Melvin Howard Tormé: The Man	3
An Appraisal	4
A Selective Chronology	6
Notes	11

PART 2: RECORDING SESSIONS

1942–1946 Jewel and Decca	13
1946–1947 Musicraft	15
1948–1952 Capitol	26
1953–1954 Coral	35
1955–1957 Bethlehem, Decca, Philips and Tops	37
1958–1961 Verve	44
1962–1967 Atlantic and Columbia	51
1968–1982 Liberty, Capitol, London, Atlantic, Century, Gryphon, Finesse and Flair	62
1982-1996 Concord Jazz and Telarc	66

PART 3: RECORD ISSUES

Singles 78 and 45 rpm	77
EPs and MPs	86
LPs (albums)	88

Tapes	121
CDs	124

PART 4: FILMS AND VIDEOS

Drama and Documentary	157
Musical Stage Performances	159
Television Shows	159
Songs in Films	159
The Judy Garland Show	160
The Mel-Tones Soundies	163

PART 5: BOOKS

Tormé as Author	165
Tormé as Contributor	165
Tormé as Subject	165

PART 6: MISCELLANY

The Hit Parade	167
Desert Island Discs	167
Nominations and Awards	168

Appendix 1: Alternative Takes	169
Appendix 2: A Discographical Problem	171
Indexes:	
Songs Recorded by Mel Tormé	173
Musicians	183

PREFACE

I know of only two published discographies of Mel Tormé: the one that I helped to compile for *Jazz Records 1942–62* (Jepsen) in the 1970s and the one published in 1990 by W. Bruyninckx in his *Vocalists Discography* Volume 4 (Si–Z). In addition, there is a very useful listing of records in Mel Tormé's autobiography, *It Wasn't All Velvet*. Further valuable sources of information are the volumes on *The Clef/Verve Labels*, *The Atlantic Label* and *The Decca Label* by Michel Ruppli. Where I show different data from any of these sources, I am of the belief that my information is more accurate.

Some of my information has come from record sleeves and some from published discographies of artists such as Artie Shaw and Peggy Lee. I also have noted information from all the usual discographical sources: reviews, articles, sales lists, advertisements etc. In all these cases, I have tried to verify the information.

A recent source of information that I used is the computer-based "Complete Catalog of 45's" compiled by Charlie Holz (USA). This proved valuable for discovering 45 rpm singles and verifying the existence of those that I already knew.

The Internet also provides an unending source of information but it is largely fragmentary, and one needs to conduct additional research to complete the details. The amount of information on Judy Garland, on whose 1963-64 television show Mel Tormé worked, is vast and very detailed.

I also acknowledge the help that I received from Derek Mahony (UK) of the Sinatra Music Society, who checked through an early draft version and made many useful additions and comments.

Tony Middleton (UK) has kindly checked my information against the Musicraft work sheets and the Decca and Capitol data that are in his possession. As a result he has provided missing dates and master numbers in several cases.

The article on Artie Shaw on Musicraft by Luiz Carlos do Nascimento Silva with a supplement by Art Zimmerman that appeared in the *Journal of the IAJRC*, Winter 1998 issue, has provided personnel and dates to confirm or supplement those I already had obtained.

Jack Mirtle (Canada) provided some Capitol session sheets and these were very useful. Michel Ruppli (France) checked the

Capitol and Musicraft material against his files and provided some missing dates and locations.

Finally I must thank Tony Cox (UK) for a lot of help and support, even to the extent of lending me some 78s that I had not been able to obtain otherwise.

Others who provided valuable information include:

> Gerry Atkinson (UK)
> Roy Belson (UK)
> Peter Burgis (Australia)
> Mark Cantor (USA)
> Derek Coller (UK)
> Bill Daniels (USA)
> Mike Ellis (UK)
> Fabian Grob (Germany)
> Dick March (UK)
> Dan Mather (USA)
> Ray Purslow (UK)
> Dieter Salemann (Germany)
> Kay Sealey (UK)
> Brian Thomas (UK)

If you have any kind of addition, no matter how small, or any corrections, no matter how minor, I shall be delighted to receive them courtesy of the publisher, but please tell me the source of your information. I shall incorporate corrections and additions and acknowledge them in any future versions of this discography.

PART 1

INTRODUCTION

Melvin Howard Tormé: The Man

Melvin Howard Torme was born in Chicago on September 13, 1925, and died in Los Angeles on June 5, 1999. His father was an immigrant from Russia with the family name Torma but on entry to the United States of America, the Immigration Authority wrote it as Torme. In Chicago, it was normally pronounced Torm-ee. Melvin adopted the name Mel Tormé for professional purposes.

MARRIAGES AND CHILDREN

From February 1949 to 1955 Mel Tormé was married to Candy Toxton. They had two children: Steven, 1953; and Melissa, 1955. Candy Toxton's real name was Florence Tockstein; she acted under the stage name of "Susan Perry." From October 1956 to 1966 Tormé was married to Arlene Miles. They had one child, Tracy, in 1959. Tormé was married to Janette Scott from May 1966 to 1977. Their children were Daisy Ann, 1969; and James, 1973. From October 1984 to his death, Tormé's spouse was Ali Severson. They had no children. Tormé and Severson lived together for some years before they married and this has given rise to the misapprehension that they were married at an earlier date, usually given as 1980. Severson had two children by a previous marriage, Carrie and Kurt, and these became step-children to Tormé when their mother married him.

LIFESTYLE AND INTERESTS

Mel Tormé was a non-smoker. He never drank hard liquor (spirits) and his consumption of wine was largely confined as an accompaniment to meals. He had a self-confessed addiction for chocolate and, according to Rich Little, was too fond of jelly doughnuts.

His passions were motion picture films, model trains and hand guns and the Old West. He was expert in these subjects. He also had a lasting interest in sports cars, notably the British MG and Jaguar models. His favorite composers outside the jazz field were Frederick Delius and Percy Grainger.

An Appraisal

For various reasons, I missed the Mel Tormé tour of Britain that resulted from the popularity of "Mountain Greenery" in 1956, and it was not until I obtained the Bethlehem recordings that I first heard him, even on record. By that time his recordings for Decca, Musicraft and Capitol were deleted from the catalogs and I only obtained them second-hand, later on. Despite this late start, I became a Mel Tormé enthusiast from that time. The years have done nothing to diminish my admiration and I believe that his voice improved as he aged. Certainly the voice was faultless on his final tours of Britain in the early 1990s, and the recorded evidence of his recordings in 1996 just before his stroke confirms this view.

Tormé is remarkable in that he was an accomplished vocalist, pianist, drummer and arranger in the musical field, but one can also add song writer and author (of two novels and several non-fiction books) to his credits. He is, in addition, an acknowledged and renowned expert on hand guns and motion pictures as well as the writer of scripts for television programs. There again, this omits his early careers as a child actor on radio and as a performer in movie films. His life, his work, his style and his opinions have been comprehensively covered in a variety of books and elsewhere but no one seems to have considered him as a person and a performer.

Although I did not have the opportunity to meet Mel Tormé myself, I am pleased to have been given permission to recount two stories originally told to me by Tony Cox, a friend and fellow Tormé enthusiast. Tony worked for the B.B.C. and was present when Tormé was a guest on the Cyril Stapleton *Show Band Show* on the B.B.C. in July 1956 during the "Mountain Greenery" visit to the UK. After the rehearsal, there was a period before the actual recording would begin. Mel Tormé was sitting at the piano talking to a couple of people and Tony went over and introduced himself as an admirer of Tormé's earlier work. Tormé's reaction was one of delight and he spent the next half an hour or so chatting to Tony about his early days, especially working with Artie Shaw, and illustrating points by playing excerpts from the songs on the piano. This went on until the performers were called for the recording session to begin. Tony remembers the episode with great pleasure as Mel was so approachable and so willing to discuss music in general. During the same tour, Tormé recorded five or six 15-minute programs for B.B.C. Radio with a small group of local musicians and Tony was again present. The programs were all recorded on the same day and Tony was impressed by the way that Tormé took the musicians through the tunes that were to be recorded and set the tempos, keys and arrangements just as one professional musician to another.

Gabrielle Clawson and Eileen Branch have also told me how easy it was to talk to Mel when they met him during one of his more recent visits to the UK. Eileen reports that "we met him after the concert and he was really nice to us. When we went to New York in 1984 for the Kool Jazz Festival Tribute to Basie we attended a concert at Carnegie Hall by Mel Tormé. We were backstage after the Concert when Mel Tormé came out of his dressing room. He suddenly spotted us and said 'What are you two girls doing in New York?' He actually remembered us and then asked us if we had come over specifically for the Tribute to Basie. He asked us to walk with him to his car at the stage door and even then he was in no rush to get away. What a nice man and how sad that we will never and see him 'live in concert' again."

I spoke to Henry Mackenzie of the Ted Heath Orchestra in September 1999 and he said that he well remembered the Ted Heath Decca session with Mel Tormé in September 1956 and recalled it as having been a very happy session.

Something that I have witnessed myself is Mel Tormé's approach to performing. I first saw him at the London Hippodrome during that venue's incarnation as a supper club in 1967. His spot was for one hour and I have never known 60 minutes to pass so quickly. We got the full works, with Mel singing, playing piano and performing on drums. We got an encore but I had the impression that, given the chance, he would have done several more. Some years later, I saw him at the Drury Lane Theatre with the Syd Lawrence Orchestra. The Orchestra played the first set and then accompanied Mel in the second half at the end of which there were a couple of encores. It was obvious that the audience wanted more and Mel apologized for the fact that they had not rehearsed any other songs. He said he would, if the audience wanted, be happy to sing another song accompanying himself on piano. Having got a roar of approval, he set off and members of the orchestra joined in on what became a 30-minute jam session. I think it only ended when the stage staff became restive.

These two experiences showed me that Tormé just loved to perform. Perhaps the greatest example came during the tour in 1991 that the B.B.C. arranged for Mel and George Shearing, supported by the B.B.C. Big Band. They visited half a dozen cities and the B.B.C. made recordings of the concerts for later broadcast. The concert at the Royal Festival Hall goes down in my memory as the finest concert that I have ever attended although I have seen dozens of shows by many of the mega-stars of popular music. The plan for the concert was that, after a warm-up period of about thirty minutes, there would be an hour that would be recorded and then would come an encore that was not to be used in the broadcast. What actually happened was that after the encore the audience did not want to leave. Tormé led Shearing back onto the stage and they gave the audience three quarters of an hour more of absolute magic. They both loved to perform and the audience loved them for doing it.

He rarely made a derogatory remark about other people except where he felt that they had acted unprofessionally or failed to live up to promises that they had made. For him, to honor one's word was of paramount importance.

His stroke in 1966 put an end to his career just when it seemed that his voice would last for ever. It seemed at first that he might recover from the stroke sufficiently to return to performing but a second stoke made that impossible. His passing in June 1999 leaves jazz and popular music sadly depleted but his legacy of recordings is something that we all can cherish.

An interesting aspect of the relatively inexpensive cost of producing CDs is that lately, we have seen many of Tormé's recordings become available once more. Half of the early Jewel coupling is in the Rhino set and a few of the American Decca sides have appeared on CDs. The Musicraft sessions both with Artie Shaw and with Tormé solo are available on Musicraft CDs issued by Discovery, while a selection of the Artie Shaw sides is available on President and several other labels. The Capitols are not available in any systematic form and *The California Suite* remains unissued on CD but most of the other recordings from this period are on a variety of CDs from Capitol and other EMI labels, and a complete CD was licensed to Disky of Holland. Coral has issued very little on CD in the USA and UK but the original albums have been issued on CD in Japan. The original Crescendo LP album was released on CD in the USA with the addition of most of the previously unissued tracks but, surprisingly, one of the original tracks was omitted. The Bethlehem recordings including the *Porgy and Bess* set have been available on Bethlehem CDs but now seem to have been deleted although a further series of reissues has begun to appear recently through Rhino under the Avenue Jazz banner. While the British Decca sides have been released on a CD coupled with some tracks by Matt Monro, the recording for Philips is not yet on CD. A period suffering from serious neglect is Mel's time at Verve and Atlantic but even here, some infilling is taking place. Verve has released straight reissues of a few of the original LP albums, often with a couple of extra tracks, but seems to prefer concocting compilations either of Tormé alone or with other artists. You have to go to Japan for the Atlantic material except for a compilation on Atlantic/Curb, now deleted, and the *Songs of New York* album which has been issued in the USA, as has a recent compilation on Rhino while the two "live" Atlantic albums have been given a lease of life by Collectors' Choice Music. Columbia has issued everything that Tormé had recorded for them as two CDs that include several previously unissued sides.

The 1969-70 albums for Capitol and Liberty have not been transferred to CD in the USA but odd tracks have turned up in compilations. The one-album recordings for Tops, Flair and Finesse are available on CD and the albums originally made for Gryphon have turned up on various labels. The Concord and Telarc recordings have remained in print, while many of the sessions that were either of broadcast or of transcription origin have appeared on a variety of labels including Audiophile, Hindsight, Mr. Music and Stash.

If you want a representative selection of Tormé's work then the Rhino 4-CD box set is the best one to get as it covers his whole career except for the Concord period and it has a fine booklet with discographical information and lots of photographs. The Readers' Digest set is markedly inferior. If you want a wider selection of Tormé's work it is easy enough to assemble a collection of CDs that will do the job moderately well but a systematic coverage is not yet possible. However, new CDs are appearing constantly and the number of compilation issues with just an odd Tormé track or two defies belief. Never a week goes by without one appearing somewhere.

A Selective Chronology

There is little need to provide a full biography of Mel Tormé in this publication because his autobiography, *It Wasn't All Velvet* (Viking/Penguin, 1988), tells his story better than anyone else could do, and his subsequent book *My Singing Teachers* (Oxford University Press, 1994) tells of the singers whom he admires and were an influence on his style. If you want a description and analysis of his style then you can do no better than to read Will Friedwald's book *Jazz Singing* (Collier/Macmillan, 1992). A more biographical approach is adopted by Bruce Crowther and Mike Pinfold in their book with the confusingly similar title *Singing Jazz* (Blandford/Cassell, 1997). This latter book also quotes extensively from a few of the interviews that Tormé has given over the years. Finally, *American Singers — Twenty Seven Portraits in Song* by Whitney Balliett (University Press, 1988) has an essay that is a preview of his autobiography but with some perceptive additions by Balliett. In lieu of a full biography, here are some of the highlights of the career of Mel Tormé:

1929: Coon-Sanders Orchestra at the Blackhawk in Chicago. Mel sang "You're Driving Me Crazy" with the band and then performed regularly on Monday nights for $15 per night for almost six months. This was followed by engagements at the Oriental Gardens with Louis Panico and at the College Inn of the Hotel Sherman with Frankie Masters and with the orchestra of Buddy Rogers.

1932/33: Performed with children's companies around Chicago including one with band leader Paul Ash. Appeared in a film with Ash singing "Whose Sweet Patootie Are You?"

1934/39: Won a singing contest at the Chicago World's Fair. Joined the cast of the radio series "Song of the City" playing the part of Jimmy the Newsboy. This was followed by work on many other radio programs in Chicago, including "The Romance of Helen Trent," "Mary Marlin," "Mary Noble, Backstage Wife," "Jack Armstrong, the All-American Boy," "Little Orphan Annie," "It Can Be Done" (with Edgar A. Guest) and "Lights Out" (with Arch Oboler). He obtained a scholarship to "The Jack and Jill Players" Drama School.

1939: His voice "broke" and work became scarce.

1940: In October he auditioned on drums for Harry James. He played "Lament to Love," his own composition. He was offered a job as "specialty" drummer and vocalist.

1941: In April, the offer from Harry James was withdrawn as Tormé had not finished school and would have needed a full-time tutor while on the road. In June, the Harry James recording of "Lament to Love" was released and became a hit. It was also recorded by Sonny Dunham, Lanny Ross and Les Brown and was broadcast by Gene Krupa and many other bands.

1942: August, joined the Chico Marx Orchestra in Los Angeles as vocalist and specialty drummer. He wrote "Stranger in Town." Took over from George Wettling on drums when Wettling was drafted.

1943: The Chico Marx band folded in July. Made "Higher and Higher" with Frank Sinatra at R.K.O. Studios. Went on to make "Pardon My Rhythm." Was introduced to a young vocal group called "The School Kids" with whom he sang and for whom he began to write arrangements. Les Baxter replaced Shelley "Diz" Disruhd in "The School Kids." Tormé made "Let's Go Steady." The School Kids changed their name to The Mel-Tones and, with Tormé, began to work regularly on AFRS radio programs. Tormé was offered the drum chair in the orchestras of Gene Krupa and Stan Kenton.

1944: Spring, drafted into the U.S. Army. Discharged after two months by reason of his flat feet. Continued to work with the Mel-Tones at military camps and on radio. Signed by Warner Bros. Studios and appeared in *Night and Day*.

1945: Worked on the Hires Root Beer Show on radio. Met Bob Wells. Obtained a contract with Decca Records and recorded with the Mel-Tones on a Bing Crosby recording. Bob Wells and Tormé signed a contract with the Burke and Van Heusen Song Company as song writers. They wrote the title songs for "Abie's Irish Rose" and "Magic Town" as well as writing "County Fair" for the film *So Dear to My Heart*. They also wrote "The Christmas Song" which became a hit recording for Nat King Cole.

1946: Worked on the Fitch Bandwagon radio program. Mel Tormé and The Mel-Tones signed a recording contract with the Musicraft label. Tormé offered a job as drummer with the Tommy Dorsey Orchestra. Made recordings with Artie Shaw. The Mel-Tones completed their last engagement with Tormé in November. Tormé began a solo career. Fred Robbins, the New York disc-jockey, named him "The Velvet Fog."

1947: Wrote, with Bob Wells, for the musical *Break It Up*. Signed to appear in *Good News* with June Allyson and Peter Lawford. May, missed the finale, "Varsity Drag" sequence, because he was opening at the "Copa" in New York City. His three-week engagement was extended to nine weeks. In August he performed on the Toni Home Permanent radio program with the Walter Gross group including Tony Mattola on guitar.

1948: MGM took up an option for two motion pictures a year. Mid-year, worked on *Words and Music*. Joined Capitol Records. Worked on *The Mel Tormé Show* on radio during the summer. The Mel-Tones also took part in the program.

1949: February, married Candy Toxton. Worked at the Paramount Theatre in NYC with Buddy Rich. Later in the year worked on *The Duchess of Idaho*. Worked on *The Mel Tormé Show* on NBC sponsored by Philip Morris Company. Wrote *The California Suite* which was recorded by Capitol and issued as their first 12-inch popular music LP album.

1950: Al Pellegrini joined Tormé as accompanist on piano and clarinet.

1951: Appeared at the Paramount Theatre in NYC with Ella Fitzgerald and the Sam Donahue band. Began writing articles for *Speed Age*, *Car Life*, *Guns*, *Metronome*, and *Down Beat* magazines. March, appeared on *Spotlight Bands* (Kriesler Bandstand) with Benny Goodman and Teddy Wilson. Appeared on the summer replacement show *TV's Top Tunes* with Peggy Lee. In September, started a CBS in-house pilot afternoon chat show to evaluate color transmission systems. This led to *The Mel Tormé Show* on CBS black & white TV. This ran until the spring of 1953 and featured Peggy King, Kaye Ballard and The Mellowlarks.

1953: Appeared with Teresa Brewer on *Summertime U.S.A.*, a summer replacement for the Jane Froman TV show and this lasted until September. Joined Coral Records. Made albums and singles.

1954: Highly successful album recorded in a live performance at the Crescendo Club.

1955: A novel, *Dollarhide*, published under the pen-name Wesley Butler Whyatt. Obtained release from Coral to join Bethlehem Records. First visit to Australia in September with broadcasts on ABC. Al Pellegrini left on the return to the USA.

1956: First album with Marty Paich for Bethlehem in January. Alan Dell played "Mountain Greenery" from the Coral Crescendo album on BBC and it became a hit in the UK. Tormé visited the UK for the first time and made appearances in variety theaters throughout the

UK. During the visit he made several broadcasts for the BBC and made records in London for British Decca. Married Arlene Miles.

1957: Appeared in "The Comedian," a *Playhouse 90* production on CBS TV and was nominated for best supporting actor but the category was canceled. It did however result in an appearance in *The Fearmakers* for Goldwyn Studios with Dana Andrews. Made the *Porgy and Bess* album for Bethlehem. Made a second UK tour in the summer and recorded an album for Philips.

1958: Appeared in a number of films including *The Big Operator* (MGM, with Mickey Rooney), *Girls Town* (MGM, with Paul Anka) and *The Private Lives of Adam and Eve* (MGM, with Mickey Rooney and Mamie Van Doren). Return visit to Australia with Ella Fitzgerald. Bethlehem ceased operation and Tormé joined Verve Records.

1960: Appeared in the film *Walk Like a Dragon* (Paramount, with Jack Lord).

1961: Another tour in Europe and the final album for Verve was recorded in London with British arrangers and musicians.

1962: Joined Atlantic Records. "Comin' Home Baby" was a hit, reaching No. 19 in the charts.

1963-64: Worked on the Judy Garland TV series. Learned to fly light aircraft.

1964: A further tour of Europe.

1965: December, appeared at Basin Street East in NYC opposite Duke Ellington; this gave rise to the great Tormé-Ellington billing dispute.

1965-66: Wrote articles for the Arts and Leisure section of the *New York Times*.

1966: May, married Janette Scott.

1967: June, appeared at *The Talk of the Town* in London. Wrote an episode called "The Frozen Image" for the *Run for Your Life* TV series. Conceived *The Singers* TV series for which he wrote the musical material. Wrote another article for *Guns* magazine.

1969: Wrote "The Handy Man" episode for *The Virginian* TV series (Universal). It was filmed in December.

1970: Dale Sheets became his manager. *The Other Side of the Rainbow* published. Hosted a TV jazz special, *One Night Stand*, with Gene Krupa, Buddy Rich, Gerry Mulligan and Lionel Hampton.

1971: Host and "line producer" for the TV series *It Was a Very Good Year*. This was a year by year review that ran for 17 episodes.

1973: Took the lead in a TV movie, *The Snowman*, which was filmed in Utah. Appeared on the Monsanto TV program with Benny Goodman.

1974: May, on holiday in England. Appeared for the second time on the "Muscular Dystrophy Telethon" with Jerry Lewis.

1975: Performed at "Buddy's Place" in NYC with Buddy Rich. Started writing a novel eventually published in 1978 as *Wynner*.

1976: January, gained the Edison Award in Holland as the best male vocalist. February, appeared at the Grammy Awards with Ella Fitzgerald and was nominated for a Grammy as best arranger for the Gershwin Medley on the *Mel Tormé: Live at the Maisonette* album. Signed with Gryphon Records. May, appeared with Buddy Rich at the Waldolf Astoria hotel in NYC. June, made a return engagement at "The Talk of the Town," London. Was a guest on the BBC "Desert Island Discs" radio program. July, sang in Philadelphia as part of the American Bicentennial celebrations. August, separation from Janette Scott. September, appeared at the Concord Jazz Festival. October, met Ali Severson.

1977: Won second Edison Award as best male vocalist. June, to London and recorded at Olympic Studios with Chris Gunning. Concert at Carnegie Hall, NYC, for George Wein; performed with George Shearing and Gerry Mulligan. First appearance at Marty's, NYC.

1980: March, three concerts at Carnegie Hall, NYC, as "Mel Tormé and Friends."

1982: 15th April, concert with George Shearing issued on Concord as *An Evening with Mel Tormé and George Shearing*. The album was nominated and won Tormé the Grammy for best male vocalist.

1983: The segment with Mel Tormé on the *20/20* TV program won the Emmy for best documentary profile. March, concert with Shearing issued as "Top Drawer" on Concord, gained Tormé his 13th nomination as best jazz vocalist. He won the award.

1984: October, married Ali Severson. Seven appearances on the *Night Court* TV series.

1985: Nominated as the best jazz vocalist for the album with George Shearing, *An Evening at Charlie's*, but lost the award to Joe Williams.

1986: The first album with Rob McConnell made the album chart.

1988: Autobiography *It Wasn't All Velvet* published.

1990: August, was a guest on the *John Dunn Show* on BBC radio. September, made broadcasts on the BBC radio program *Record Choice*. Appeared in an episode of the *Seinfeld* TV series.

1995: Recorded the title song for the TV series *Joe's Apartment* (with Don Ho). Appeared in an episode of *Sliders* TV show (screened 31 May 1996)

1996: June, asked by the group the Presidents of the United States of America to record a track for the group's new album. Appeared with the Honolulu Symphony in Hawaii. August 8th, Tormé had a stroke. Left hospital in November but returned in December with pneumonia. He was discharged again in 1997.

1999: Lifetime Achievement Award from the National Academy of Recording Arts and Sciences. His funeral service was held at the Westwood Village Memorial Park and was attended by his family, his show business friends and his fans.

Notes

GENERAL NOTES

For convenience, I have divided the listing into parts. Each part is self-contained but complements the others.

In listing the recordings, my intention has been to show only American and British issues unless there is a particular reason to include others. For example, where a Japanese issue was the only LP or CD issue then it would be included. This was easy enough when I started on the discography, but it is now increasingly difficult. Towards the end of the life of LPs and, more especially, since the era of the CD, the major producers have tended to make records in one location for distribution throughout a much wider area. For example, EMI and Polygram tend to make records in one country for distribution throughout Europe. Records made available in Europe can also turn out to be either direct imports from the USA or locally made or even a mixture of the two. Every attempt has been made to be consistent in the listings.

NOTES ON RECORD ISSUES

Where singles have been issued on both 78 and 45 rpm with the same catalog number but with different prefixes, these are shown, for example, as 78-/ 45-1234. In many cases, the 78 rpm version has no prefix and so the numbers are shown as 9-/ 1234, meaning 1234 for 78 rpm and 9-1234 for 45 rpm. Similarly, where mono and stereo records have been issued with the same catalog number but with different prefixes, this is shown, for example, as ABM-/ ABS-12345, meaning two records with numbers ABM-12345 and ABS-12345. This method is never used for equivalent issues on LP and cassette or CD and cassette; the catalog numbers are always shown in full.

There is a good deal of confusion over the numerical prefixes of the Capitol singles (78 and 45 rpm) series. I am listing what I have seen myself or had reported reliably to me. Most singles in the 1948–1952 period were issued both on 78 rpm and 45 rpm. The 57- series which is used for the 78 rpm releases may have a prefix of 54- for the 45 rpm issues. Once the 57- prefix was dropped, the 45 rpm issue has the same number as the 78 rpm issue but with an F- prefix. Only 57-591 does not seem to have been issued on 45 rpm but the same two titles are on 54-583. Some issues (particularly those in the 1700 and 1800 series) are listed in the Capitol logs as having a 5- prefix but the discs themselves do not show this prefix. The significance of the prefix is not known but has been suggested as a book keeping indicator by Capitol that the record was issued on 78 and 45 rpm. This 5- prefix has shown up in other discographies presumably because the information was taken from the Capitol log rather than from the discs themselves. The only record labels that are not listed in full are

Great Voices of the Century which is abbreviated to **GVOC**
His Master's Voice which is abbreviated to **HMV**
Music for Pleasure which is abbreviated to **MFP**
Reader's Digest Music which is abbreviated to **Read**
Vogue Coral which is abbreviated to **VgCrl.**

RECORDING LOCATIONS AND DATES

Recording locations are generally well known but Columbia Records, in particular, has been including contradictory information in the notes to some of its recent CD issues. I have assumed that Tormé did not fly back and forth across America between takes at the sessions, but it is always possible that he did!

Some recording dates are known accurately from previously published information in books, on record sleeves and on CD inserts. Some sessions present more of a problem. The recording dates for the Artie Shaw Musicraft records, in particular, have been the subject of a great deal of confusion. I have taken the accurate dates provided by Discovery Records when they reissued the material on the Musicraft LPs and CDs although these are far from complete. The Musicraft work sheets owned by Tony Middleton also provided dates for many of the sessions. The information published by Luiz Carlos do Nascimento Silva and Art Zimmerman in the *Journal of the IAJRC* provided accurate dates for the sides issued on the Musicraft 78s but several alternate takes have been reported on subsequent microgroove issues and the dates for these are not certain. I have only concerned myself with the dates and takes of the Shaw recordings where Tormé is present. The rest of the dates throughout the discography remain my best estimates based on the information that I have been able to obtain.

MASTER NUMBERS AND TAKES

Wherever possible the master numbers and takes are taken from the actual records. The take number on Musicraft, where it is found on the record, does correspond with the take on the work sheet that is marked as "Okay" for release. Similarly on Capitol, at least until mid 1950, the takes agree with the Capitol ledgers. On Columbia, the 45 rpm singles have stamper numbers rather than the master numbers, and so the information I have listed has come from the information that Columbia has published.

COVERAGE OF THE PARTS

Part 2: Recording Sessions. This part lists sessions producing two kinds of recordings. Firstly, commercial recordings including those of live performances that were recorded with the intent to issue them. Secondly, motion pictures and broadcasts on radio or television including transcriptions for use on these media. These are only listed where they have been issued on commercial records even where these issues are illegal.

In Part 2, a session reference number has been allocated to each session. These reference numbers are used in the indexes for location purposes.

Part 3: The Record Issues. This part is a listing of the issued records (78, 45 and 33 rpm), cassette and other audio tapes and compact discs. The listing includes track listings of multi-track records.

Part 4: Films and Videos. These are the films made for distribution to cinemas (movie theaters) or for broadcast on television. Also included are television shows, but only those of which a video has been made commercially available.

Part 5: Books. These are the books of which Mel Tormé is the author or to which he has contributed.

Part 6: Miscellany. This part contains some miscellaneous information such as the "hits" made by Mel Tormé and the awards that he won or for which he was nominated.

Appendix 1 discusses alternative takes that have been issued for two Artie Shaw recordings in which Mel Tormé was involved. Appendix 2 presents a curious discographical problem involving Johnny Blowers and Mel Tormé.

Following the two appendices are two indexes. The Song Title Index is an alphabetical listing of all the songs in Part 2, and the Musicians Index is an alphabetical listing of all the artists who participated in the recording sessions in Part 2. Numbers refer to the relevant sessions.

PART 2

RECORDING SESSIONS

1942–1946 Jewel and Decca

SESSION 421220 (Broadcast, Blackhawk restaurant, Chicago, 20th December 1942) CHICO MARX ORCHESTRA. Personnel (*Note 1*) Chico Marx, leader & occasional piano; Marty Marsala, Irving Goodman, trumpets; Chuck Maxon, Elmer Schneider, trombones; Gabe Galinas, Vernon Yokum, alto-saxes; Howard Dietterman, Emmett Carls, tenor-saxes; Harry Sopp, baritone-sax; Marty Napoleon, piano; Johnny Frigo, bass; George Wettling, drums; Mel Tormé, vocal; Skip Nelson, vocal; Kim Kimberly, vocal; and probably, Bobby Clark, trumpet; Barney Kessel, guitar.

Abraham (vcl MT) (*Note 2*) LaserLight 15 767; Murray Hill 931680
Velvet Moon (vcl SN) (*) LaserLight 15 767
Pagliacci (Vesti la Giubba) (*Note 3*) LaserLight 15 767; Murray Hill 931680
Swing Stuff (*) LaserLight 15 767
Beer Barrel Polka (Marx, piano) (*) LaserLight 15 767
Mr. Five by Five (vcl KK) (*) LaserLight 15 767; Murray Hill 931680
Chicago Strut (*) LaserLight 15 767.
This broadcast was on transcription AFRS Bandwagon No. 8.

Note 1: This personnel is from a review in Down Beat (issue of 15th November 1942) plus Clark and Kessel who are mentioned by Mel Tormé in various publications.
Note 2: Abraham was arranged by Fred Norman.
Note 3: Tormé plays the drum solo on this tune.
(*) Tormé is not present on these items from this broadcast.

SESSION 430001 (Hollywood, August/October 1943) HIGHER AND HIGHER (film sound track). Musical director: Constantin Bakaleinikoff. Music played by The RKO Radio Pictures Studio Orchestra conducted by Constantin Bakaleinikoff. Music arranged and orchestrated by Gene Rose. The other members of the cast who sing on the soundtrack include Marcy Maguire, Grace Hartman, Mary Wickes, Leon Errol and Dooley Wilson. Mel Tormé is present as a member of the

cast and performs, vocally, on these musical items.
It's a Most Important Affair (*Note 1*) Hollywood Soundstage HS411
I'm a Debutante Hollywood Soundstage HS411
Disgustingly Rich (*Note 1*) Hollywood Soundstage HS411
You're on Your Own (*Note 1*) Hollywood Soundstage HS411
Minuet in Boogie (*Notes 1 & 2*) Hollywood Soundstage HS411; Rhino R2 75481
Mrs. Whiffen (*Notes 1 & 3*) Rhino R2 75481.

Note 1: Tormé is audible individually on these items.
Note 2: Tormé also plays piano on this tune.
Note 3: This is an outtake, not used in the final release of the film.
Note 4: The items on Hollywood Soundstage HS411 except "Disgustingly Rich" also on Great Movie Themes CD 60004.

SESSION 440001 (Hollywood, 1944 [*Note 2*]) THE MEL-TONES with Orchestra. The Mel-Tones are: Bernie Parke, Les Baxter, Betty Beveridge and Ginny O'Connor with unknown accompaniment (*Note 1*).
White Christmas Jewel GS-4000
Where or When Jewel GS-4000, Rhino R2 71589.

Note 1: The accompaniment on "Where or When" is a small string section, a flute and a rhythm section including piano/celeste and string bass. Tormé is not individually audible on this side.
Note 2: The date of this session has been given as being as early as 1942, presumably because "White Christmas" dates from that year, but Mel Tormé did not join the "School Kids" until the end of 1943 and they did not adopt the name 'Mel Tormé and the Mel-Tones' until 1944.

SESSION 440002 (Unknown location and date [?Los Angeles 1944?]) LEON EDGAR and the Mel-Tones (probably the same personnel as 440001).
Who'll Be the Fool Jewel GS-3001
unknown title Jewel GS-3001.

Note 1: this issue appears in an undated check list (but probably ca 1964/65) of "Mel Torme on American Releases" complied by Jim Hayes and John C. Irwin. I have seen this record listed nowhere else and thus have not been able to confirm its existence.

SESSION 440621A (Los Angeles, 21st June 1944) ELLA MAE MORSE. Ella Mae Morse, vocal; Paul Geil, Charles Griffard, Billy May and John Silva, trumpets; William Atkinson, Burton Johnson, Abe Lincoln, Dale Nicholls and James Skiles, trombones; Samuel Rice, tuba; Russell Cheever, clarinet; Clyde Hylton, Fred Stulce and Les Robinson, alto-saxes; King Guion and Karl Leaf, tenor-saxes; Clyde Rogers, baritone-sax; Ted Repay, piano; Barney Kessel, guitar; Stan Fletcher, bass; Mel Tormé, drums.
258-3 **The Patty Cake Man** Capitol 163; CDP 7 95288 2; Bear Family BCD 16117-1
259-2 **Hello Suzanne** Capitol 176; Bear Family BCD 16117-1
260 (see below)
261-2 **Take Care of You for Me** Capitol (Note 2); Bear Family BCD 16117-1.

Note 1: Personnel from Bear Family Records.
Note 2: There was no Capitol issue of this master.
Bear Family gives the take of master 258 as -2.

SESSION 440621B (Los Angeles, 21st June 1944) JOHNNY MERCER. Johnny Mercer, vocal with the same accompaniment as above.
260 **Sam's Got Him** Capitol 164.

SESSION 440901 (Los Angeles, September 1944) MEL TORMÉ AND HIS

MEL-TONES, (same personnel as 440001) with Eddie LaRue's Quartet (piano/celeste, guitar, bass and drums).

L3636A **A Stranger in Town** World 7579; Decca 18653; Coral 60071, 9-60071, Brunswick 03831; Music Club MCCD198, MCTC198; Rhino R2 71589; Pulse PLS CD 342

L3637A **You've Laughed at Me for the Last Time** World 7588; Decca 18653; Coral 60071, 9-60071; Brunswick 03831; Music Club MCCD198, MCTC198

L3758A **Night Must Fall** World 6959; Decca 7

L3759A **I'm Down to My Last Dream** World 6968; Decca 7

Guilty World Transcriptions
unknown title World Transcriptions.

Note 1: The Decca files give a date of 5th October 1944 for masters L3636/3637 and 23rd March 1945 for L3758/3759 but these are almost certainly the dates when the World masters were transferred for issue on the Decca label.

Note 2: Decca 18653 and 7 as Mel Tormé and his Mel-Tones, Vocal with Instrumental Accompaniment.

SESSION 450427 (Los Angeles, 27th April 1945) EUGENIE BAIRD (vocal) with Mel Tormé and His Mel-Tones (same personnel as 440001). Vocal with instrumental accompaniment (piano, guitar and bass).

L3817A **Am I Blue** Decca 18707; Music Club MCCD198, MCTC198

L3818A **I Fall in Love Too Easily** Decca 18707.

SESSION 450503 (Broadcast Los Angeles, 1945) MEL TORMÉ with Bob Burns and His Orchestra.
Juanita Biac BRAD 10529
Straighten Up and Fly Right Biac BRAD 10529.

SESSION 450913 (Los Angeles, 13th September 1945) BING CROSBY (vocal) with Mel Tormé and his Mel-Tones (same personnel as 440001) and Instrumental Accompaniment (Buddy Cole, piano; Dave Barbour, guitar; Phil Stephens, bass; Nick Fatool, drums (*Note 1*).

L3965A **Day by Day** Decca 18746; Brunswick 03731; Music Club MCCD198, MCTC198; Rhino R2 71589; MCA MCLD 19377; Blue Moon BMCD 3014; Pulse PLS CD 34

L3966A **Prove It by the Things You Do** Decca 18746; Brunswick 03731; MCA MCFM2775, MCLD 19377.

Note 1: The personnel for the instrumental accompaniment is as given by Rhino and on MCA MCLD 19377. Previously the guitarist has been given as Les Paul.

SESSION 460001 (Broadcast, Los Angeles, 1946) MEL TORMÉ with John Scott Trotter and His Orchestra.
Saint Louis Blues Biac BRAD 10529
On the Atchison Topeka and the Sante Fe Biac BRAD 10529
East Side, West Side Biac BRAD 10529.

1946–1947 Musicraft

SESSION 460319 (Los Angeles, 19th March 1946) MEL TORMÉ AND THE MEL-TONES with Sonny Burke and His Orchestra. Sonny Burke, leader and arranger; Charles Griffard, Clyde Hurley, Mannie Klein, Ray Linn, trumpets; William Atkinson, Francis Howard, Les Jenkins, Si Zentner, trombones; Mahlon Clark, Jack Dumont, Deacon Dunn, Chuck Gentry, Don Raffell, woodwinds; Ann Mason, harp; Milt Raskin, piano & celeste; Al Hendrickson, guitar; Phil Stephens, bass; Nick Fatool, drums. The Mel-Tones are: Bernie Parke, Les

Baxter, Betty Beveridge and Ginny O'-Connor (Note 1).

5427-3 **There's No One But You** Musicraft 363 MVS510, MVSCD60; GVOC GVC 2005

5428-3 **Willow Road** Musicraft 363, 495, MVS510, MVSCD60; Rhino R2 71589; GVOC GVC 2005; Pulse PLS CD 342

5429-1 **That's Where I Came In** Musicraft 15111, MVS510, MVSCD54; GVOC GVC 2005.

Note 1: Richard Sears in his book "V-discs — A History and Discography" gives the Mel-Tones personnel for the Musicraft sessions with Shaw as Bob Decker, Ellis Decker, Allen Copeland and Bob Parker. The reason for this claim is not known but as contemporary reports in Down Beat give the personnel above and the same personnel is quoted by Musicraft, I have taken this personnel in preference to the one given by Sears.

SESSION 460430 (Los Angeles, 30th April 1946) ARTIE SHAW AND HIS ORCHESTRA. Vocal by Mel Tormé (MT) or Mel Tormé and The Mel-Tones (MTM). Artie Shaw, clarinet and leader; Mannie Klein, Ray Linn, Zeke Zarchy, Clyde Hurley, trumpets; Elmer Smithers, Ollie Wilson, Hoyt Bohannon, trombones; Les Robinson, Heine Beau, Deacon Dunn, Don Rafell, Chuck Gentry, saxes; David Frisina, Nicholas Pisani, Sam Cytron, Peter Ellis, George Kast, Mark Levent, Walter Edelstein, Mischa Russell, William Bloom, violins; David Sterkin, Sam Freed, Stanley Spiegelman, violas; Fred Goerner, Charles Gates, Nicholas Ochi-Albi, cellos; Tommy Todd, piano; Al Hendrickson, guitar; Phil Stephens, bass; Nick Fatool, drums. Sonny Burke, arranger. Mel-Tones personnel as for 460319.

5467 **They Can't Convince Me** (*Note 1*)
5473-4 **I Got the Sun in the Morning** (MTM) Musicraft 365, MVS503, MVSCD50; MGM 10730, E/SE 4240; Lion L70058; Vernon MVM 503; Sutton SU295; Tiara TMT7560,TST560; President PLCD 557; GVOC GVC 2005; Pulse PLS CD 342

5474-4 **Along with Me** (MT) (*Note 2*) Musicraft 365, MVS503, MVSCD50; Allegro 4030, 1466; Society SOC-982; Presto PRE685; Boulevard 4025; President PLCD 557; GVOC GVC 2005

*Note 1: A version of They Can't Convince Me (master **5467**) has been attributed to this session or to one on the previous day, with a second version, master **5647**, from the 10th September 1946 session. Musicraft MVS503 claims to use master 5467 while MVS507 claims master 5647. However, master 5467 is actually by Kitty Kallen and was recorded on 29th April 1946. I therefore believe that both the issued takes of "They Can't Convince Me" derive from the 10th September 1946 session.*

Note 2: "Along With Me" (master 5474) has been listed as issued on some copies of MGM 10730 as a backing to "I Got The Sun In The Morning" (5473) but this is not confirmed. The normal backing to 5473 on MGM 10730 is "There's No Business Like Show Business" (5803).

SESSION 460530 (Broadcast, [Note 2] Los Angeles, April/May 1946 [Note 3]) BOYD RAEBURN AND HIS MUSICIANS with Mel Tormé and His Mel-Tones. Boyd Raeburn, leader and bass-sax; Ray Linn, Dale Pierce, Nelson Shelladay, Frank Beach, trumpets; Hal Smith, Freddy Zito, Ollie Wilson, trombones; Lloyd Otto, Evan Vail, French-horns; Wilbur Schwartz, alto-sax & clarinet; Harry Klee, alto-sax and flute; Julie Jacobs, tenor-sax, oboe and English horn; Gus McReynolds, tenor-, alto-sax and flute; Ralph Lee, tenor-sax and bassoon; Hy Mandel, baritone-sax; Dodo Marmarosa, piano; Tony Rizzi, guitar; Harry Babasin, bass; Jackie Mills, drums. Conducted by George Handy. (*Note 1*) The Mel-Tones are Bernie Parke,

Les Baxter, Betty Beveridge and Ginny O'Connor.
Old Man River First Heard FHR-1974-8; Joyce LP-5010; Hep CD-1
That's Where I Came In First Heard FHR-1974-8; Joyce LP-5010; Hep CD-1.

Note 1: Boyd Raeburn had disbanded his permanent orchestra in December 1945 and thereafter used studio and session musicians until he opened at Club Morocco in June 1946. The personnel of the band therefore varied from date to date. The personnel given is the considered opinion of Dieter Salemann and Fabian Grob based on research on Dodo Marmarosa. See the note following session 460319 regarding the composition of the Mel-Tones.

Note 2: These two sides come from AFRS Jubilee 188. The remainder of the program is by the Raeburn band and does not involve Mel Tormé.

Note 3: Richard Sears in his "V-discs: A History and Discography" gives the date as mid–April 1946. Hep has taken this date from Sears. First Heard gives its source as a "Sponsor's Invitation Broadcast" on 26th August 1946. Joyce gives the source as an AFRS Jubilee program of December 1945. Dieter Salemann and Fabian Grob have determined the date as no later than May 1946 as the Metronome June 1946 issue mentions the fact that George Handy's Tone Poem had been performed at a concert, probably the one that AFRS recorded for issue in the Jubilee series.

SESSION 460604 (Los Angeles, 4th June 1946) MEL TORMÉ (MT) or MEL TORMÉ AND HIS MEL-TONES (MTM) with Sonny Burke and His Orchestra. Sonny Burke, leader and arranger; Clyde Hurley, Ray Linn, George Wendt, Zeke Zarchy, trumpets; Francis Howard, Ed Kusby, Elmer Smithers, Si Zentner, trombones; Chuck Gentry, Skeets Herfurt, Harry Klee, Don Raffell, Babe Russin, reeds; Gail Laughton, harp; Milt Raskin, piano; Al Hendrickson, guitar; Phil Stephens, bass; Nick Fatool, drums. Mel-Tones personnel as for 460319.

5509-2 **South America, Take It Away** (MTM) Musicraft 381, MVS510, MVSCD60; GVOC GVC 2005

5510-3 **Try a Little Tenderness** (MTM) Musicraft 381, 495, MVS510, MVSCD60; Tiara TST515; Egmont EGM8119; GVOC GVC 2005; Pulse PLS CD 342

5511-3 **It Happened in Monterey** (MTM) Musicraft 397, MVS510, MVSCD54; Sutton SU/SSU-281; GVOC GVC 2005; Pulse PLS CD 342

5512-3 **Born to Be Blue** (MT) Musicraft 397, MVS510; Rhino R2 71589; GVOC GVC 2005; Pulse PLS CD 342

SESSION 460606 (Los Angeles, 6th June 1946) ARTIE SHAW AND HIS ORCHESTRA vocal by Mel Tormé (MT) or Mel Tormé and the Mel-Tones (MTM). Artie Shaw, clarinet and leader; Fred Fox, Jack Kirksmith, James Decker, Harry Parshal, French horns; Chuck Gentry, Herman Bernardinelli, Joe Krechler, Skeets Herfurt, Harold Lawson, saxes, Gordon Pope, oboe; Harold Lewis, flute; Jules Seder, Charles Graver, bassoons; Marshall Sosson, James Cathcart, Morris King, Mark Levent, Joseph Chassman, Vincenzo Pometti, George Barres, Marvin Limonick, James Getzoff, Howard Halbert, Oscar Wasserberger, Eugene Lamas, violins; David Sterkin, Stanley Spiegelman, Harry Rumpler, Alvin Dinkin, violas; Julius Tannenbaum, Fred Goerner, Edgar Lustgarten, Kurt Reher, cellos; Gail Laughton, harp; Mark McIntyre, piano; Dave Barbour, guitar; Nat Gangursky, Manny Stein, Art Shapiro, basses; Lou Singer, drums; Dick Jones, arranger for 5541 & 5543; Sonny Burke, arranger for 5542; Artie Shaw and Lennie Hayton, arrangers for 5545. Mel-Tones personnel as for 460319

5541 **I've Got You Under My Skin** (*)

Musicraft rejected and remade 25th June 1946

5542 **Get Out of Town** (MT) Musicraft rejected and remade 25th June 1946

5543 **Night and Day** (*) Musicraft rejected and remade 25th June 1946

5544 **You Do Something to Me** (*) Musicraft 391, MVS503, MVSCD51

5545 **Begin the Beguine** (*) Musicraft rejected and remade 13th June 1946

5546 **My Heart Belongs to Daddy** (*) Musicraft rejected and remade 13th June 1946

5547-3 **In the Still of the Night** (*) Musicraft 390, MVS503, MVSCD51

5548 **What Is This Thing Called Love** (MTM) Musicraft rejected and remade 19th June 1946

(*) Tormé is not present on these other titles recorded at this session, and for which only the Musicraft issues, if any, are shown.

SESSION 460619 (Los Angeles, 19th June 1946) ARTIE SHAW AND HIS ORCHESTRA vocal by Mel Tormé and the Mel-Tones (MTM). Artie Shaw, clarinet and leader; Zeke Zarchy, Clyde Hurley, Mannie Klein, Ray Linn, trumpets; Si Zentner, Elmer Smithers, Joe Howard, trombones; Skeets Herfurt, Joe Krechler, Harold Lawson, Don Raffell, Chuck Gentry, saxes; Marshall Sosson, Mischa Russell, George Kast, Harry Bluestone, Howard Halbert, Eugene Lamas, Dan Lube, Nick Pisani, Olcott Vail, violins; Paul Robyn, Stanley Spiegelman, Sam Freed, violas; Cy Bernard, Fred Goerner, Edgar Lustgarten, cellos; Milt Raskin, piano; Dave Barbour, guitar; Art Shapiro, bass; Nick Fatool, drums; Dick Jones, arranger for 5543; Sonny Burke, arranger for 5548. Mel-Tones personnel as for 460319

5543-4 **Night and Day** (*) Musicraft 389, MVS503, MVSCD51

5548-3 **What Is This Thing Called Love** (MTM) (*Note 2*) Musicraft 390, MVS507, MVSCD50; Parlophone R3032; MGM 10612, K30243, E517, X1042, EPC-3, Lion L70058; V-Disc 751-A; President PLCD 557

5548-take? **What Is This Thing Called Love** (MTM) (*Note 2*) Everest FS248

(*) *Tormé is not present on this other title recorded at this session, and for which only the Musicraft issues are shown. Two takes are known to have been issued of this tune.*

Note 1: Musicraft 390 shows no master number in the wax for 5548 but this master number appears on the label. Parlophone R3032, which seems to be a dubbed master, shows 5548 in the wax twice as the master number.

Note 2: There are two issued takes of "What Is This Thing Called Love," details of the differences are given in Appendix 1. It is possible that one of the takes was recorded at the Shaw session of 11th June but this is unlikely as Torme and the Mel-Tones do not seem to have been involved at that session. It is not known, at present, which take is used on Allegro LP4023, LP4107, LP1466; Rondolette L-1755 and A-852; Golden Tone GT-4098; Galaxy 4852; Tops LP-975; Ember EMB3328 and FA2015; MGM S/SE4240, C990; Vernon MVM503; Rhino R2 71589; Avid AMSC 692; Classic Popular CDCD 1158; World Record Club R-23; Pulse PLS CD 342 and GVOC GVC 2005

SESSION 460625 (Los Angeles, 25th June 1946) ARTIE SHAW AND HIS ORCHESTRA vocal by Mel Tormé (MT). Artie Shaw, clarinet and leader; Vince DeRosa, Jack Kirksmith, Richard Perissi, James Stagliano, French horns; Herman Bernardinelli, Chuck Gentry, Skeets Herfurt, Harold Lawson, Jack Mayhew, woodwinds; Harold Lewis, flute; Gordon Pope, oboe; Charles Graver, Jules Seder, bassoon; Harry Bluestone, Sam Cytron, Peter Ellis, David Frisina, Howard Halbert, George Kast,

Morris King, Eugene Lamas, Nick Pisani, Mischa Russell, Marshall Sosson, Olcott Vail, violins; Sam Freed, Maurice Perlmutter, Paul Robyn, David Sterkin, violas; Cy Bernard, Fred Goerner, Edgar Lustgarten, Nicolas Ochi-Albi, cellos; Kathryn Thompson, harp; Mark McIntyre, piano; Dave Barbour, guitar; Nat Gangursky, Artie Shapiro, Manny Stein, basses; Lou Singer, drums. Dick Jones, arranger for 5541; Sonny Burke, arranger for 5542.

5541-4 **I've Got You Under My Skin** (*) Musicraft 392, MVS507, MVSCD50

5542-4 **Get Out of Town** (MT) Musicraft 389, MVS507, MVSCD50; Allegro 4023, 4107, 1405; MGM K30245, E517, X1042, EPC-3; Royale 18151; Lion L70058; Rondolette L-1755, A-852; Tops LP-975; Golden Tone GT-4098; Tiara TMT7517, TST517; Vernon MVM503; Parlophone R3074; Society SOC983; Presto PRE681; ARC ARC 67; World Record Club R-23; Rhino R2 71589; President PLCD 557; Pulse PLS CD 342.

(*) *Tormé is not present on this other title recorded at this session, and for which only the Musicraft issues are shown.*

SESSION 460816 (Los Angeles, 16th August 1946) ARTIE SHAW AND HIS ORCHESTRA vocal by Mel Tormé (MT) or Mel Tormé and the Mel-Tones (MTM). Artie Shaw, clarinet and leader; Clyde Hurley, Mannie Klein, Ray Linn, Zeke Zarchey, trumpets; Ed Kusby, Elmer Smithers, Ollie Wilson, trombones; Chuck Gentry, Harry Klee, Les Robinson, Don Raffell, Babe Russin, reeds; Harry Bluestone, Sam Cytron, Sam Freed, David Frisina, Howard Halbert, George Kast, Nick Pisani, Mischa Russell, Marshall Sosson, violins; Paul Robyn, Stanley Spiegelman, David Sterkin, violas; Fred Goerner, Arthur Kafton, Nicolas Ochi-Albi, cellos; Dodo Marmarosa, piano; Al Hendrickson, guitar; Phil Stephens, bass; Lou Singer, drums. Sonny Burke, arranger for 5629 & 5636. Mel Tormé and Sonny Burke, arrangers for 5635. The Mel-Tones personnel is as for 460319.

5629-2 **For You, for Me, for Evermore** (MT) Musicraft 412, MVS507, MVSCD50; Allegro 1405; Rondolette A852; Presto PRE681; Society SOC-982; Boulevard 4025; Rhino R2 71589; President PLCD 557; GVOC GVC 2005; Pulse PLS CD 342

Masters 5630–34 were recorded on 28th July 1946 and do not involve Tormé.

5635-4 **Changing My Tune** (MTM) Musicraft 412, MVS507, MVSCD50; Allegro 1405; Parlophone R3100; Vernon MVM503; Society SOC983; Presto PRE681; President PLCD 557; GVOC GVC 2005; Pulse PLS CD 342; Avid AMSC 641

5636 **Love for Sale** (*) (*Note 1*) Musicraft rejected and remade on 10th September 1946.

(*) *Tormé is not present on this title*

Note 1: "Love for Sale" has also been listed as master 5631 but 5636 appears both in the wax and on the label of Musicraft 391.

SESSION 460910 (Los Angeles, 10th September 1946) ARTIE SHAW AND HIS ORCHESTRA vocal by Mel Tormé (MT) or Mel Tormé and the Mel-Tones (MTM). Artie Shaw, clarinet and leader; Ray Linn, Zeke Zarchey, Clyde Hurley, Manny Klein, trumpets; Si Zentner, Ed Kusby, Joe Howard, trombones; Skeets Herfurt, Harry Klee, Babe Russin, Don Raffell, Morton Friedman, saxes; Harry Bluestone, Marshall Sosson, Mischa Russell, Nick Pisani, Olcott Vail, George Kast, Peter Ellis, Howard Halbert, Eugene Lamas, Sam Cytron, violins; David Sterkin, Stanley Spiegelman, Paul Robyn, violas; Cy Bernard, Fred Goerner, Arthur Krafton, cellos; Milt Raskin, piano; Allan Reuss, guitar; Art Shapiro, bass; Nick Fatool, drums. Sonny Burke, arranger for all but 5652. The Mel-Tones personnel is as for 460319.

5636-2 **Love for Sale** (*) (*Note 1*) Musicraft 391, MVS507, MVSCD50

5647-take? **They Can't Convince Me** (MT) Musicraft MVS503; President PLCD 557

5647-3 **They Can't Convince Me** (MT) Musicraft 441, MVS507, MVSCD50; Parlophone R3067; Allegro 1405; Presto PRE685; Society SOC983; President PLCD 557

5648 **Guilty** (MTM) Musicraft rejected and remade on 19th September 1946

5649 **The Anniversary Song** (*) Musicraft rejected and remade on 19th September 1946

5650 **And So to Bed** (MTM) Musicraft rejected and remade on 18th October 1946

5651 **Connecticut** (*) Musicraft rejected and remade on 18th October 1946.

(*) Tormé is not present on these other titles recorded at this session.

Note 1: "Love for Sale" has also been listed as master 5631 but 5636 appears both in the wax and on the label of Musicraft 391.

Note 2: Another version of "They Can't Convince Me" (master 5467) has been attributed to the Artie Shaw session of 30th April 1946 with a second version, master 5647, from the above session. This information is incorrect. There is only one version and it belongs to this session, but there are two issued takes of this version; see Appendix 1 for details of the differences.

Note 3: "They Can't Convince Me" also appears on Rondolette A-852 and GVOC GVC 2005 but the take that is used is not known.

SESSION 460919 (Los Angeles, 19th September 1946) ARTIE SHAW AND HIS ORCHESTRA vocal by Mel Tormé and the Mel-Tones (MTM). Artie Shaw, clarinet and leader; Ray Linn, Zeke Zarchey, Clyde Hurley, Manny Klein, trumpets; Si Zentner, Ed Kusby, Joe Howard, Carl Loeffler, trombones; Skeets Herfurt, Harry Klee, Babe Russin, Don Raffell, Morton Friedman, saxes; Harry Bluestone, Marshall Sosson, Mischa Russell, Nicholas Pisani, Olcott Vail, George Kast, Peter Ellis, Howard Halbert, Eugene Lamas, Walter Edelstein, violins; David Sterkin, Stanley Spiegelman, Paul Robyn, violas; Cy Bernard, Fred Goerner, Arthur Krafton, cellos; Milt Raskin, piano; Allan Reuss, guitar; Art Shapiro, bass; Nick Fatool, drums. Sonny Burke, arranger for both titles. The Mel-Tones personnel is as for 460319.

5648-2B **Guilty** (MTM) Musicraft 428, MVS507, MVSCD51; Allegro 4030, 1405; Parlophone R3042; Rondolette A852; Presto PRE681; Tops 975; Galaxy 4852; Golden Tone GT-4098; Sutton SU/SSU 381; ARC ARC 67; President PLCD 557; Ember EMB3328, FA2015; Hollywood Nites HNC 0049; GVOC GVC 2005; Pulse PLS CD 342

5649-2J **The Anniversary Song** (*) Musicraft 428, MVS507, MVSCD51.

(*) Tormé is not present on this other title recorded at this session, and for which only the Musicraft issues are given.

SESSION 461017 (Los Angeles, 17th or 18th October 1946) ARTIE SHAW AND HIS ORCHESTRA vocal by Mel Tormé (MT) or Mel Tormé and the Mel-Tones (MTM). Artie Shaw, clarinet and leader; Ray Linn, Zeke Zarchey, Frank Beach, Manny Klein, trumpets; Bill Schaefer, Ed Kusby, Joe Howard, Elmer Smithers, trombones; Skeets Herfurt, Harry Klee, Babe Russin, Bob Lawson, Harold Lawson, saxes; Sam Freed, Harry Bluestone, Morris King, Lewis Elias, Mischa Russell, Nick Pisani, Olcott Vail, George Kast, Alex Law, Edgar Berman, Sam Cytron, Walter Edelstein, violins; David Sterkin, Maurice Perlmutter, Harry Weiss, violas; Cy Bernard, Fred Goerner, Jack Sewell, cellos; Dodo Marmarosa, piano; Allan Reuss, guitar; Phil Stephens, bass; Nick Fatool, drums. Sonny Burke, arranger for all titles. The Mel-Tones personnel is as for 460319.

5650-2 **And So to Bed** (MTM) Musicraft 441, MVS507, MVSCD50; Allegro

1466; Parlophone R3054; President PLCD 557; GVOC GVC 2005; Pulse PLS CD 342

5651-2 **Connecticut** (*) Musicraft 445, MVS507, MVSCD50

5701-2 **Don't You Believe It Dear** (MTM) Musicraft 445, MVS507, MVSCD50; Parlophone R3080; Presto PRE681; President PLCD 557; GVOC GVC 2005; Pulse PLS CD 342

5702 **It's the Same Old Dream** (MT) Musicraft rejected and remade on 8th November 1946

5703 **I Believe** (MT) Musicraft rejected and remade on 8th November 1946

5704 **When You're Around** (*) Musicraft rejected and remade on 8th November 1946.

(*) *Tormé is not present on these other titles recorded at this session, and for which only the Musicraft issues, if any, are given.*

Take -1 of 5701 has been reported to have been issued on Musicraft 445 but this is not yet confirmed.

The AFM copy of the contract for this session shows the date as 17th October while the Musicraft log sheet shows the 18th. It is not possible to establish which is correct.

SESSION 461018 (Los Angeles, 18th October 1946 [*Notes 3 & 4*]) MEL TORMÉ with the Mel-Tones (MTM) same personnel as for 460319. With Ray Linn and His Orchestra (*Note 2*) Personnel unknown but instrumentation is 1 trumpet, 1 trombone, 5 reeds and 4 rhythm. Arrangers: 5800 & 5803, Ray Conniff; 5801 & 5802, Harold Mooney.

5800-2A **One for My Baby** Musicraft 15107; Sutton SU/SSU-281

5801-113 **A Little Kiss Each Morning** (A Little Kiss Each Night) Musicraft 15107, MVS2005, MVSCD60; MGM EP591, E552, K30356; GVOC GVC 2005

5802-4 **Dream Awhile** (MTM) Musicraft 15099, MVS510; MGM 10844, EP562; Sutton SU/SSU-281; GVOC GVC 2005

5803-6-B **There's No Business Like Show Business** (MTM) (*Note 5*) Musicraft 15099, 15111, MVS510, MVSCD54; MGM 10730, 922, 45-MGM-922; Lion L70058; GVOC GVC 2005.

Note 1: Master 5801. The master number in the wax of the Musicraft 78 is handwritten and appears as -1 13 but in comparison with the other Musicraft takes it is probably a poorly written -1 B.

Note 2: The sleeve of Musicraft MVS510 erroneously gives SONNY BURKE and his Orchestra for 5803.

Note 3: The Musicraft worksheet for master 5800 gives the recording date as 18th October 1946. While this makes no sense as far as the master number is concerned, it has to be accepted as correct. The sleeve of Musicraft MVS2005 gives the date of 5801 as 27th November 1946 and this does make sense of the master number in the Musicraft sequence. The date has also been given as 17th November.

Note 4: Against masters 5800-2 and 5801-1 on the Musicraft work sheets it says "Okay (Mel to be dubbed)" and against 5803 -4 and -5 there is "To be dubbed with MT solo" and on 5803-6 is "Okay. To be dubbed with MT solo." At this time, masters were cut into acetate blanks rather than on tape and the technique of overdubbing was in its infancy. The probability is that the instrumental tracks, including, where relevant, the contributions of the Mel-Tones were cut on 18th October with the Tormé vocals added later, probably on 27th November.

Note 5: MGM 10730 and Lion L70058 erroneously credit this side to Artie Shaw and his Orchestra. The credit on MGM 922 is correct.

SESSION 461108 (Los Angeles, 8th or 9th November 1946 [*Note 1*]) ARTIE SHAW AND HIS ORCHESTRA vocal by

Mel Tormé (MT). Artie Shaw, clarinet and leader; Ray Linn, Zeke Zarchey, Frank Beach, Manny Klein, trumpets; Si Zentner, Ed Kusby, Joe Howard, Bill Schaefer, trombones; Skeets Herfurt, Harry Klee, Babe Russin, Herbie Haymer, Bob Lawson, saxes; Sam Freed, Felix Slatkin, Morris King, Harry Bluestone, Marshall Sosson, Mischa Russell, Nick Pisani, Olcott Vail, George Kast, Peter Ellis, Howard Halbert, Sam Cytron, violins; David Sterkin, Maurice Perlmutter, Stanley Spiegelman, violas; Cy Bernard, Fred Goerner, Jack Sewell, cellos; Dodo Marmarosa, piano; Dave Barbour, guitar; Art Shapiro, bass; Nick Fatool, drums. Sonny Burke, arranger for all titles.

5702-7 **It's the Same Old Dream** (MT) Musicraft 492, MVS507, MVSCD51; Allegro 1466; Parlophone R3067; Presto PRE685; President PLCD 557; GVOC GVC 2005

5703-3 **I Believe** (MT) Musicraft 492, MVS507, MVSCD51; Allegro 1405; Parlophone R3054; Presto PRE681; Society SOC-982; Rondolette A-852; President PLCD 557; GVOC GVC 2005

5704 **When You're Around** (*) Musicraft 512, MVS507, MVSCD51.

(*) *Tormé is not present on this title, for which only the Musicraft issues are given.*

Note 1: The AFM copy of the contract for the session gives 9th November while the Musicraft log sheets give 8th November. It is not possible to establish which is correct.

SESSION 461127 For the session usually dated 27th November 1946 see the session on 18th October 1946 (Session 461018).

SESSION 461129 (Los Angeles, 29th November 1946) MEL TORMÉ with Sonny Burke and His Orchestra. Sonny Burke, leader and arranger; Ray Linn, trumpet; Si Zentner, trombone; Skeets Herfurt, Harry Klee, Bob Dawson, Don Raffell, Babe Russin, reeds; Edward Bergman, Harry Bluestone, Walter Edelstein, Jacques Gasselin, Anthony Olson, Nick Pisani, Felix Slatkin, Olcott Vail, violins; Gail Laughton, harp; Dodo Marmarosa, piano; Dave Barbour, guitar; Lewis Popp, bass; Nick Fatool, drums. Harold Mooney, arranger for 5805.

5805-3 **It's Dreamtime** Musicraft 15102, MVS508, MVSCD54; Parlophone R3094; Rhino R2 71589; Read RC7-012-1; Pulse PLS CD 342

5806-5 **You're Driving Me Crazy!** Musicraft 15102, 595, MVS2000, MVSCD54; Pulse PLS CD 342

5807-3 **Who Cares What People Say** Musicraft 15104, MVS2000, MVSCD54

5808-1 **I'm Yours** Musicraft 15104, MVS2000, MVSCD54; Parlophone R3094; MGM EP562.

SESSION 470201 (Hollywood, February/April 1947) GOOD NEWS (film sound track). Musical director: Lennie Hayton. Music played by The M-G-M Studio Orchestra conducted by Lennie Hayton. Artists heard in the film are Patricia Marshall (PM), Peter Lawford (PL), June Allyson (JA), Joan McCracken (JM), M-G-M Studio Chorus (MSC), The Williams Brothers (WB) Mel Tormé is audible in these selections from the film sound track:

Be a Ladies' Man (with PL, WB) (*Note 3*) Sountrak STK-111; Rhino R2 75481

Lucky in Love (with PM, PL, JA, JM, MSC) (*Note 2*) Sountrak STK-111; Rhino R2 75481

The Best Things in Life Are Free (with PL) (*Note 1*) Sountrak STK-111; Rhino R2 75481

Just Imagine (with JA) Sountrak STK-111

Just Imagine (**outtake**) (with JA) (*Note 4*) Rhino R2 75481

Lucky in Love (reprise) (outtake) (*Note 5*) Rhino R2 75481.

The items on Sountrak STK-111 are also on Sony AK-47025.

Note 1: recorded 3rd March 1947. Arranged and orchestrated by Robert Franklyn

Note 2: recorded 5th March 1947. Arranged and orchestrated by Robert Franklyn and Conrad Salinger

Note 3: on Sountrak as "Be A Lady's' Man." On Sony as "He's A Ladies Man." Recorded 16th April 1947. Arranged by Kay Thompson. Orchestrated by Wally Heglin. Tormé also plays ukulele.

Note 4: not used in the released version of the film. Recorded 16th April 1947. Arranged and orchestrated by Lennie Hayton

Note 5: not used in the released version of the film. Recorded 5th March 1947. Arranged and orchestrated by Robert Franklyn and Conrad Salinger

SESSION 470531 (Broadcast, New York City, 31st May 1947) WNEW SATURDAY NIGHT SWING SESSION. Roy Eldridge, trumpet & vocal; Flip Phillips, tenor-sax; Mike Coluccio, piano & vibes; Al Casey, guitar; Eddie Safranski, bass; Specs Powell, drums; Mel Tormé, vocal or -1, drums:

WS 5012 **Honeysuckle Rose** (vcl, RE, MT) Vox 16029; Polydor 580089

WS 5013 **Flip and Jazz Pt 1** (*) Vox 16027; Polydor 580087

WS 5014 **Flip and Jazz Pt 2** (*) Vox 16028; Polydor 580087

WS 5015 **Flip and Jazz Pt 3** (*) Vox 16029; Polydor 580088

WS 5016 **How High the Moon** (-1) Vox 16028; Polydor 580089

WS 5017 **Lover** (*) Vox 16027; Polydor 580088

Buck Still Jumps (*) unissued on 78 rpm.

(*) Tormé is not present on these other titles from this broadcast.

All seven titles also on Esoteric ESJ2, Vogue LDE007, and Counterpoint CPT549, and all except "Buck Still Jumps" also on Everest FS231.

SESSION 470601 (New York City [*Note 1*], June 1947) MEL TORMÉ with Walter Gross and His Orchestra. Personnel unknown. Instrumentation includes flute and rhythm.

Untraced **It's Easy to Remember** Musicraft (Note 2), MVS2005, MVSCD60; GVOC GVC 2005

5879-4 **Kokomo, Indiana** Musicraft 15109, MVS508, MVSCD54

5880-2 **How Long Has This Been Going On** Musicraft 15109, MVS2005, MVSCD60; Avid AMSC 640; GVOC GVC 2005

5881-2 **Boulevard of Memories** Musicraft 15114, MVS508.

Note 1: Walter Gross was Musical Director of Mel Tormé's radio program for the Toni Home Permanent company on NBC in New York. It is therefore probable that this session was recorded in New York City. If so, the guitar player is Tony Mottola.

Note 2: there was no 78 rpm Musicraft issue of this title. The master number is probably 5878.

SESSION 470901 (Los Angeles, September 1947) MEL TORMÉ with Orchestra (*Note 1*).

5886-3 **I Can't Give You Anything But Love, Baby** (*) Musicraft 528, MVS2000, MVSCD60; MGM K30357, E552, 922, 45-MGM-922; Halo 50243; Royale EP246; Allegro Elite 4117; GVOC GVC 2005

5887-4 **Three Little Words** Musicraft 528, MVS508, MVSCD60; Halo 50243; Allegro Elite 4117; GVOC GVC 2005

5888-2 **...and Mimi** (*) Musicraft 15114, MVS2005

5889-1 **My Baby Just Cares for Me** Musicraft 589, MVS2000, MVSCD54

5890-- **I'll Always Be in Love with You** (*) Musicraft 529, MVS2005

5891 **untraced**

5892-- **Love, You Funny Thing** Musicraft 529, MVS2000; MGM K 30356, EP562, E552; Royale EP246.

*Note 1: The accompaniment on this session is actually by **Page Cavanaugh & His Trio**. The personnel of the Trio is Page Cavanaugh, piano and (*) harp, Al Viola, guitar, Lloyd Pratt, bass.*

SESSION 470902 (Los Angeles, September 1947) MEL TORMÉ with Orchestra (*Note 1*).
5893 **The Day You Came Along** Musicraft 530, MVS2005, MVSCD60; GVOC GVC 2005
5894 **The Best Things in Life Are Free** Musicraft 15118, MVS2005, MVSCD60; MGM K 30356, EP591, E552; GVOC GVC 2005
5895 **What Are You Doing New Year's Eve** Musicraft 15116, MVS2005
5896 **Ballerina** Musicraft 15116, MVS2005
5897 **untraced**
5898 **Magic Town** Musicraft 15118, MVS2005
5899 **If I Had a Girl Like You** Musicraft 573, MVS2000; Halo 50243; Royale EP246; Allegro Elite 4117
5900 **Fine and Dandy** Musicraft 530, MVS510; GVOC GVC 2005.

*Note 1: The accompaniment is actually by **Page Cavanaugh & His Trio**. The personnel of the Trio are Page Cavanaugh, piano and, except 5899, harp, Al Viola, guitar, Lloyd Pratt, bass.*

SESSION 471001 (Los Angeles, 1947) MEL TORMÉ with the Page Cavanaugh Trio (Page Cavanaugh, piano and harp, Al Viola, guitar, Lloyd Pratt, bass).
MM0933 **How Are Things in Glocca Morra** Macgregor 381/2; Glendale GL6007
MM0933 **April Showers** Macgregor 381/2; Glendale GL6018; LaserLight 12223; Star Line SLC-61005
MM0933 **April in Paris** Macgregor 381/2; Glendale GL6007; LaserLight 12224
MM0933 **This Can't Be Love** Macgregor 381/2; Glendale GL6018
MM0934 **Isn't This a Lovely Day** Macgregor 381/2; Glendale GL6007; LaserLight 12223
MM0934 **September Song** (omit gtr & bass) Macgregor 381/2; Glendale GL6018
MM0934 **County Fair** Macgregor 381/2; Glendale GL6018; LaserLight 12222; Star Line SLC-61005
MM0934 **Makin' Whoopee** Macgregor 381/2;
MM0934 **You're the Cream in My Coffee** Macgregor 381/2.

SESSION 471002 (Los Angeles, 1947). Same.
MM0937 **Stranger in Town** Macgregor 387/8; Glendale GL6007
MM0937 **I Can't Get Started with You** Macgregor 387/8; Glendale GL6007
MM0937 **They Didn't Believe Me** Macgregor 387/8; Glendale GL6018
MM0937 **They Can't Take That Away From Me** (omit guitar) Macgregor 387/8; Glendale GL6018
MM0937 **You Ought to Be in Pictures** Macgregor 387/8
MM0938 **My Funny Valentine** (omit guitar & bass) Macgregor 387/8; Glendale GL6018
MM0938 **Country Boy** Macgregor 387/8; Glendale GL6007
MM0938 **How Long Has This Been Going On** Macgregor 387/8; Glendale GL6007
MM0938 **How High the Moon** Macgregor 387/8
MM0938 **The Best Things in Life Are Free** Macgregor 387/8; Glendale GL6018.

SESSION 471003 (Los Angeles, 1947) MEL TORMÉ accompanied by THE DAVE BARBOUR FOUR: Buddy Cole, piano; Dave Barbour, guitar; unknown harp and bass.
MM0970 **It's Easy to Remember** Macgregor 431/2; Glendale GL6018; LaserLight 12224; Star Line SLC-61005

MM0970 **I Cover the Waterfront** Macgregor 431/2; Glendale GL6007; Pickwick PMTD 16009; LaserLight 15381, 12224; Star Line SLC-61005; Giants of Jazz CD 53343

MM0970 **The Blues** Macgregor 431/2; Glendale GL6007; LaserLight 12223; Giants of Jazz CD 53343

MM0971 **Gone with the Wind** Macgregor 431/2; Glendale GL6007; Pickwick PMTD 16009; LaserLight 15381, 12223; Star Line SLC-61005; Giants of Jazz CD 53343

MM0971 **When It's Sleepy Time Down South** Macgregor 431/2; Glendale GL6007; LaserLight 12223; Star Line SLC-61005; Giants of Jazz CD 53343

MM0971 **Cottage for Sale** Macgregor 431/2; Glendale GL6007; Pickwick PMTD 16009; LaserLight 15381, 12224; Star Line SLC-61005; Giants of Jazz CD 53343.

SESSION 471004 (Los Angeles, 1947) MEL TORMÉ accompanied by THE DAVE BARBOUR FOUR; same personnel as last.

MM0977 **Love Me or Leave Me** Macgregor 433, 188; Glendale GL6018; Pickwick PMTD 16009; LaserLight 15381, 12222; Star Line SLC-61005; Rhino R2 71589; Giants of Jazz CD53343

MM0977 **Blues in the Night** Macgregor 433; Glendale GL6018; LaserLight 12222; Star Line SLC-61005; Giants of Jazz CD 53343

MM0977 **Don't Take Your Love from Me** Macgregor 433; Glendale GL6018; Pickwick PMTD 16009; LaserLight 15381, 12222; Star Line SLC-61005; Giants of Jazz CD 53343

MM0977 **Three Little Words** Macgregor 433, 188; Rhino R2 71589; Giants of Jazz CD 53343.

SESSION 471114 (Los Angeles, 14th November 1947) MEL TORMÉ with Orchestra (Musicraft 538); with HAL MOONEY AND HIS ORCHESTRA (Musicraft 573); instrumentation: 4 reeds, 4 violins, 1 viola, 1 cello, 1 horn, 1 trombone, 4 rhythm. Personnel unknown. The trombone may be Si Zentner. The guitar may be Barney Kessel.

5970-4 **Until the Real Thing Comes Along** Musicraft (*Note 1*), MVS508; MGM 10874, EP562; Tiara TST515; Egmont EGM8119

5971-5 **But Beautiful** Musicraft 538, MVS508, MVSCD54; Halo 50243

5972-5 **A Cottage for Sale** Musicraft 573, MVS2000; Parlophone R3152; MGM 10584, K 30355, E552; Halo 50243; Tiara TST515; Allegro Elite 4117; Egmont EGM 8119; Rhino R2 71589.

Note 1: There was no 78 rpm Musicraft issue of this title.

SESSION 471115 (Los Angeles, 15th November 1947) MEL TORMÉ with HAL MOONEY AND HIS ORCHESTRA: same instrumentation. Definitely Si Zentner, trombone.

5973-5 **Love Is the Sweetest Thing** Musicraft (*Note 1*), MVS2000, MVSCD60; GVOC GVC 2005

5974-3 **When Is Sometime** Musicraft (*Note 1*), MVS2005, MVSCD60; GVOC GVC 2005

5975-3 **Gone with the Wind** Musicraft 558, MVS2005; MGM 10584; Parlophone R3152; Rhino R2 71589; Pulse PLS CD 342

5976-6 **With You** Musicraft (*Note 1*), MVS508, MVSCD54.

Note 1: There was no 78 rpm Musicraft issue of this title.

SESSION 471116 (Los Angeles, 16th November 1947) MEL TORMÉ with Orchestra (Musicraft 534, 538); with HAL MOONEY AND HIS ORCHESTRA (Musicraft 558, 589); with HAROLD MOONEY AND HIS ORCHESTRA (Musicraft 5009)

Harold Mooney, leader and arranger; Manny Klein, Charles Marlowe, George Seaberg, Zeke Zarchy, trumpets; Ed Kusby, Carl Loeffer, Si Zentner, trombones; Jack Dumont, Skeets Herfurt, Harry Klee, Bob Dawson, Don Raffell, Babe Russin, reeds; Harry Bluestone, David Frisina, Erno Neufeld, Mischa Russell, Felix Slatkin, Marshall Sosson, Olcott Vail, violins; Paul Robyn, David Sterkin, violas; Cy Bernard, Eleanor Slatkin, cellos; Gail Laughton, harp; Milt Raskin, piano; Al Hendrickson, guitar; Artie Shapiro, Phil Stephens, basses; Nick Fatool, drums; Lloyd Martin, arranger for 5980; Sonny Burke, arranger for 5983.

5977-5 **I Cover the Waterfront** Musicraft 5009, MVS508, MVSCD60; MGM K 30354, E552; Halo 50243; Allegro Elite 4117; GVOC GVC 2005

5978-3 **County Fair** Musicraft 5009, 595, MVS508, MVSCD60; MGM K 30354, E552; Rhino R2 71589; Read RC7-012-1; GVOC GVC 2005; Pulse PLS CD 342

5979-10 **A Foggy Day** Musicraft 589, MVS508, MVSCD54; MGM 10874; Read RC7-012-1

5980-3 **Making Whoopee** (*Note 1*) Musicraft 534, MVS508, MVSCD54; Parlophone R3138; MGM 10844, EP591; Halo 50243; Allegro Elite 4117; Rhino R2 71589; Read RC7-012-1; Pulse PLS CD 342

5981-4 **Little White Lies** Musicraft 558, MVS2000, MVSCD60; Parlophone R3131; MGM K 30355, E552, EP591; Halo 50243; Allegro Elite 4117; GVOC GVC 2005

5982-3 **Do It Again** Musicraft 534, MVS508, MVSCD54; Parlophone R3138; Halo 50243; Royale EP246; Allegro Elite 4117

5983-4 **Night and Day** Musicraft 538, MVS510, MVSCD54; Parlophone R3131; Halo 50243; Rhino R2 71589; Read RC7-012-1; GVOC GVC 2005; Pulse PLS CD 342.

Note 1: as "Making Whoopee" on Musicraft 534 but "Makin' Whoopee" on Musicraft LP and CD, on Parlophone 78, Allegro Elite LP and on Rhino CD.

1948–1952 Capitol

SESSION 480202 (Hollywood, 2nd February 1948) **WORDS AND MUSIC** (Film soundtrack); Mel Tormé, accompanied by the M-G-M Studio Orchestra conducted by Lennie Hayton. Musical director: Lennie Hayton. Arranged and orchestrated by Conrad Salinger.

Blue Moon JJA 1982-2; Rhino R2 75481.

Note 1: JJA 1982-2 contains other musical excerpts recorded for the soundtrack of the film but no other item includes Tormé. The official soundtrack album issued by M-G-M in the "Silver Screen Soundtrack Series" (UK catalog number — 2353 033) does not include Tormé's "Blue Moon" nor does it even mention him on the sleeve.

SESSION 480706 (Hollywood, 6th July 1948) **THE MEL TORMÉ SHOW** (NBC radio program). MEL TORMÉ with THE MEL-TONES (MTM), JANET WALDO (vocal), BARBARA EILER (vocal) and SYDNEY MILLER (vocal) with Orchestra conducted by DEAN ELLIOTT. The Mel-Tones are: Virginia Maxey, Bernie Parke, Les Baxter, Sheldon "Diz" Disruhd and Ralph Brewster.

You're Driving Me Crazy Sounds Great Live SG-5006; Mr. Music MMCD-7005; GVOC GVC 2005

Pythagoras, How You Stagger Us (with MTM) (*Note 1*) Sounds Great Live SG-5006; Mr. Music MMCD-7005; GVOC GVC 2005

It's Dark on Observatory Hill Sounds Great Live SG-5006; Mr. Music MMCD-7005

Hooray for Love (with JW) Mr. Music MMCD-7006.

All the titles on Sounds Great Live SG-5006 also on Jasmine JASM 2529 and JASMC 2529.
*Note 1: Pythagoras... as **Geometric Blues** on Mr. Music.*

SESSION 480713 (Hollywood, 13th July 1948). Same.

The French Lesson (with BE) Sounds Great Live SG-5006; Mr. Music MMCD-7005

You're the Cream in My Coffee (with MTM) Sounds Great Live SG-5012 Mr. Music MMCD-7005

Fine and Dandy Sounds Great Live SG-5012; Mr. Music MMCD-7006

It's Magic Mr. Music MMCD-7006.

The title on Sounds Great Live SG-5006 also on Jasmine JASM 2529 and JASMC 2529.

SESSION 480810 (Hollywood, 10th August 1948). Same.

That Old Black Magic Mr. Music MMCD-7005

When the Red Red Robin Comes Bob Bob Bobbing Along (with MTM) Sounds Great Live SG-5006; Mr. Music MMCD-7005; GVOC GVC 2005

Friendship (with SM) Mr. Music MMCD-7006.

The title on Sounds Great Live SG-5006 also on Jasmine JASM 2529 and JASMC 2529.

SESSION 480817 (Hollywood, 17th August 1948). Same.

Maybe You'll Be There Mr. Music MMCD-7005

Brahm's Lullaby Sounds Great Live SG-5006; Mr. Music MMCD-7005; GVOC GVC 2005

It's the Sentimental Thing to Do Sounds Great Live SG-5012; Mr. Music MMCD-7006

Wrap Your Troubles in Dreams Sounds Great Live SG-5012; Mr. Music MMCD-7006; LaserLight 12224

Back in Your Own Back Yard (with MTM) Sounds Great Live SG-5012; Mr. Music MMCD-7006; LaserLight 12222.

The title on Sounds Great Live SG-5006 also on Jasmine JASM 2529 and JASMC 2529.

SESSION 480824 (Hollywood, 24th August 1948). Same.

Dear Old Fairmont (with MTM) Sounds Great Live SG-5006; Mr. Music MMCD-7005

Blues in the Night Mr. Music MMCD-7006

Dear Old Fairmont (reprise) (with MTM) Sounds Great Live SG-5006; Mr. Music MMCD-7006.

*All the titles on Sounds Great Live SG-5006 also on Jasmine JASM 2529 and JASMC 2529. Both versions of Dear Old Fairmont as **Fairmont College** on Mr. Music.*

SESSION 480831 (Hollywood, 31st August 1948). Same.

Mountain Greenery (with JW) Mr. Music MMCD-7005

Wish I May, Wish I Might (with MTM) Sounds Great Live SG-5006; Mr. Music MMCD-7005; GVOC GVC 2005

Malt Shop Special (with MTM) (Note 1) Sounds Great Live SG-5006; Mr. Music MMCD-7006; LaserLight 12224; GVOC GVC 2005.

All the titles on Sounds Great Live SG-5006 also on Jasmine JASM 2529 and JASMC 2529.
*Note 1: Malt Shop Special as **Lover's Delight** on Mr. Music and LaserLight.*

SESSION 480907 (Hollywood, 7th September 1948). Same.

I've Got the Sun in the Morning and the Moon at Night (with MTM) Sounds Great Live SG-5006; Mr. Music MMCD-7005; GVOC GVC 2005
Get Out and Get Under Sounds Great Live SG-5012; Mr. Music MMCD-7006
This Is the Moment Mr. Music MMCD-7006.

The title on Sounds Great Live SG-5006 also on Jasmine JASM 2529 and JASMC 2529.

SESSION 480914 (Hollywood, 14th September 1948). Same.
It's a Most Unusual Day (with MTM) Sounds Great Live SG-5006; Mr. Music MMCD-7005; GVOC GVC 2005
I Gotta Right to Sing the Blues Mr. Music MMCD-7005
Isn't It Romantic? (with JW) Sounds Great Live SG-5012; Mr. Music MMCD-7006.

The title on Sounds Great Live SG-5006 also on Jasmine JASM 2529 and JASMC 2529.

SESSION 480921 (Hollywood, 21st September 1948). Same.
Everything Happens to Me Sounds Great Live SG-5006; Mr. Music MMCD-7005; GVOC GVC 2005
What Is This Thing Called Love? (with MTM) Sounds Great Live SG-5012; Mr. Music MMCD-7006
Let's Fall in Love Sounds Great Live SG-5012; Mr. Music MMCD-7006.

The title on Sounds Great Live SG-5006 also on Jasmine JASM 2529 and JASMC 2529.

SESSION 480928 (Hollywood, 28th September 1948). Same.
The Money Song (with MTM) Sounds Great Live SG-5012; Mr. Music MMCD-7006; LaserLight 12223
Ah, But It Happens Sounds Great Live SG-5012; Mr. Music MMCD-7006
A Fine Romance (with JW) Sounds Great Live SG-5012; Mr. Music MMCD-7006; LaserLight 12223.

SESSION 481005 (Hollywood, 5th October 1948). Same.
Here I'll Stay Mr. Music MMCD-7005
I Get Along Without You Very Well Sounds Great Live SG-5012; Mr. Music MMCD-7006
How High the Moon Sounds Great Live SG-5012; Mr. Music MMCD-7006; Rhino R2 71589.

SESSION 481012 (Hollywood, 12th October 1948). Same.
You're the Top (with JW) Sounds Great Live SG-5006; Mr. Music MMCD-7005
On a Slow Boat to China Sounds Great Live SG-5006; Mr. Music MMCD-7005; GVOC GVC 2005.

The titles on Sounds Great Live SG-5006 also on Jasmine JASM 2529 and JASMC 2529.

SESSION 490001 (Los Angeles, circa 1949) **MEL TORMÉ** accompanied by Harry Sosnik and his Orchestra.
Because of You LaserLight 12222
Something's Gotta Give LaserLight 12222
Johnny One Note LaserLight 12222
Luck Be a Lady LaserLight 12222.

SESSION 490113 (Los Angeles, 13th January 1949) **MEL TORMÉ** with orchestra conducted by SONNY BURKE (personnel similar to the next session). Strings added on 3868 and 3869.
3866-4 **Do-Do-Do** (*Note 2*) Capitol F-/1177, CL13448, CDEMS 1447, 0777 7 99426 2 6, 0777 7 89941-2 1; MFP MFP1112
3867-1 **Goodbye** Capitol (*Note 4*). CDP 7243 8 31775-2 3, 72434-94749-0-1
3868-2 **She's a Home Girl** Capitol 15379, CL13131

3869-4 **There Isn't Any Special Reason** Capitol F-/54-583, 57-591, ST23869, CL13148.

Note 1: The take number for master 3869 is shown as -1 on the Capitol Performer's sheet but is -4 on the disc.

Note 2: Some of the titles listed above may have been made or remade at the next session.

Note 3: The notes to CDP 0777 7 89941-2 1, give this title as "previously unissued" but it is identical to the versions issued earlier.

Note 4: There was no 78 or 45 rpm issue of this title.

SESSION 490117 (Los Angeles, 17th January 1949) **MEL TORMÉ** with orchestra conducted by SONNY BURKE. Sonny Burke, leader and arranger; Ziggy Elman, Paul Geil, Ray Linn, George Seaberg, trumpets; Walter Benson, Francis Howard, Ed Kusby, Si Zentner, trombones; Skeets Herfurt, Harry Klee, Bob Lawson, Don Raffell, Babe Russin, reeds; Walter Weschler, piano; Barney Kessel, guitar; Larry Breen, bass; Alvin Stoller, drums.

3870-2 **Careless Hands** Capitol 15379, ST23869, ST24585, 72434-94749-0-1, CL13094, 0777 7 89941-2 1; Rhino R2 71589; Disky TC 885732; Read RC7-012-1

3871- **Stomping at the Savoy** (*Note 2*) Capitol ST23869, 0777 7 89941-2 1; Ranwood 8270-2; Read RC7-012-1

3872-5 **You're Getting to Be a Habit with Me** Capitol 54-583, 57-591, F-/1402, ST23869, 0777 7 89941-2 1, CL13123, CDEMS 1447, 0777 7 99426 2 6; MFP MFP1112, CDMFP6217, 7243 8 53503 2 0, CDDLD 1299, 7243 8 36547 2 7, CDMFP 6282, MFP 94349-2; Ranwood 8270-2; Disky TC 885732; Read RC7-012-1; Cdcard CD536.

Note 1: Some of the titles listed above may have been made originally at the previous session.

Note 2: There was no 78/45 rpm issue of this title.

SESSION 490221 (New York City, 21st February 1949) **MEL TORMÉ** with ORCHESTRA conducted by PETE RUGOLO. Personnel unknown but the instrumentation includes strings and French-horn.

3411-4 **Blue Moon** Capitol 15428, F-/1662, ST23368, ST23869, ST24585, 72434-94749-0-1, CL13123, EST23368, 0777 7 89941-2 1, CDEMS 1447, 0777 7 99426 2 6, CDP7-98478-2; MFP MFP1112, CDMFP6217, CDDLD 1299, 7243 8 36547 2 7, 7243 8 53503 2 0, 494 3502, 7243 4 94350 2 5; Rhino R2 71589; Ranwood 8270-2; Disky TC 885732; Read RC7-012-1; Cdcard CD537; St. Michael 9599 222

3412-5 **Again** Capitol 15428, ST23869, ST24585, 72434-94749-0-1, CL13094, CDEMS 1447, 0777 7 99426 2 6; MFP MFP1112, CDDLD 1299, 7243 8 36547 2 7; Rhino R2 71589; Disky TC 885732; Read RC7-012-1.

SESSION 490521 (Los Angeles, 21st May 1949) **MEL TORMÉ** with FRANK DEVOL AND HIS ORCHESTRA. Frank DeVol, leader and arranger; Ray Linn, Uan Rasey, Joe Triscari, trumpets; Francis Howard, Tommy Pederson, Collen Satterwhite, trombones; Huntington Burdick, French horn; Skeets Herfurt, Jerome Kasper, Jules Kinsler, Roland Pirozzi, Ernest (Ted) Romersa, woodwinds; June Weiland, harp; Arnold Ross, celeste; Barney Kessel, guitar; Harry Babasin, bass; Milt Holland, bongos and gong; unknown vocal group. Arrangements by Frank DeVol.

4476-3 **The Four Winds and the Seven Seas** Capitol 57-/54-671, ST23869, CL13148, 72434-94749-0-1, CDEMS 1447, 0777 7 99426 2 6; MFP MFP1112; Curb D2-77618; Rhino R2 71589; Disky TC 885732; Read RC7-012-1

4477-2 **It's Too Late Now** Capitol 57-/54-671, ST23869, CL13131, 0777 7 89941-2 1, CDEMS 1447, 0777 7 99426 2 6; Read RC7-012-1.

SESSION 490826 (Los Angeles, 26th August 1949) **MEL TORMÉ** accompanied by FRANK DEVOL AND HIS ORCHESTRA. Full personnel unknown but includes Arnold Ross, piano and Barney Kessel, guitar. A vocal group is present on 4916. Arrangements by DeVol.

4916-5 **The Meadows of Heaven** Capitol 57-/54-743, CL13232

4917-4 **Sonny Boy** Capitol 57-/54-743, ST23869, CL13232, CDP 0777 7 89941-2 1; MFP CDMFP6217, 7243 8 53503 2 0; Ranwood 8270-2

4918-8 **Oh, You Beautiful Doll** Capitol 57-/54-751, ST23869, CL13292, 0777 7 89941-2 1, CDEMS 1447, 0777 7 99426 2 6; MFP MFP1112, CDMFP6217, 7243 8 53503 2 0; Ranwood 8270-2; Disky TC 885732; Read RC7-012-1

4919-4 **There's a Broken Heart (For Every Light on Broadway)** Capitol 57-/54-751, ST23869, CL13292.

Note 1: Capitol 57-/54-751. This is also reported as 57-/54-752 but this is incorrect. 751 has also been listed as Frank DeVol's "Lotta Pizzicato"/"Southwest Territory."

SESSION 491021 (Los Angeles, 21st October 1949) **MEL TORMÉ with** FRANK DEVOL AND HIS ORCHESTRA (5176); and the Mel-Tones (MTM) with FRANK DEVOL AND HIS ORCHESTRA (5177). The personnels of the Mel-Tones and the orchestra are unknown but the Mel-Tones are probably the same as for the next session. Arrangements by DeVol.

5176- 6 **The Blossoms on the Bough** Capitol 57-/54-775, ST23869, CL13244

5177- 6 **Don't Do Something to Someone Else (That You Wouldn't Want Done to You)** (MTM) Capitol 57-/54-775, ST23869, CL13244.

SESSION 491024 (Hollywood, 24th October 1949) **DUCHESS OF IDAHO** (Film soundtrack) MEL TORMÉ with the M-G-M Studio Orchestra conducted by George Stoll. Arranged and orchestrated by Wally Hegin.

Warm Hands, Cold Heart (*note 1*) Rhino R2 75481.

Note 1: This is an outtake, i.e., it was not used in the released version of the film

SESSION 491101 (Los Angeles, November 1949) **MEL TORMÉ** with his Mel-Tones and Chorus. Orchestra conducted by Hal Mooney. Chorus conducted by Jud Conlon. The Mel-Tones are Loulie-Jean Norman, Ginny O'Connor, Bernie Parke and Les Baxter. Featured voices: the Easterner, "Susan Melton" (Peggy Lee); the 'Extra' Girl, Ginny O'Connor. Chorus: the Jud Conlon Rhythmaires and the Starlighters. Arrangements for Orchestra: Hal Mooney, Dick Jones, Paul Villepique, Neal Hefti and Billy May. Arrangements for the Mel-Tones: Mel Tormé. Arrangements for the Chorus: Jud Conlon. Orchestra personnel: Conrad Gozzo, Uan Rasey, George Seaberg, Joe Triscari, trumpets; Francis Howard, Ed Kusby, Si Zentner, trombones; Skeets Herfurt, alto-sax and clarinet; Jules Jacob, Jules Kinsler, Bob Lawson, alto- and tenor-saxes; Chuck Gentry, baritone-sax; Buddy Neal, piano; Allan Reuss, guitar; Phil Stephens, bass; Irv Cottler, drums; Ralph Hansell, vibes; plus strings.

The California Suite Capitol P200, LCT6004. Comprising:

5463 **Mountain Desert Theme** (instrumental), **The Golden West** (MT and Chorus), **We Think the West Coast Is the Best Coast:** Part 1 (MT and Chorus)

5464 **We Think the West Coast Is the Best Coast:** Part 2 (MT, PL, Mel-Tones and Chorus)

5465 **Coney Island** (PL) (*Note 1*), **The Miami Waltz** (PL)

5466 **They Go to San Diego** (*Note 3*) (MT & Mel-Tones)

5467 **Sunday Night in San Fernando** (MT & Chorus)

5468 Got the Gate on the Golden Gate (*Note 2*) (PL, MT & Mel-Tones)

5469 Prelude to "Poor Little 'Extra' Girl" (MT, GOC & Chorus)

5470 Poor Little "Extra" Girl (MT), **We Think the West Coast Is the Best Coast** (reprise) (PL, MT & Chorus), **Mountain Desert Theme** (closing) (Chorus).

Also issued in an album set of four 12-inch 78s with the catalog number EDD200 and a set of three 7-inch 45s with the catalog number KCF200. The complete suite also on Discovery DS-910. The four 78s are numbered 8-28004 to 8-28007 (with master numbers as above) and are auto-coupled so that side 1 is backed with side 8, 2 with 7, 3 with 6 and 4 with 5. The 45s are numbered 6F-28004 to 6F-28006 with master numbers 5470 to 5475 and are auto-coupled.

None of the individual titles is listed on the US Capitol issues which simply have "Mel Tormé's California Suite" sides 1 & 2 (on the LP) and sides 1 to 8 (on the 78s). The titles do, however, appear on the UK Capitol LP labels and on the Discovery labels and sleeve. The LPs are not banded into individual songs.

Note 1: This song arranged by Billy May.

Note 2: This song arranged by Neil Hefti and recorded 11th November 1949. Also issued on Capitol 72434-94749-0-1, Music for Pleasure CDMFP 6162, 7243 8 32763 2 5, Rhino R2 71589, Read RC7-012-1 and City Songs — San Francisco.

Note 3: This song also issued on City Songs — Southern California.

SESSION 491116 (Los Angeles, 16th November 1949) **PEGGY LEE AND MEL TORMÉ** with the Mellomen and Orchestral Accompaniment (*Note 1*).

5217-4 Bless You (For the Good That's in You) Capitol F-/ 791, CL13241

5218-3 The Old Master Painter Capitol F-/ 791, CL13241, ST23869, CDP 7 93195 2, 72434-94749-0-1, CDEMS 1447, 0777 7 99426 2 6; Disky TC 885732; Read RC7-012-1.

Note 1: The orchestra leader is given as Lou Busch on the Capitol log sheets. The notes for Capitol CDEMS 1447/ 0777 7 99426 2 6 credit Lou Busch as the orchestra leader but the notes for Capitol CDP 7 93195 2 mistakenly give the leader as Dave Barbour. The vocal group is wrongly credited in the notes of CDEMS 1447/ 0777 7 99426 2 6 as the Mellow Men.

SESSION 491219 (Los Angeles, 19th December 1949 [*Note 1*]) **MEL TORMÉ** with the Mel-Tones (MTM) with orchestra conducted by Harold Mooney (master 5324 only) or, orchestra conducted by Harold Mooney. Mel-Tones personnel probably the same as last entry. Orchestra personnel: Harold Mooney, leader and arrangements; Uan Rasey, Joe Triscari, Zeke Zarchy, trumpets; Karl Loeffler, Bill Schaefer, Si Zentner, trombones; Gus Bivona, Mort Friedman, Alex Gershunoff, Harry Schuchman, saxes; Milt Raskin, piano; George Van Eps, guitar; John Ryan, bass; Alvin Stoller, drums. Strings added on 5324.

5324-7 I Hadn't Anyone Till You (MTM) (*Note 2*) Capitol F-/ 880, ST23869, CL13291, CDEMS 1447, 0777 7 99426 2 6, 0777 7 89941-2 1; MFP CDMFP6217, 7243 8 53503 2 0; Read RC7-012-1

5325-6 The Queen of Hearts Is Missing Capitol F-/ 825, CL13322

5326- Geordie Capitol unissued

5327-7 Cross Your Heart Capitol F-/ 880, ST23869; Rhino R2 71589; Read RC7-012-1

5328-4 There's an "X" in the Middle of Texas Capitol F-/ 825.

Note 1: The recording date for this session has also been given as 6th March 1950 but the December date is confirmed by the Capitol log sheets.

Note 2: The take for master 5324 is shown as -2 on the Capitol Performer's sheet but is -7 on the disc.

SESSION 500331 (New York City, 31st March 1950) **MEL TORMÉ** with Pete Rugolo and his Orchestra and vocal group. The vocal group is the Dave Lambert Octet. The same personnel as for the next session. The titles made at the next session (3rd April 1950) are reported to have been originally recorded but rejected at this session. The March session is not listed in the Capitol files.

SESSION 500403 (New York City, 3rd April 1950) **MEL TORMÉ** with Pete Rugolo and his Orchestra and vocal group. The vocal group is the Dave Lambert Octet (DLO) Pete Rugolo, leader and arrangements; Tony Faso, Louis Mucci, trumpets; Kai Winding, trombone; Al Richman, French horn; Eddie Brown, Sid Cooper, Mannie Thaler, Milt Yaner, woodwinds; Tom Alonje, Maurice Brown, Stank Karpenia, Leo Kruczek, Morris Lefkowitz, Ray Sabinsky, Phil Soloman, Lew Stone, Sandor Szatmert, George Zornig, strings; Teddy Napoleon, piano; Barry Galbraith, guitar; Eddie Safranski, bass; Mel Zelnick, drums. The personnel of the vocal group is unknown but will include Dave Lambert.

5707 **Skylark** Capitol F-/ 1291, CL13851, CDEMS 1447, 0777 7 99426 2 6, 0777 7 89941-2 1; MFP MFP1112, CDMFP6217, 7243 8 53503 2 0, CDDL 1230, 0 777 7 80615 2 6; Ranwood 8270-2; Read RC7-012-1

5708 **Lullaby of the Leaves** (DLO) Capitol F-/ 1291, CL13675, CDEMS 1447, 0777 7 99426 2 6, 0777 7 89941-2 1; MFP MFP1112; Disky TC 885732; Read RC7-012-1

5709-5 **The Piccolino** (DLO) Capitol F-/ 1000, CL13291; MFP MFP1112, CDMFP6217, 7243 8 53503 2 0

5710-2 **Bewitched** (DLO) Capitol F-/ 1000, F-/ 1662, CL13322, 72434-94749-0-1, CDEMS 1447, 0777 7 99426 2 6, 0777 7 89941-2 1; Rhino R2 71589; Ranwood 8270-2; MFP CDMFP6217, 7243 8 53503 2 0, CDDL 1236, 0777 7 80618 2 3, CDDLD 1299, 7243 8 36547 2 7; Disky TC 885732; Read RC7-012-1; Cdcard CD538.

Note 1: The date of 5709 and 5710 has also been reported as 4th April 1950 but the 3rd is given on the Capitol log sheets.

Note 2: A two or three second excerpt from "Bewitched" is used to introduce the biography narrated by Jack Perkins on Capitol 72434-94749-0-1.

SESSION 500811 (New York City, 11th August 1950) **MEL TORMÉ** accompanied by Orchestra conducted by Pete Rugolo with (MTM) the Mel-Tones.

6378-6 **Recipe for Romance** (MTM) Capitol F-/ 1177, CL13448, 0777 7 89941-2 1; MFP CDMFP 6217, 7243 8 53503 2 0

6379- **Just in Case We Have to Say Goodbye** Capitol unissued

6365-5 **I Owe a Kiss to a Girl in Iowa** Capitol F-/ 1237

6495-5 **Say No More** Capitol F-/ 1237.

Note 1: The date for the last two titles has also been given as 20th August but the Capitol log gives the 11th. There is no explanation of the discontinuity in the master number sequence.

SESSION 500824 (Los Angeles, 23rd and 24th August 1950) **MEL TORMÉ** Accompanied by Al Pellegrini, piano; Vincent Terri, guitar; Phil Stephens, bass; Irma Louise Clow, harp. On 1001, Tormé, plays brushes on a single snare drum.

1001 **April Showers** Camay CA-3034-S

1002 **Trouble Is a Girl** Camay CA-3034-S

1003 **Blue Room** Camay CA-3034-S

1004 **You're Driving Me Crazy** Camay CA-3034-S

1005 **You Ought to Be in Pictures**
Camay CA-3036-A

Note 1: These tracks were made as Snader film transcriptions for use on television. The visual material was filmed on the afternoon of the 23rd August and in the morning of the 24th August. The soundtracks were made on the afternoon of the 24th.

Note 2: All the tracks are available on Swingtime Video (US)— catalog number untraced. Tracks 1001, 1002, 1004 & 1005 are on Charly Video (UK) VID JAM 18 and tracks 1001, 1003, 1004 & 1005 are on MCEC Virgin Storyville (UK) VVD757.

Note 3: The Camay LP comes with different sleeves for mono (CA-3034) and stereo (CA-3034-S) and the LPs have, correspondingly, stampers CA-3040 A and B mono or A and B stereo in the wax but the labels have CA-3034-S whether they are on mono records or on stereo ones.

SESSION 500831 (Los Angeles, 31st August 1950) **MEL TORMÉ** Accompanied by the Red Norvo Trio (Norvo, vibes and piano; Tal Farlow, guitar; Charles Mingus, bass).

6553-3 **I've Got a Feeling I'm Falling** Capitol CDEMS 1447, 0777 7 99426 2 6, 0777 7 89941-2 1; MFP CDMFP6217, 7243 8 53503 2 0; Disky TC 885732; Read RC7-012-1

6566-7 **The Carioca** Capitol CDEMS 1447, 0777 7 99426 2 6

6567-1 **On a Little Street in Singapore** Capitol CDEMS 1447, 0777 7 99426 2 6; Disky TC 885732

6568- **I Like to Recognize the Tune** Capitol CDEMS 1447, 0777 7 99426 2 6; 7243 8 29384 2 2; 72434-94749-0-1.

Note 1: These four titles were not issued in 78 or 45 rpm form.

Note 2: The Capitol log shows all the titles were recorded on the same day and there is no explanation for the discontinuity in the master number sequence.

SESSION 510105 (Los Angeles, 5th January 1951) **MEL TORMÉ** with orchestra conducted by Pete Rugolo.

6977-1 **Around the World** Capitol F-/ 1383, CL13495; Ranwood 8270-2

6978-5 **The Sidewalk Shufflers** Capitol F-/ 1383, CL13495

6979 **A Lonesome Cup of Coffee** (Note 1) Capitol 72434-94749-0-1

6980-7 **Sailin' Away on the Henry Clay** Capitol F-/ 1402.

Note 1: There was no 78/45 rpm issue of this title.

SESSION 510201 (Los Angeles, 1st February 1951) **MEL TORMÉ** with orchestra conducted by Pete Rugolo.

7051 **Come Out Singing** Capitol unissued.

SESSION 510409A (New York City, 9th April 1951) **MEL TORMÉ** with Orchestra conducted by Joe Lipman (*Note 1*). Chris Griffin, Dale McMickle, Louis Mucci, trumpets; Lou McGarity, Buddy Morrow, Billy Rauch, trombones; Ed Beck, Bernie Kaufman, Toots Mondello, Stan Webb, reeds; Al Pellegrini, piano; Bob Haggart, bass; Bunny Shawker, drums.

6291-2 **Who Sends You Orchids?** Capitol F-/ 1598

6292-3 **(I'm Sending You a) Bundle of Love** Capitol F-/ 1524.

Note 1: The name of this musician has been given as Lippman but Lipman is correct.

SESSION 510409B (New York City, 9th April 1951) **MEL TORMÉ** with Orchestra conducted by Sid Feller same or similar personnel to previous session.

6293-4 **The World Is Your Balloon** Capitol F-/ 1524

6294-2 **You Locked My Heart** Capitol F-/ 1598, CL13591.

SESSION 510626 (New York City, 26th

June 1951) **MEL TORMÉ** with Orchestra and Chorus conducted by Nelson Riddle. Includes strings on 7272/7273.

7272 **The One for Me** Capitol F-/ 1712

7273 **Love Is Such a Cheat (The Gypsy Song)** Capitol F-/ 1712, 72434-94749-0-1, CL13591

7274 **My Buddy** Capitol F-/ 1761, CDEMS 1447, 0777 7 99426 2 6, 0777 7 89941-2 1, CDP 7243 8 31774-2 4; Ranwood 8270-2; Disky TC 885732; Read RC7-012-1

7275 **Take My Heart** Capitol F-/ 1761.

SESSION 510710 (New York City, 10th July 1951) **PEGGY LEE AND MEL TORMÉ** with Orchestra Conducted by Sid Feller. Buck Clayton, Bernie Privin, trumpets; Buddy Morrow, Lou McGarity, Warren Covington, trombones; Joe Lewis, piano; Barry Galbraith, guitar; Joe Shulman, bass; Billy Exiner, drums.

7294 **Don't Fan the Flame** Capitol F-/ 1738, CL13609, CDEMS 1447, 0777 7 99426 2 6; Disky TC 885732

7295 **Telling Me Yes, Telling Me No** Capitol F-/ 1738.

SESSION 511004 (New York City, 4th October 1951) **MEL TORMÉ** at the Piano with Instrumental Accompaniment Mel Tormé, vocal and piano, accompanied by Howard Roberts, guitar; Clyde Lombardi, bass; Bunny Shawker, drums.

7735 **You're a Heavenly Thing** Capitol F-/ 1864, CL13675, CDEMS 1447, 0777 7 99426 2 6, 0777 7 89941-2 1; MFP MFP1112; Read RC7-012-1

7736 **Heart and Soul** (*Note 1*) Capitol CDEMS 1447, 0777 7 99426 2 6, 0777 7 89941-2 1, 7243 8 32592 2 9; Ranwood 8270-2; Disky TC 885732; Read RC7-012-1; Cdcard CD539.

Note 1: there was no 78/45 rpm issue of this title.

SESSION 511015 (New York City, 15th October 1951) **MEL TORMÉ** at the Piano with Instrumental Accompaniment. Mel Tormé, vocal and piano, accompanied by Mary Osborne, guitar; Clyde Lombardi, bass; Bunny Shawker, drums.

7749 **I Love Each Move You Make** (*Note 1*) Capitol 0777 7 89941-2 1; Read RC7-012-1

7750 **Foolish Little Rumors** Capitol F-/ 1864.

Note 1: There was no 78/45 rpm issue of this title.

SESSION 520513 (Los Angeles, 15th May 1952) **MEL TORMÉ** with vocal group and orchestra conducted by Harold Mooney. Omit the vocal group on 10175/10176.

10108 **A Stranger in Town** Capitol F-/ 2529, CDEMS 1447 0777 7 99426 2 6; Curb D2-77618; Disky TC 885732; Read RC7-012-1

10109 **Don't Leave Me** Capitol F-/ 2131

10110 **Around the Corner** Capitol unissued

10175 **It Made You Happy When You Made Me Cry** Capitol F-/ 2529

10176 **Black Moonlight** Capitol F-/ 2131, CL13851; MFP MFP1112, CDMFP6217, 7243 8 53503 2 0.

Note 1: All five titles are from the one session despite the gap in the master sequence. The recording date has also been given as the 13th of May.

SESSION 520926 (New York City, 26th September 1952) **MEL TORMÉ** with chorus (*Note 1*) and orchestra conducted by Al Pellegrini.

20046 **Anywhere I Wander** Capitol F-/ 2263, 72434-94749-0-1, CL13837; Ranwood 8270-2; Read RC7-012-1

20047 **Shenandoah Valley** Capitol (*Note 2*); Ranwood 8270-2

20048 **Casually** Capitol F-/ 2263, CL13837.

Note 1: The chorus has been reported to be the

Jud Conlon Singers but this is unlikely if the session took place in New York City.

Note 2: There is no Capitol issue of this title.

1953–1954 Coral

SESSION 531001 (New York City, 1st October 1953) MEL TORMÉ with Orchestra and Chorus directed by Neal Hefti.

85292 T3A **Just One More Chance** Coral 9-/ 61136, CRL57044

85293 T1A **The Anything Can Happen Mambo** Coral 9-/ 61136; Music Club MCCD 198, MCTC 198

85294 A1 **Blue Skies** Coral 9-/ 61089, CRL57044; Decca DL75188; MCA Coral CDL-8016

85295 A1 **Oo-Ya-Ya** Coral 9-/ 61089.

Note 1: The two titles on Coral CRL57044, are also on Vocalian VL73905, VgCrl LVA9032 and Jasmine JASM1004.

SESSION 531231 (New York City, unknown date) MEL TORMÉ with Sy Oliver and his Orchestra.

Yes Indeed Coral untraced/unissued.

Note 1: This recording is listed in Tormé's autobiography but I have found no trace of it. It is not listed in the Decca NYC log. I wonder if it has been listed as the result of a faulty recollection of the Verve version (9th March 1961), which is not listed in the autobiography although it was certainly recorded and issued.

SESSION 540802 (Los Angeles, 2nd August 1954) MEL TORMÉ with Orchestra directed by George Cates. George Cates, leader; Johnny Best, Conrad Gozzo, Manny Klein or Shorty Sherock, trumpets; Ed Kusby, Lloyd Ulyate, (Note 2), trombones; Georgie Auld, Benny Carter, Matty Matlock, Babe Russin, reeds; Al Pellegrini, piano; Allan Reuss, guitar; Joe Comfort, bass; Nick Fatool or Alvin Stoller, drums. Arrangers: 7770 & 7771, Benny Carter, others unknown.

L7770 **Tutti Frutti** Coral CRL57044, 9-/ 61263

L7771 **It Don't Mean a Thing** Coral CRL57044, 9-/ 61452; VgCrl Q72202; Rhino R2 71589; Capitol 72434-94749-0-1

L7772 **Rose O'Day** Coral CRL57044, 9-/ 61452; Music Club MCCD 198, MCTC 198

L7773 **Hold Tight** Coral CRL57044; Music Club MCCD 198, MCTC 198

L7774 **I'se a Muggin'** Coral CRL57044, 9-/ 61263.

Note 1: The five titles on Coral CRL57044 are also on VgCrl LVA9032, Jasmine JASM1004 and Coral MVCM-275. All except L7774 are also on Vocalian VL73905.

Note 2: The notes for the Rhino issue of L7771, include "Ted Vesely, unknown (instrument)" in the personnel but Vesely was a well-known trombonist and is likely to play that instrument here.

Note 3: Vogue Coral Q72202 issued on both 78 and 45 rpm.

SESSION 540803 (Los Angeles, 3rd August 1954) MEL TORMÉ with Orchestra directed by (GC) George Cates or (SB) Sonny Burke same personnel as last. Arrangers, 7775, Billy May, others unknown.

L7775 **All of You** (GC) Coral CRL57044, 9-/ 61294; VgCrlQ72202; Music Club MCCD 198, MCTC 198; Rhino R2 71589; Crimson CRIMIDCD11

L7776 **Spellbound** (GC) Coral CRL57044, 9-/ 61294; Music Club MCCD 198, MCTC 198

L7777 **Cement Mixer** (SB) Coral CRL57044

L7778 **The Flat Foot Floogie** (SB) Coral CRL57044

L7779 **The Hut-Sut Song** (GC) Coral

CRL57044; Music Club MCCD 198, MCTC 198.

Note 1: The five titles on Coral CRL57044 are also on VgCrl LVA9032, Jasmine JASM1004 and Coral MVCM-275. All except L7778 are also on Vocalian VL73905.

Note 2: Vogue Coral Q72202 issued on both 78 and 45 rpm.

SESSION 541201 (Hollywood, circa December 1954) **JERRY GRAY AND HIS BAND OF THE DAY with MEL TORMÉ.** Jerry Gray, leader; with a personnel including Graham Young, Carlton McBeath, Whitney Thomas, trumpets; Jimmy Priddy, John Halliburton, Bob Fitzpatrick, trombones; Joe Estren, clarinet & alto-sax; Riley Weston, alto-sax; Jack Montrose, Ronny Perry, tenor-saxes; Jack Du Long, baritone-sax; Marty Paich, piano; John Mosher, bass; Jimmy Pratt, drums; Mel Tormé, vocals. Compere, Jimmy Wallington.

    Theme — **Desert Serenade** Magic DAWE85

    You Ought to Be in Pictures (vcl MT) Magic DAWE85

    Interview (Wallington with Tormé) Magic DAWE85

    All of You (vcl MT) Magic DAWE85

    Coronado Cruise Magic DAWE85

    I Cover the Waterfront (vcl MT) Magic DAWE85

    Theme — **Desert Serenade** Magic DAWE85.

Note 1: These are taken from a 15-minute US Navy recruiting radio program: Stand by for Music, Program No. 17.

Note 2: Johnny Best, trumpet; Paul Tanner, trombone; Jack Ferrier, tenor-sax; have also been suggested as members of the orchestra but Best and Tanner had definitely left the band by the time of this session.

SESSION 541215 (The Crescendo Club, Los Angeles, 15th December 1954)

MEL TORMÉ with the Al Pellegrini Trio. Mel Tormé, vocal and * piano; Al Pellegrini, # piano or $ clarinet; James Dupre, bass; Richard Shanahan, drums or % bongos.

87592 # **From This Moment On** Coral CRL57012; VgCrl FEP2028?; MCA GRP-16172, MCBD 19533

    # **September Song** MCA GRP-16172; MCA GRP 97482

87593 # **That Old Black Magic** Coral CRL57012; VgCrl Q72159, FEP2026; MCA GRP-16172; Music Club MCCD 198, MCTC 198; Rhino R2 71589

87594 *$% **Get Out of Town** Coral CRL57012; VgCrl FEP2026; MCA GRP-16172, MCBD 19533

    *$ **My Shining Hour** MCA GRP-16172

87595 *$ **Goody Goody** Coral CRL57012, 9-/ 61507; VgCrl FEP2026, Q72185; MCA GRP-16172, MCLD 19235; Rhino R2 71589

87601 *$ **County Fair** Coral CRL57012; VgCrl FEP2028; MCA GRP-16172; Music Club MCCD 198, MCTC 198

87602 *$ **The Christmas Song** Coral CRL57012, CRL57355; VgCrl FEP2028; MCA GRP-16172; Music Club MCCD 198, MCTC 198

    # **A Stranger in Town** MCA GRP-16172

    *$ **I Wish I Were in Love Again** MCA GRP-16172

    # **Moonlight in Vermont** MCA GRP-16172

87605 *$ **Bernie's Tune** Coral CRL57012, 9-/ 61709; VgCrl FEP2027; MCA GRP-16172; Rhino R2 71589

87596 *$ **(Our) Love Is Here to Stay** Coral CRL57012; VgCrl FEP2026, Q72185; MCA GRP-16172

87598 *$% **(That) Old Devil Moon** Coral CRL57012; VgCrl FEP2027 MCA GRP-16172

87597 # **Blue Moon** Coral CRL57012, EP94075; VgCrl Q72159; MCA GRP-16172; Music Club MCCD 198, MCTC 198

    # **Have You Met Miss Jones?** MCA GRP-16172

87603 *$ **Jeepers Creepers** Coral CRL57012, 9-/ 61507; VgCrl Q72150, FEP2028; MCA GRP-16172, MCLD 19232

87600 # **Mountain Greenery** Coral CRL57012, CRL57228, 9-/ 61709, EP94075; VgCrl FEP2027, LVA9060, Q72150; MCA GRP-16172; Music Club MCCD 198, MCTC 198; Rhino R2 71589

Imagination MCA GRP-16172

87599 # **Get Happy** Coral CRL57012; VgCrl FEP2027; MCA GRP-16172

87604 # **You're Driving Me Crazy** Coral CRL57012; VgCrl FEP2027; Music Club MCCD 198, MCTC 198.

Note 1: The fourteen titles on Coral CRL57012 are also on VgCrl LVA9004. All fourteen except 87602 are also on Coral CP40 and MCA MCL1683. All the issued titles from MCA GRP-16172 plus 87604 are also on Coral MVCM-274.

Note 2: only the titles issued on the Coral album were allocated master numbers.

Note 3: the Vogue Coral singles (Q72000 series) were issued on both 78 and 45 rpm.

550112 (Los Angeles, 12th January 1955) MEL TORMÉ AND THE MEL-TONES with Orchestra arranged and conducted by George Cates.

L8911 **How** Coral 9-/ 61588; VgCrl Q72217

L8912 **My Rosemarie** Coral 9-/ 61588; VgCrl Q72217; Music Club MCCD 198, MCTC 198.

Both titles also on AFR & tvS P6443.
Note 2.411: Vogue Coral Q72217 was issued on both 78 and 45 rpm.

550301 (Los Angeles, circa 1955) MEL TORMÉ with the Buzz Adlam Orchestra.
You Ought to Be in Pictures LaserLight 12222
I Hadn't Anyone Till You LaserLight 12222
Baby, Don't You Go 'Way Mad LaserLight 12223
Isn't It a Lovely Day LaserLight 12224
You're the Cream in My Coffee LaserLight 12224.

Note 1: These are almost certainly from a broadcast.

1955–1957 Bethlehem, Decca (UK), Philips (UK) & Tops

550302 Los Angeles, circa 1955 THESE DESPERATE HOURS. MEL TORMÉ with Orchestra conducted by Marty Paich.
These Desperate Hours Rhino R2 75481.
This was taken from the soundtrack of a promotion for the film "These Desperate Hours".

SESSION 550828 (Los Angeles, 28th, 29th & 30th August 1955) MEL TORMÉ Orchestra conducted by Al Pellegrini. A collective personnel for the orchestra over the three days is: Frank Beach, trumpet; John Cave, French horn; Harry Klee, Eddie Rosa, Ethmer Roten, Wilbur Schwartz, flutes; Chuck Gentry or Bill Ulyate, bass clarinet; Cheryll Butterman or Corky Hale, harp; Marty Paich, piano & celeste; Al Hendrickson, guitar; Monty Budwig or Red Mitchell, bass; Irv Cottler drums and percussion; Israel Baker, Anatol Kaminsky, Marvin Limonick, Eudice Shapiro, Paul Shure, Felix Slatkin, violins; Virginia Majewski, viola; Kurt Reher or Eleanor Slatkin, cello; The normal instrumentation on these sessions included only two flutes and five strings. Arrangers: 1: Marty Paich; 2: Sandy Courage; 3: Andre Previn; 4: Al Pellegrini; 5: Russell Garcia; 6: Hal Mooney.

I Got It Bad and That Ain't Good (1) Bethlehem BCP34; Rhino R2 71589
Till the Clouds Roll By (2) Bethlehem BCP34
Isn't It Romantic (3) Bethlehem BCP34; Rhino R2 71589

I Know Why (4) Bethlehem BCP34; Parlophone GEP8773
You Leave Me Breathless (3) Bethlehem BCP34; Parlophone GEP8773
Stay As Sweet As You Are (5) Bethlehem BCP34; Parlophone GEP8773
All This and Heaven Too (1) Bethlehem BCP34; Parlophone GEP8773; Rhino R2 71589
How Long Has This Been Going On (3) Bethlehem BCP34
Polka Dots and Moonbeams (5) (Note 3) Bethlehem BCP34; Prism PLAC 467, PLATCD 467
I Found a Million Dollar Baby (3) Bethlehem BCP34
Wonderful One (5) Bethlehem BCP34
It's a Blue World (6) Bethlehem BCP34; Prism PLAC 466, PLATCD 466.

Note 1: All the titles on Bethlehem BCP34 also on Bethlehem BR-5015/BCP-34 (CD), London HAN2016, Affinity AFF138, and Charly CDGR 135.
Note 2: All the titles on Bethlehem BCP34 are also on a CD in the 3 CD set Rhino/Avenue Jazz 75961.
Note 3: The Prism issues of this tune are labeled as "Polka Dust and Moonbeams".

SESSION 551129 (Concert, City Hall, Brisbane, Queensland, Australia 29th November 1955) **MEL TORMÉ** accompanied by an orchestra.
Walking My Baby Back Home Kingfisher STAR-23
It's a Blue World Kingfisher STAR-23
Love Walked In Kingfisher STAR-23.

Note 1: These are taken from the Ford Radio Show. Date from Peter Burgis of Kingfisher Cassettes.
Note 2: The director of the orchestra is probably Al Pellegrini or, less likely, Bob Gibson.

SESSION 560116 (Los Angeles, 16th, 18th & 20th January 1956) **MEL TORMÉ** accompanied by the Marty Paich Dek-tette. Collective personnel for the Dek-tette over the three days is: Pete Candoli, Don Fagerquist, trumpet; Bob Enevoldsen, valve-trombone; Vince De Rosa or John Cave, French horn; Bud Shank, alto-sax; Bob Cooper or Jack Montrose, tenor-sax; Jack du Long, baritone-sax; Red Mitchell, bass; Albert Pollan, tuba; Mel Lewis, drums; Marty Paich, leader, arranger, piano.
Lulu's Back in Town Bethlehem BCP52, 45-11008; Parlophone GEP8790; London HLN8305, EZ-N19039; Rhino R2 71589; Charly CDGR 200-2
Lullaby of Birdland Bethlehem BCP52; London HLN8322, EZ-N19039; Rhino R2 71589
The Lady Is a Tramp Bethlehem BCP52; Parlophone GEP8790; London HLN8305; Rhino R2 71589; MFP CDMFP6217, 7243 8 53503 2 0
The Carioca Bethlehem BCP52; Parlophone GEP8790; London EZ-N19039; Rhino R2 71589
I Like to Recognize the Tune Bethlehem BCP52
Fascinating Rhythm Bethlehem BCP52; London EZ-N19039; Rhino R2 71589
I Love to Watch the Moonlight Bethlehem BCP52; London HLN8322
When the Sun Comes Out Bethlehem BCP52
The Blues Bethlehem BCP52; Rhino R2 71589
Keeping Myself for You Bethlehem BCP52, 45-11008
When April Comes Again Bethlehem BCP52
Sing for Your Supper Bethlehem BCP52.

Note 1: All the titles on Bethlehem BCP52 also on Bethlehem BCP-6042, BR-5007/BCP-52 (CD), London LTZ-N15009, Polydor 545110, Affinity AFF85, CDCHARLY 5, Avenue Jazz R2 75732.
Note 2: All the titles on Bethlehem BCP52 are also on a CD in the 3 CD set Rhino/Avenue Jazz 75961.

Note 3: The London singles (HLN 8000 series) were issued on both 78 and 45 rpm.

SESSION 560501 (Hollywood, May 1956) **PORGY AND BESS** This is a recording of the opera *Porgy and Bess* with Mel Tormé taking the part of Porgy. The accompaniment to Tormé's musical items is normally by the Bethlehem Orchestra but on one item, he is accompanied by the Stan Levey Quartet (Howard McGhee, trumpet; Ralph Sharon, piano; Max Bennett, bass; Stan Levey, drums). A vocal group, the Pat Moran Quartet (Pat Moran, John Doling, Bev Kelly, John Whited), is heard on some items. The collective personnel for the Bethlehem Orchestra is Maynard Ferguson, Ray Linn, Frank Beach, Buddy Childers, Uan Rasey, Howard McGhee, Don Fagerquist, trumpets; Tommy Pederson, Lloyd Ulyate, Joe Howard, Herbie Harper, Frank Rosolino, Bob Enevoldsen, trombones; Sam Most, flute; Bill Holman, tenor-sax & clarinet; Claude Williamson, Ralph Sharon, piano; Alvin Stoller, Irv Kluger, vibes, typani and drums; Stan Levey, drums; John Cave, Vince DeRosa, French horns; Albert Pollan, tuba; Felix Slatkin, Irma Neumann, Erno Neufelf, Eudice Shapiro, Paul Shure, Marvin Limonick, Israel Baker, Marshall Sosson, Gerald Vinci, Nathan Ross, violins; Alvin Dinkin, Paul Robyn, viola; Eleanor Slatkin, cello. Russ Garcia, leader and arranger.

MEL TORMÉ with FRANCES FAYE (ff), GEORGE KIRBY (gk), LOULIE-JEAN NORMAN (ljn), THE PAT MORAN QUARTET (pmq), the Bethlehem Chorus (tbc) and the Bethlehem Orchestra (arranged and conducted by Russell Garcia) or Stan Levey Quartet (slq).

Porgy's Return from Begging Bethlehem EXLP-1
They Pass by Singing Bethlehem EXLP-1
Overflow (tbc) (*Note 2*) Bethlehem EXLP-1
I Can't Puzzle This Thing Out Bethlehem EXLP-1
I Got Plenty of Nothing (tbc, slq) (*Notes 2, 3 & 4*) Bethlehem EXLP-1
The Divorce Scene (ff, gk, pmq) (*Notes 1 & 2*) Bethlehem EXLP-1
The Buzzard Song Bethlehem EXLP-1
Bess, You Is My Woman Now (ff) (*Notes 2, 3 & 5*) Bethlehem EXLP-1
I Want to Stay Here/I Love You Porgy (ff) (*Notes 2 & 3*) Bethlehem EXLP-1
Oh Lawd, What Am I Gonna Do (ff, gk, pmq) Bethlehem EXLP-1
Bess, Oh Where's My Bess (ljn) (*Notes 2 & 3*) Bethlehem EXLP-1
Oh Lawd, I'm on My Way (*Notes 2, 3 & 6*) Bethlehem EXLP-1.

Only those tracks that involve Tormé are given above (including those where he only speaks). The full content of the work is given in Part 3.3 under Bethlehem EXLP-1.

Note 1: "The Divorce Scene" is sometimes called "The Law Scene".

Note 2: Also on Bethlehem BCP-6009.

Note 3: Also on Bethlehem BCP6040, BR-5004/BCP-6040 (CD), and Ember CEL900.

Note 4: Also on Bethlehem BCP6031, BX4015, Parlophone PMC1114 and Rhino R2 71589. This track recorded on 8th May 1956.

Note 5: These titles are also on Bethlehem EXLP-1-SP (a single 10-inch LP).

Note 6: Also on Ember SE8000.

Note 7: Bethlehem EXLP-1 is a three record set.

Note 8: All the material on EXLP-1 also on Bethlehem 3BP-1 (3 LP set) & BR-5014-2/EXLP-1 (2 CD set). The insert of the CD set shows the catalog number as BR-5014-3/EXLP-1.

Note 9: All the material from EXLP-1 also on Avenue Jazz 75828 with alternative titling: Porgy's Return From Begging as Evenin' Ladies, Hello Boys. / No, No,

Brother, Porgy Ain't Soft on No Woman / The Divorce Scene as Mornin', Lawyer, Looking for Somebody? / I Want to Stay Here as Porgy, I Hates to Go.

SESSION 560921 (London, 21st September 1956) **MEL TORMÉ** with **TED HEATH AND HIS MUSIC**. Bobby Pratt, Bert Ezzard, Duncan Campbell, Eddie Blair, trumpets; Wally Smith, Don Lusher, Ric Kennedy, Ted Heath, trombones; Les Gilbert, Ronnie Chamberlain, alto-sax; Henry Mackenzie, tenor-sax and clarinet; Red Price, tenor-sax; Ken Kiddier, baritone-sax; Frank Horrox, piano; Johnny Hawksworth, bass; Ronnie Verrell, drums.

DR 22457-T1 **Walkin' Shoes** Decca F10800, 45F10800, DFE6384, DPA3078; London 1699; Eclipse 820 642-2

DR 22458-T1 **The Cuckoo in the Clock** Decca F10800, 45F10800, DFE6384; London 1699; Eclipse 820 642-2.

Note 1: Decca used a DRX prefix for 78 rpm stampers and DRF for 45 rpm stampers.

SESSION 560922 (London, 22nd September 1956) **MEL TORMÉ** with **CYRIL STAPLETON AND HIS ORCHESTRA**.

DR 22459 **Shenandoah Valley** Decca DFE6384; London 1700; Eclipse 820 642-2

DR 22460 **Hooray for Love** Decca DFE6384; London 1700; Eclipse 820 642-2.

SESSION 560924 (London, 24th September 1956) **MEL TORMÉ** with **THE ROLAND SHAW ORCHESTRA**.

DR 22461-T1 **Waltz for Young Lovers** Decca F10809, 45F10809; London 1701; Eclipse 820 642-2

DR 22462-T1 **I Don't Want to Walk Without You** Decca F10809, 45F10809; London 1701; Eclipse 820 642-2.

Note 1: Decca used a DRX prefix for 78 rpm stampers and DRF for 45 rpm stampers.

SESSION 561101 (Los Angeles, 10th & 11th November 1956) **MEL TORMÉ** accompanied by the Marty Paich Dek-tette Pete Candoli, Don Fagerquist, trumpets; Bob Enevoldsen, valve-trombone and tenor-sax; Vince De Rosa, French horn; Herb Geller, alto-sax; Jack Montrose, tenor-sax; Jack du Long, baritone-sax; Max Bennett, bass; Albert Pollan, tuba; Alvin Stoller, drums & percussion; Marty Paich, leader, arranger and possibly piano.

A Foggy Day Bethlehem BCP6013; London EZ-N19027; Rhino R2 71589

Nice Work If You Can Get It Bethlehem BCP6013; Parlophone GEP8830; London EZ-N19027; Rhino R2 71589; Crimson CRIMIDCD11

The Way You Look Tonight Bethlehem BCP6013; Parlophone GEP8830; London EZ-N10927; Rhino R2 71589

A Fine Romance Bethlehem BCP6013; London EZ-N19027

Cheek to Cheek Bethlehem BCP6013; London EZ-N19028; Rhino R2 71589

Something's Gotta Give Bethlehem BCP6013; Parlophone GEP8830; London EZ-N19028; Rhino R2 71589

Let's Call the Whole Thing Off Bethlehem BCP6013; London EZ-N19028

They Can't Take That Away from Me Bethlehem BCP6013; London EZ-N19028

Top Hat, White Tie and Tails Bethlehem BCP6013

The Piccolino Bethlehem BCP6013

Let's Face the Music and Dance Bethlehem BCP6013; Parlophone GEP8830

They All Laughed Bethlehem BCP6013.

Note 1: All the titles on Bethlehem BCP6013 also on Bethlehem BCP-6022, BR-5003/BCP6013 (CD), 30082 (shown as 20-30082 on the insert of the CD), London LTZ-N15076, Affinity AFF107, TCAFF 107 and Affinity CDCHARLY 96.

Note 2: All the titles on Bethlehem BCP6013 are also on a CD in the 3 CD set Rhino/Avenue Jazz 75961.

SESSION 561201 (Los Angeles, 1956-57) **MEL TORMÉ** with the Marty Paich

Dektette. Personnel uncertain but probably Pete Candoli, Don Fagerquist, trumpets; Bob Enevoldsen, valve-trombone; Vince De Rosa or John Cave, French horn; Bud Shank, alto-sax and flute; Bob Cooper or Jack Montrose, tenor-sax; Jack du Long, baritone-sax; Red Mitchell, bass; Albert Pollan, tuba; Mel Lewis, drums & percussion; Marty Paich, leader, arranger and sometimes piano.

Lulu's Back in Town Stash ST252, ST-CD-4
When the Sun Comes Out Stash ST252, ST-CD-4
From Now On (*Note 1*)Stash ST252
The Lady Is a Tramp Stash ST252, ST-CD-4.

Note 1: omit Tormé, Paich plays piano.

SESSION 561202 (Los Angeles, probably from this period) **MEL TORMÉ** with the Marty Paich Orchestra.
Don't Get Around Much Anymore LaserLight 12223.

SESSION 570222 (Two shows at the Crescendo Club, Los Angeles, 22nd February 1957) **MEL TORMÉ** accompanied by the MARTY PAICH GROUP. Don Fagerquist, trumpet; Marty Paich, leader, piano and accordion, Larry Bunker, vibes & bongos; Max Bennett, bass; Mel Lewis, drums.

It's Only a Paper Moon Bethlehem BCP6020
What Is This Thing Called Love Bethlehem BCP6020
One for My Baby Bethlehem BCP6020
Love Is Just a Bug Bethlehem BCP6020
A Nightingale Sang in Berkeley Square Bethlehem BCP6020
Just One of Those Things Bethlehem BCP6020; Rhino R2 71589
The Boy Next Door Bethlehem BCP6020
Lover Come Back to Me Bethlehem BCP6020
Looking at You Bethlehem BCP6020
(Love Is) The Tender Trap Bethlehem BCP6020
I'm Beginning to See the Light Bethlehem BCP6020; Rhino R2 71589
Autumn Leaves (*Note 4*) Bethlehem BCP6020, BCP6031; Rhino R2 71589; MFP CDMFP6217, 7243 8 53503 2 0
Manhattan Bethlehem BCP6031
It's All Right with Me (*Note 7*) Bethlehem BCP6031; Rhino R2 71589
(Here I Go Again), Taking a Chance on Love (*Note 8*) Bethlehem BCP6031
Home by the Sea Bethlehem BCP6031
It's Delovely Bethlehem BCP6031; MFP CDMFP6217, 7243 8 53503 2 0
Tenderly Bethlehem BCP6031; MFP CDMFP6217, 7243 8 53503 2 0
I Wish I Were in Love Again Bethlehem BCP6031; MFP CDMFP6217, 7243 8 53503 2 0
Nobody's Heart (*Note 9*)Bethlehem BCP6031.

Note 1: There are two versions of BCP6031 ("Songs for Any Taste"). The first has a cover picture with shelves of cheese, sausages and fruit. The second has a jar and plate of sweetmeats and a glass.

Note 2: The titles on BCP6020 are also on Parlophone PMC1096

Note 3: All titles on BCP6031 (first version) are also on Parlophone PMC1114.

Note 4: The complete performance of "Autumn Leaves" consists of a spoken introduction, some singing in mock Maurice Chevalier style in French and heavily accented English and then a complete version in French. BCP6020 has only the final French version lasting about 1 minute 30 seconds while BCP6031 (first version) and the MFP issues have the complete performance including the part that is on BCP6020. The full version lasts about 3 minutes 03 seconds. The second version of BCP6031 has only the introduction and mock Chevalier segment lasting about 1 minute 30 seconds.

Note 5: All the titles from BCP6031 (2nd version) are also on Bethlehem BX4015 but in a different order.

Note 6: All the titles from BCP6020 and BX4015 are on Affinity AFF(D) 100 (a 2 LP album) and CDCHARLY60 (a CD). On these issues "Autumn Leaves" is in two parts. One, the intro and "Chevalier" performance and, two, the final French version; these parts appear separately. There is no single complete version on these issues.

Note 7: As "It's Alright with Me" on the Affinity issues.

Note 8: Shown as "Here I Go Again" on the front of Bethlehem BCP6031 (second version) and front of BX4015 but "Taking a Chance on Love" on the label and on the rear of the sleeve of both these issues. "Here I Go Again" is, of course, the first line of the song.

Note 9: Accompaniment is by Tormé's own piano.

SESSION 570311 (Los Angeles, 11th & 13th March 1957) **MEL TORMÉ** accompanied by the Bethlehem Orchestra and Chorus, directed, arranged and conducted by Marty Paich. Pete Candoli, Don Fagerquist, trumpets; Bob Enevoldsen, valve-trombone; Vince De Rosa, French horn; Albert Pollan, tuba; Ronnie Lang, Ted Nash, Dave Pell, woodwinds; Marty Paich, leader, arranger, piano and celeste; Barney Kessel, guitar; Max Bennett, bass; Mel Lewis, Alvin Stoller, drums and percussion; Marvin Limonick, Erno Neufeld, Irma Neumann, Paul Shure, Felix Slatkin, Marshall Sosson, violins; Alvin Dinkin, Paul Robyn, violas; Edgar Lustgarten, Eleanor Slatkin, cellos; Stella Castellucci, Richard Cornell, harps.

California Suite (Tormé) Bethlehem BCP6016. The suite comprises these items:
Overture (Mountain-Desert Theme)
The Golden West
We Think the West Coast Is the Best Coast in the Land
East Coast (Coney Island Theme and Atlantic City Waltz)
They Go to San Diego
Sunday Night in San Fernando
Manhattan, Manhattan
San Francisco (I Met My Love at the Golden Gate)
Hollywood (Prelude to "Poor Little Extra Girl")
Poor Little Extra Girl (Note 2)
We Think the West Coast Is the Best Coast in the Land
Finale (Mountain-Desert Theme).

Note 1: The complete suite is also on Bethlehem BX4016, XLP-4016/BR-5026 (CD) and Parlophone PMC1137.

Note 2: Also on Rhino R2 71589.

SESSION 570701 (London, Summer 1957) **MEL TORMÉ** accompanied by Wally Stott and his Orchestra.
Limehouse Blues Philips BBL7205, BBE12181
A Nightingale Sang in Berkeley Square Philips BBL7205, BBE12181; Rhino R2 71589
The White Cliffs of Dover Philips BBL7205, BBE12181, PB1045
London Pride Philips BBL7205, BBE12181
I've Got a Lovely Bunch of Coconuts Philips BBL7205, PB1045
These Foolish Things (Torme, piano) Philips BBL7205; Rhino R2 71589
Georgie Philips BBL7205
My One and Only Highland Fling Philips BBL7205
Danny Boy Philips BBL7205
Let There Be Love Philips BBL7205
Greensleeves Philips BBL7205
Try a Little Tenderness (arr: Colin Beaton) Philips BBL7205; Rhino R2 71589
Ev'ry Which Way Philips PB728
Time Was Philips PB728.

Note 1: All 14 titles also on Apex AX5.

SESSION 571101 (Los Angeles, November 1957) **MEL TORMÉ** accompanied by Orchestra conducted by Marty Paich. Don Fagerquist, trumpet; Vince De Rosa, French horn; Ronnie Lang, clarinet, alto-sax, baritone-sax; Hynie Gunkler, clarinet, alto-sax; Bob Enevoldsen, bass-clarinet, tenor-sax; Marty Paich, piano, celeste, arranger; Bill Pitman, guitar; Joe Mondragon, bass; Mel Lewis, drums; Stella Castellucci, harp.

  1. **I'm Getting Sentimental Over You** Tops L1615
  2. **I Can't Believe That You're in Love with Me** Tops L1615
  3. **I've Got the World on a String** Tops L1615
  4. **Between the Devil and the Deep Blue Sea** Tops L1615
  5. **I Let a Song Go Out of My Heart** Tops L1615
  6. **I Can't Give You Anything But Love** Tops L1615

SESSION 571102 (Los Angeles, November 1957) Same but add 6 violins, 2 viola and cello.

  7. **Something to Live For** Tops L1615
  8. **I Don't Stand a Ghost of a Chance with You** Tops L1615
  9. **Prelude to a Kiss** Tops L1615
  10. **I Surrender Dear** Tops L1615
  11. **Don't Worry 'Bout Me** Tops L1615
  12. **One Morning in May** Tops L1615

Note 1: This has to be one of the most reissued sets of all time. On the original issue, the songs are linked by dialogue by Tormé and Barbara Ruick. This dialogue is often removed from the subsequent issues. Details are given for individual records in Part 3 (the Record Listing section) of this discography. The sessions were recorded in stereo but the Tops issue seems to have been released only in mono.

Note 2: All titles from Tops L1615 also on Gala GLP301, Mayfair 9615-S, Westerfield 1005-10021, Fresh Sounds FSR-CD 109, Rockin' Chair unnumbered (uses the same stamper as FRS-CD 109), Simitar 55002 and Giants of Jazz CD 53343. (Rockin' Chair is a Spanish issue and is not listed in Part 3).

Note 3: Other issues: • 1: Allegro ALL740, Fontana 6438022, Strand SL1076, SLS1076, Bulldog BDL1017, Hall of Fame GP701, Oscar Disco OS098, Bomar RD104, Classic Jazz CDCD1076, Fat Boy FATCD164, Pickwick PMTD 16009, LaserLight 15381, PRI SPL 9, Telehouse TS772, Vari/Sonics 3510, Members Edition UAE 30652, Big Band Era Vol. 1, Michelle MICH 5601. • 2: Allegro ALL740, Fontana 6438022, Strand SL1076, SLS1076, Bulldog BDL1017, Hall of Fame GP701, Bomar RD104, Classic Jazz CDCD1076, Fat Boy FATCD164, Pickwick PMTD 16009, LaserLight 15381, PRI SPL 9, Telehouse TS772, Vari/Sonics 3510, Members Edition UAE 30652, Big Band Era Vol. 9, Michelle MICH 5609. • 3: Allegro ALL740, Fontana 6438022, Strand SL1076, SLS1076, Bulldog BDL1017, Oscar Disco OS098, Bomar RD104, Classic Jazz CDCD1076, Fat Boy FATCD164, Pickwick PMTD 16009, LaserLight 15381, PRI SPL 9, Telehouse TS772, Vari/Sonics 3510, Members Edition UAE 30652, Big Band Era Vol. 5, Michelle MICH 5605. • 4: Allegro ALL740, Fontana 6438022, Strand SL1076, SLS1076, Bulldog BDL1017, Hall of Fame GP701, Oscar Disco OS098, Bomar RD104, Classic Jazz CDCD1076, Fat Boy FATCD164, Pickwick PMTD 16009, LaserLight 15381, PRI SPL 9, Telehouse TS772, Members Edition UAE 30652; Big Band Era Vol. 3, Michelle MICH 5603. • 5: Strand SL1076, SLS1076, Bulldog BDL1017, Hall of Fame GP701 (as 'Out of My Heart'), Oscar Disco OS098, Classic Jazz CDCD1076, Fat Boy FATCD164, PRI SPL 9; Rhino R2 71589, Members Edition UAE 30652. • 6: Allegro ALL740, Fontana 6438022,

Crown 5347, Summit ATL4123, unknown label DRLP1225, Strand SL1076, SLS1076, Bulldog BDL1017, Oscar Disco OS098, Bomar RD104, Classic Jazz CDCD1076, Fat Boy FATCD164, Pickwick PMTD 16009, LaserLight 15381, Telehouse TS772, Members Edition UAE 30652, Big Band Era Vol. 10, Michelle MICH 5610. • *7: Hall of Fame GP701 (as 'Things to Live For'), Pickwick PMTD 16009, LaserLight 15381, PRI SPL 9.* • *8: Allegro ALL740, Fontana 6438022, Crown 5347, Summit ATL4123, unknown label DRLP1225, Hall of Fame GP701, Philips 6612056, Pickwick PMTD 16009, LaserLight 15381, Telehouse TS772, Vari/Sonics 3510, Big Band Era Vol. 4, Michelle MICH 5604.* • *9: Allegro ALL740, Fontana 6438022, Strand SL1076, SLS1076, Bulldog BDL1017, Hall of Fame GP701, Classic Jazz CDCD1076, Fat Boy FATCD164, Pickwick PMTD 16009, LaserLight 15381, Telehouse TS772; Rhino R2 71589, Members Edition UAE 30652.* • *10: Allegro ALL740, Fontana 6438022, Crown 5347, Summit ATL4123, unknown label DRLP1225, Strand SL1076, SLS1076, Bulldog BDL1017, Hall of Fame GP701, Oscar Disco OS098, Bomar RD104, Classic Jazz CDCD1076, Fat Boy FATCD164, Pickwick PMTD 16009, LaserLight 15381, PRI SPL 9, Telehouse TS772, Vari/Sonics 3510, Members Edition UAE 30652, Big Band Era Vol. 2, Michelle MICH 5602.* • *11: Allegro ALL740, Fontana 6438022, Crown 5347, Summit ATL4123, unknown label DRLP1225, Strand SL1076, SLS1076, Bulldog BDL1017, Hall of Fame GP701, Oscar Disco OS098, Classic Jazz CDCD1076, Fat Boy FATCD164, Pickwick PMTD 16009, LaserLight 15381, Telehouse TS772, Members Edition UAE 30652, Big Band Era Vol. 7, Michelle MICH 5607.* • *12: Allegro ALL740, Fontana 6438022, Strand SL1076, SLS1076, Bulldog BDL1017, Hall of Fame GP701, Oscar Disco OS098, Classic Jazz CDCD1076, Fat Boy FATCD164, Pickwick PMTD 16009, LaserLight 15381, PRI SPL 9, Telehouse TS772, Members Edition UAE 30652.*

Oscar Disco is Italian and is not listed in Part 3.

1958–1961 Verve

SESSION 580505 (Los Angeles, 5th May 1958 [*Note 1*]) **CHARLIE BARNET AND HIS ORCHESTRA with MEL TORMÉ** (vocal). Ray Triscari, John Audino, Al Porcino, Joe Triscari, Jack Hohman, trumpets; Juan Tizol, valve trombone; Frank Lane, Lew McCreary, Walt Mahzline, trombones; Charlie Barnet, alto-, tenor- and soprano-saxes; Bob Jung, alto-sax; Lanny Morgan, alto- and baritone-sax; Dave Madden, Jack Kernan, tenor-saxes; Bob Dawes, baritone-sax; Buddy Motsinger, piano; Harry Babasin, bass; Jack Sperling, drums.

Redskin Rhumba (*) Joyce LP1081
Cherokee (*) Joyce LP1081; Calliope CAL3026
Bakiff (*) Joyce LP1081; Calliope CAL3026
Cross My Heart (MT) Joyce LP1081; Calliope CAL3026
Looking at You (MT) Joyce LP1081; Calliope CAL3026
Lemon Twist (*) Joyce LP1081; Calliope CAL3026
Skyliner (*) Joyce LP1081.

Note 1: These tracks are from a Bobby Troup "Stars of Jazz" TV program. 5th May was the transmission date. The recording may have been made some days before.

Note 2: (*) Tormé is not present on these tracks.

SESSION 580626 (Los Angeles, 26th

June 1958 [*Note 1*]) MEL TORMÉ accompanied by Orchestra conducted by Marty Paich. Frank Beach, Marion Childers, Richard Collins, Jack Sheldon, trumpets; George Roberts, Frank Rosolino, trombones; Vince De Rosa, Richard Perissi, French horns; John Kitzmiller, tuba; Med Flory, Dave Pell, Bill Perkins, Bud Shank, woodwinds; Marty Paich, piano and celeste; Joe Mondragon, bass; Shelly Manne, Alvin Stoller, drums, marimbas, bongos, timpani. Arrangements by Marty Paich.

22260-4 **Blues in the Night** Verve MGV-/MGV6-2105; Rhino R2 71589

22261-2 **Gloomy Sunday** Verve MGV-/MGV6-2105

22262-2 **That Old Feeling** Verve MGV-/MGV6-2105, MGV-8593; Read RC7-012-1

22263-10 **I Don't Want to Cry Anymore** Verve MGV-/MGV6-2105

22264-4 **House Is Haunted by the Echo of Your Last Goodbye** Verve MGV-/MGV6-2105, MGV-8593.

Note 1: The date of this session is from Ruppli. Also given elsewhere as 25th June.

Note 2: All the titles on Verve MGV-2105 also on Verve MGVS6015 and 823 010-2, HMV CLP1238 and World Record Club TP 250.

Note 3: The titles on Verve MGV-8593 also on Verve MGV6-8593.

SESSION 580628 (Los Angeles, 27th June 1958 [*Note 1*]) Same but add strings. On master 22268 accompaniment is by a solo violin. On 22270 & 22271, the accompaniment is by a solo guitar.

22265-3 **Where Can I Go Without You** Verve MGV-/MGV6-2105; Read RC7-012-1

22266-3 **I Should Care** Verve MGV-/MGV6-2105; Read RC7-012-1

22267-3 **How Did She Look** Verve MGV-/MGV6-2105, 314 521 656-2; Read RC7-012-1

22268-3 **Body and Soul** Verve MGV-/MGV6-2105, 833 282-2, 314 521 656-2; Read RC7-012-1

22269-3 **'Round Midnight** Verve MGV-/MGV6-2105, 833 282-2, 314 521 656-2; Read RC7-012-1

22270-4 **I'm Gonna Laugh You Out of My Life** Verve MGV-/MGV6-2105, MGV-8593

22271-6 **Nobody's Heart** Verve MGV-/MGV6-2105; Spectrum 552 637-2.

Note 1: The date of this session is from Ruppli. Also given elsewhere as 28th June.

Note 2: All the titles on Verve MGV-2105 also on Verve MGVS6015 and 832 010-2, HMV CLP1238 and World Record Club TP 350.

Note 3: The title on Verve MGV-8593 also on Verve MGV6-8593.

SESSION 581208 (Hollywood, 8th & 10th December 1958) MEL TORMÉ accompanied by Jimmy Rowles or Bill Miller, keyboards (piano); Vincent Terri and Allan Reuss, guitars; Phil Stephens, bass; John Cyr, vibes and percussion.

L-55877 **Where Are You?** World 513; Audiophile AP-67; Hindsight HCD 253; Soundies 4110

L-55878 **The Night We Called It a Day** World 496; Audiophile AP-67; Hindsight HCD 253; Soundies 4110

L-55879-2 **It's Easy to Remember (and So Hard to Forget)** World 513; Audiophile AP-67; Hindsight HCD 253; Soundies 4110

L-55880 **Day In, Day Out** World 496; Audiophile AP-67; Hindsight HCD 253; Soundies 4110

L-55881-2 **You Took Advantage of Me** World 525; Audiophile AP-67; Soundies 4110

L-55882 untraced

L-55883-5 **Star Eyes** World 496; Audiophile AP-67; Soundies 4110

L-55884-3 **The Christmas Song** World 513; Audiophile AP-67; Soundies 4110

L-55885-6 **I Could Have Told You** World 513; Audiophile AP-67; Hindsight HCD 253; Soundies 4110

L-55886-3 **All in Fun** World 513; Audiophile AP-67; Soundies 4110

L-55887 **Too Late Now** World 525; Audiophile AP-67; Soundies 4110

L-55888-3 **I Concentrate on You** World 496; Audiophile AP-67; Hindsight HCD 253; Soundies 4110

L-55889-2 **In Love in Vain** World 496; Audiophile AP-67; Hindsight HCD 253; Soundies 4110

L-55890-3 **Isn't It Romantic** World 525; Audiophile AP-67; Soundies 4110

L-55891-3 **Long Ago and Far Away** World 496; Audiophile AP-67; Hindsight HCD 253; Soundies 4110.

Note 1: These sessions were recorded for World Broadcasting.

SESSION 590101 (Los Angeles, circa 1959) MEL TORMÉ unknown accompaniment.

Old Folks World 534

I Understand World 534; Soundies 4110

You Make Me Feel So Young World 525; Soundies 4110

Too Darn Hot World 549; Soundies 4110

Nina World 549; Soundies 4110

Sure Thing World 549; Soundies 4110

It Never Entered My Mind World 561; Soundies 4110

I Never Had a Chance World 561; Soundies 4110

I Wish I Were in Love Again World 561; Soundies 4110

The Glory of Love World 569; Soundies 4110

Day Dreaming World 569; Soundies 4110

Time Was World 569; Soundies 4110.

Note 1: This session was recorded for World Broadcasting.

Note 2: It is possible that one of these titles is the missing master L-55882 from the previous session.

SESSION 590321 (Hollywood, 21st March 1959) MEL TORMÉ accompanied by Billy May and his Orchestra. Frank Beach, Pete Candoli, Conrad Gozzo, Mannie Klein, trumpets; Ed Kusby, Tommy Pederson, Dave Wells, Si Zentner, trombones; Red Callendar, tuba; Gene Cipriano, Chuck Gentry, Justin Gordon, Ted Nash, Bud Shank, woodwinds; Verlye Mills, harp; Jimmy Rowles, piano; Bob Gibbons, guitar; Ralph Pena, bass; Larry Bunker, Alvin Stoller, drums and marimbas. Billy May, leader and arrangements.

22754-4 **Vaya Con Dios** Verve MGV-/MGV6-2117; Rhino R2 71589; MFP CDMFP6217, 7243 8 53503 2 0

22755-4 **Six Lessons from Madame La Zonga** Verve MGV-/MGV6-2117

22756-3 **Nina** Verve MGV-/MGV6-2117

22757-7 **Frenesi** Verve MGV-/MGV6-2117, V10174; Rhino R2 71589; MFP CDMFP6217, 7243 8 53503 2 0

22758-5 **South of the Border** Verve MGV-/MGV6-2117, MGV-/MGV6-8593; MFP CDMFP6217, 7243 8 53503 2 0.

Note 1: All the titles on Verve MGV-2117 also on Verve MGVS-6058, HMV CLP1315, World Record Club T388 and Verve J25J-25136.

SESSION 590402 (Hollywood, 2nd April 1959) MEL TORMÉ accompanied by Billy May and his Orchestra. Frank Beach, Pete Candoli, Conrad Gozzo, Mannie Klein, trumpets; Ed Kusby, Tommy Pederson, Dave Wells, Si Zentner, trombones; Red Callendar, tuba; Gene Cipriano, Chuck Gentry, Justin Gordon, Ted Nash, Wilbur Schwartz, woodwinds; Verlye Mills, harp; Al Pellegrini, piano; Bob Gibbons, guitar; Buddy Clark, bass; Lou Singer, Alvin Stoller, drums, marimbas and percussion. Billy May, leader and arrangements.

22791-4 **Perfidia** Verve MGV-/MGV6-2117, MGV-/MGV6-8593; MFP CDMFP6217, 7243 8 53503 2 0

22792-7 **The Rhumba Jumps** Verve MGV-/MGV6-2117

22793-2 **At the Crossroads (Maluguena)** Verve MGV-/MGV6-2117, V10174; Rhino R2 71589

22794-3 **Cuban Love Song** Verve MGV-/MGV6-2117

22795-5 **Rosita** Verve MGV-/MGV6-2117

22796-4 **Adios** Verve MGV-/MGV6-2117

22797- **Baia** Verve MGV-/MGV6-2117.

Note 1: All the titles on Verve MGV-2117 also on Verve MGVS-6058, HMV CLP1315, World Record Club T388 and Verve J25J-25136.

SESSION 590423 (Los Angeles, 23rd, 28th, & 29th April 1959) **MEL TORMÉ** with THE MEL-TONES accompaniment by Marty Paich and his Orchestra. Jack Sheldon, trumpet; Art Pepper, alto-sax and tenor-sax; Joe Gibbons, Al Hendrickson, Barney Kessel, Bill Pitman, Tony Rizzi, guitars; Vic Feldman, vibes; Marty Paich, piano, organ and celeste; Keith Mitchell, bass; Alvin Stoller, drums. Vocal arrangements, Mel Tormé. Instrumental arrangements, Marty Paich. The Mel-Tones are Ginny O'Connor, Bernie Parke, Sue Allen and Tom Kenny.

26374-11 **Makin' Whoopee** Verve MGV-/MGV6-2120

26375-4 **What Is This Thing Called Love** Verve MGV-/MGV6-2120

26376-20 **Baubles, Bangles and Beads** Verve MGV-/MGV6-2120

26377-4 **It Happened in Monterey** (Note 2) Verve MGV-/MGV6-2120; Rhino R2 71589; Metro M-/MS-532; Read RC7-012-1; Capitol 72434-94749-0-1

26278-7 **I've Never Been in Love Before** Verve MGV-/MGV6-2120

26279-6 **Truckin'** Verve MGV-/MGV6-2120, 833 282-2; Metro M-/MS-532

26280-5 **Hit the Road to Dreamland** Verve MGV-/MGV6-2120, 553 268-2, 557 539-2; Metro M-/MS-532

26281-8 **Don't Dream of Anybody But Me** (Note 3) Verve MGV-/MGV6-2120, 314 521 656-2; Metro M-/MS-532

26282-6 **A Bunch of Blues (Keester Parade/TNT/Tiny's Blues)** Verve MGV-/MGV6-2120

26283-5 **Some Like It Hot** Verve MGV-/MGV6-2120; Metro M-/MS-532

26284-7 **A Smooth One** Verve MGV-/MGV6-2120

26285-13 **I Hadn't Anyone Till You** (Note 4) Verve MGV-/MGV6-2120, 314 521 656-2

26285-? **I Hadn't Anyone Till You** (Note 5) Verve 314 511 522-2.

Note 1: The titles on Verve MGV-2120 are also on Verve MGVS-6083, MV2675, 314 511 522-2, and HMVCLP1382.
Note 2: Recorded on 23rd April.
Note 3: Recorded on 23rd April. Also known, instrumentally, as "Li'l Darlin'".
Note 4: Recorded on 28th or 29th April.
Note 5: This version is an alternative take from that used on the original issues. It was recorded on 28th or 29th April.

SESSION 600121 (Hollywood, 21st January 1960) **MEL TORMÉ** accompaniment by the Marty Paich Orchestra. Al Porcino, trumpet; Stu Williamson, trumpet and valve trombone; Frank Rosolino, trombone; Vince De Rosa, French horn; Red Callendar, tuba; Art Pepper, alto-sax; Bill Perkins, tenor-sax; Bill Hood, baritone-sax; Marty Paich, leader, piano, arrangements; Joe Mondragon, bass; Mel Lewis, drums.

23045 **Too Close for Comfort** Verve MGV-/MGV6-2132, MGV-/MGV6-8593, 833 282-2; Rhino R2 71589; Read RC7-012-1

23046 **Once in Love with Amy** Verve MGV-/MGV6-2132, 2317076
23047 **Whatever Lola Wants** Verve MGV-/MGV6-2132, 833 282-2
23048 **Hello Young Lovers** Verve MGV-/MGV6-2132, 314 521 656-2.

Note 1: All four titles are also on Verve MGVS-6146, MV 2013, VSP17/18 (and possibly SVSP17/18), 821 581-2 and on HMV CLP1405 and CDS1330.

SESSION 600204 (Los Angeles, 4th February 1960). Same.

23071-9 **Too Darn Hot** Verve MGV-/MGV6-2132; HMV CLP1405, CDS1330; Spectrum 552 645-2
23072-5 **A Sleepin' Bee** Verve MGV-/MGV6-2132, 314 521 656-2; HMV CLP1405, CDS1330
23073-8 **All I Need Is the Girl** Verve MGV-/MGV6-2132, 2317076
23074-5 **Lonely Town** Verve MGV-/MGV6-2132, 2317076, 314 521 656-2; HMV CLP1405, CDS1330.

Note 1: All four titles are also on Verve MGVS-6146, MV 2013, VSP17/18 (and possibly SVSP17/18) and 821 581-2.

SESSION 600211 (Los Angeles, 11th February 1960). Same.

23085-19 **The Surrey with the Fringe on Top** Verve MGV-/MGV6-2132, 2317076, 833 282-2
23086-15 **On the Street Where You Live** Verve MGV-/MGV6-2132, MGV-/MGV6-8593; MGM E4243, SE4243; Read RC7-012-1
23087-5 **Just in Time** Verve MGV-/MGV6-2132, MGV-/MGV6-8593, MGV-/MGV6-8505, 2317076, 833 282-2, 314 521 656-2; MFP MFP5233
23088-4 **Old Devil Moon** Verve MGV-/MGV6-2132.

Note 1: All four titles are also on Verve MGVS-6146, MV 2013, VSP17/18 (and possibly SVSP17/18), 821 581-2 and on HMV CLP1405 and CDS1330.

SESSION 600301 (Los Angeles, March 1960). WALK LIKE A DRAGON (Film soundtrack). MEL TORMÉ unknown accompaniment.

Walk Like a Dragon Rhino R2 75481.

SESSION 600329 (Los Angeles, 29th[?] March 1960) MEL TORMÉ unknown accompaniment (supervised by Russell Garcia).

23172 **Walk Like a Dragon** Verve V10211
23173 **Poor Wayfaring Stranger** Verve V10211.

SESSION 600803 (Los Angeles, 3rd August 1960) MEL TORMÉ accompanied by Orchestra conducted by Russell Garcia. Bud Shank, alto-sax; Carl LaMango, Dan Lube, Al Neiman, violins; Kurt Reher, cello; Howard Roberts, guitar; Ralph Pena, bass; Mel Lewis, drums; Russell Garcia, leader and arrangements.

23294-6 **Moonlight in Vermont** Verve MGV-/MGV6-2144, MGV-/MGV6-8593, 2317076, 314 521 656-2
23295-5 **Moon Song** Verve MGV-/MGV6-2144; Metro M-/MS-532; HMV 45POP859
23296-7 **Moonlight Cocktail** Verve MGV-/MGV6-2144
23297-7 **Velvet Moon** (*Note 2*) Verve unissued.

Note 1: The titles on Verve MGV-/MGV6-2144 also on Verve 511 385-2, HMV CLP1445 and CSD1344, World Sound T550 and World Stereo ST550.

Note 2: The track on Verve MGV-2144 and its reissues with this title (except Verve 511 385-2), actually plays "Velvet Affair" (see session 600805). Verve 511 385-2 credits the tune as "Velvet Moon" on the inside front cover, which is a reproduction of the back of the original LP sleeve, but correctly titles the tune on the back of the sleeve.

SESSION 600804 (Los Angeles, 4th

August 1960) accompanied by Orchestra conducted by Russell Garcia. Dick Nash, Tommy Pederson, George Roberts, Tommy Shepard, trombones; Vince De Rosa, French horn; Red Callendar, tuba; Bud Shank, alto-sax, flute; Howard Roberts, guitar; Ralph Pena, bass; Mel Lewis, drums; Russell Garcia, leader and arrangements. A second flute is audible on master 23300.

23298-5 **No Moon at All** Verve MGV-/MGV6-2144

23299-5 **The Moon Was Yellow** Verve MGV-/MGV6-2144

23300-4 **Don't Let That Moon Get Away** Verve MGV-/MGV6-2144

23301- **Swingin' on the Moon** (*Note 2*) Verve MGV-/MGV6-2144; Rhino R2 71589; Read RC7-012-1.

Note 1: All four titles also on Verve 511 386-2, HMV CLP1445 and CSD1344, World Sound T550 and World Stereo ST550.
Note 2: This master was edited for release.

SESSION 600805 (Los Angeles, 5th August 1960) accompanied by Orchestra conducted by Russell Garcia. Don Fagerquist, trumpet; David Frisina, Dan Lube, Rickey Marino, William Miller, Al Neiman, Lou Raderman, Clarence Shubring, Gerald Vinci, violins; Allan Harshman, Myron Sandler, viola; George Neikug, Kurt Reher, cellos; Marcia Johnstone, harp; Pete Jolly, piano; Howard Roberts, guitar; Ralph Pena, bass; Mel Lewis, drums; Russell Garcia, leader and arrangements.

23302-2 **Blue Moon** Verve MGV-/MGV6-2144, MGV-/ MGV6-8593, 2317076, 833 282-2, 314 521 656-2; M-G-M E/SE 4238, PM-14; Metro M-/MS-522, HMV 45POP859; St. Michael CDM007

23303-3 **How High the Moon** Verve MGV-/MGV6-2144, 2317076, 314 521 656-2

23304-4 **Oh You Crazy Moon** Verve MGV-/MGV6-2144

23305-4 **I Wished on the Moon** Verve MGV-/MGV6-2144, 314 521 656-2; Metro M-/MS-532; Rhino R2 75481

23306-6 **A Velvet Affair** (*Note 2*) Verve MGV-/MGV6-2144.

Note 1: All five titles also on Verve 511 385-2, HMV CLP1445 and CSD1344, World Sound T550 and World Stereo ST550.
Note 2: Mislabeled as "Velvet Moon" on all issues except the back of the sleeve of Verve 511 385-2 where the correct title is used.

SESSION 601001 (ca. Oct. 1960) MEL TORMÉ unknown accompaniment, unknown location and date.

26828 **I'm Shootin' High** Verve 823 010-2

26829 **These Desperate Hours** Verve 823 010-2

These two titles were taken from a TV show.

SESSION 601109 (Los Angeles, 9th November 1960) **MEL TORMÉ AND MARGARET WHITING** vocals with Orchestra arranged and conducted by Russell Garcia. Unknown trumpets, trombones, flutes and tuba; Vince De Rosa, French horn; Israel Baker, Sarah Kreindler, Jack Perrer, Marshall Sosson, Heimann Weinstine, violins; Allan Harshman, Myron Sandler, violas; George Neikrug, cello; Marcia Johnstone, harp; Geoff Clarkson, piano; Howard Roberts, guitar; Don Bagley, bass; Alvin Stoller, drums and percussion; Ralph Hansell, vibes; Amerigo Marino, Tibor Zelig, Sigmund Ziebel, Olgar Zundel, unknown instruments. Russell Garcia, leader and arrangements.

23361-7 **All You Need Is a Quarter** Verve MGV-/V6-2146; HMV 7EG8721

23362-6 **Tall Hopes** Verve MGV-/V6-2146

23363-10 **Hey Look Me Over** Verve MGV-/V6-2146, V10230

23364-4 **Fireworks** Verve MGV-/V6-2146; HMV 7EG8721.

SESSION 601110 (Los Angeles, 10th November 1960). Same.
23365-8 **If Ever I Would Leave You** (*Note 1*) Verve MGV-/V6-2146
23366 **I Loved You Once in Silence** (*Note 2*) Verve MGV-/V6-2146
23367 **Our Language of Love** Verve MGV-/V6-2146, 2352171
23368 **Medley: Far Away from Home / Angelina** Verve MGV-/V6-2146; Rhino R2 71589
23369 **Cry Like the Wind** Verve MGV-/V6-2146; HMV 7EG8721
23370 **Make Someone Happy** (*Note 1*) Verve MGV-/V6-2146; HMV 7EG8721
23371 **From a Prison Cell** (*Note 2*) Verve MGV-/V6-2146
23372 **What's New at the Zoo** Verve MGV-/V6-2146, V10230; HMV 7EG8721.

Note 1: Omit Tormé.
Note 2: Omit Whiting.

SESSION 601212 (Los Angeles, 12th December 1960) MEL TORMÉ with Johnny Mandel's Orchestra. Jack Sheldon and two others, trumpets; Frank Rosolino and another, trombone; Stu Williamson, valve trombone; three unknown, French horns; Joe Maini, alto-sax; Teddy Edwards, tenor-sax; Bill Perkins, baritone-sax; another, saxophone; Jimmy Rowles, piano; Al Hendrickson, guitar; Joe Mondragon, bass; Shelly Manne, drums; Johnny Mandel, conductor and arrangements.
23400-10 **Reminiscing in Tempo** Verve MGV-2153
23401-7 **Don't Get Around Much Anymore** Verve MGV-2153, 833 282-2
23402-8 **Just a Sittin' and a Rockin'** Verve MGV-2153, 2317076
23403-6 **I'm Gonna Go Fishin'** Verve MGV-2153, MGV-/MGV6-8593
23404-6 **Take the "A" Train** Verve MGV-2153, 833 282-2
23405-4 **I Like the Sunrise** Verve MGV-2153, MGV-/MGV6-8593.

Note 1: All six titles also on Verve V6-2153, MGV-/MGV6-8491, VLP9027, SVLP9027, 823 248-2; VSPVerve VSP17/18 and possibly SVSP17/18.

SESSION 610202 (Los Angeles, 2nd February 1961) MEL TORMÉ with Johnny Mandel's Orchestra. John Anderson, Don Fagerquist, Jack Sheldon, Ray Triscari, trumpets; Joe Howard, Dick Nash, Richard Noel, trombones; Stu Williamson, valve trombone; Joe Maini, alto-sax; Teddy Edwards, tenor-sax; Bill Perkins, tenor-sax; Chuck Gentry, baritone-sax; Charlie Kennedy, alto-sax; Jimmy Rowles, piano; Al Hendrickson, guitar; Joe Mondragon, bass; Shelly Manne, drums; Johnny Mandel, conductor and arrangements.
23477-4 **Oh What a Night for Love** (*Note 2*) Verve MGV-2153, 2317076; Franklin Mint FM006
23478-2 **Down for Double** Verve MGV-2153; Smithsonian RD-113
23479-4 **Sent for You Yesterday and Here You Come Today** Verve MGV-2153, 833 282-2; Rhino R2 71589
23480-2 **I'm Gonna Move to the Outskirts of Town** Verve MGV-2153; Rhino R2 71589
23481-1 **Blue and Sentimental** Verve MGV-2153, 833 282-2, 314 521 656-2
23482-1 **In the Evening When the Sun Goes Down** Verve MGV-2153, 2317076.

Note 1: All six titles also on Verve V6-2153, MGV-/MGV6-8491, VLP9027, SVLP9027, 823 248-2; VSPVerve VSP17/18 and possibly SVSP17/18.
Note 2: Also known, instrumentally, as "Softly with Feeling."

SESSION 610309 (New York City, 9th March 1961) MEL TORMÉ with the Sy Oliver Orchestra.
23520 **Her Face** Verve 10232, VS505, 823 010-2
23521 **He's Got the Whole World in His Hands** Verve unissued

23522 **Yes Indeed** Verve 10232, VS505, 823 010-2.

SESSION 610701 (London, 18th – 21st July 1961) MEL TORMÉ accompanied by Tony Osborne and Orchestra.
A Stranger in Town Verve V-8440, 833 282-2
Born to Be Blue Verve V-8440, 833 282-2, 314 521 656-2
Dancing in the Dark Verve V-8440.

Note 1: All three titles also on Verve V6-8440, J25J-25135, POJC-2665, HMV CLP1584 and CSD1442.
Note 2: The notes of 314 521 656-2 give the recording date of "Born to Be Blue" as 2nd February 1961 but this is certainly incorrect.

SESSION 610702 (London, 18th – 21st July 1961) MEL TORMÉ accompanied by Wally Stott and Orchestra.
I Guess I'll Have to Change My Plan Verve V-8440, 2317076
County Fair Verve V-8440; Metro M-/MS-532
Alone Together Verve V-8440, 314 521 656-2
Welcome to the Club Verve V-8440, 833 282-2
7XSM 1375 **The Christmas Song** Verve V-8440, MGV-/MGV6-8593, 2317076, 833 282-2; MGM 1144; Rhino R2 71589; Capitol 72434-94749-0-1.

Note 1: All five titles also on Verve V6-8440, J25J-25135, POJC-2665, HMV CLP1584 and CSD1442.

SESSION 610703 (London, 18th – 21st July 1961) MEL TORMÉ accompanied by Geoff Love and his Orchestra.
7XSM 1376 **A Shine on Your Shoes** Verve V-8440, 2317076; MGM 1144
By Myself Verve V-8440, 2317076; Rhino R2 71589
You and the Night and the Music Verve V-8440, MGV-/MGV6-8593.

Note 1: All three titles also on Verve V6-8440, J25J-25135, POJC-2665, HMV CLP1584 and CSD1442.
Note 2: The name of the orchestra leader is misspelled "Jeff Love" on the sleeve of Verve V-/V6-8440 and POJC-2665 but is correct on the labels. The same misspelling occurs in the notes of Rhino R2 71589.

SESSION 610909 (Los Angeles, 9th September 1961) MEL TORMÉ with studio orchestra directed by Carl Brandt. Joe Graves, trumpet; Ed Kusby, trombone; Skeets Herfurt, reeds; Allen Reuss, guitar; Verlye Mills, harp; Carl Brandt, piano; Ira Westley, bass and tuba; Chester Ricord and Ralph Hansell, percussion.
Gone with the Wind (Note 1) Stash ST-CD-4
That Old Feeling Stash ST-CD-4.

Note 1: Tormé, piano; replaces Brandt on this title.
Note 2: Stash ST-CD-4 erroneously credits the Shorty Rogers titles from 13th May 1963 to this session and the subsequent reissue on Viper's Nest of "'Round Midnight" from that session is wrongly attributed to this date also.

1962–1967 Atlantic and Columbia

SESSION 620324 (The Red Hill Club, Pennsauken, PA, 24th March 1962) MEL TORMÉ accompanied by the Jimmy Wisner Trio (Jimmy Wisner, piano; Ace Tesone, bass; Dave Levin, drums).

A-6102 **Shakin' the Blues Away** Atlantic 8066, 80066
A-6103 **In Other Words** Atlantic 8066
A-6104 **It's All Right with Me** unissued

A-6105 **London Pride** unissued
A-6106 **Medley** unissued
A-6107 **Angel Eyes** unissued
A-6108 **Medley: Porgy and Bess** unissued
A-6109 **Love Is Just Around the Corner** Atlantic 8066; Rhino R2 75481
A-6110 **Breezing Along with the Breeze** unissued
A-6111 **Misty** unissued
A-6112 **Hey, Look Me Over** unissued
A-6113 **(Ah, the Apple Trees) When the World Was Young** Atlantic 8066; Rhino R2 71589
A-6114 **Anything Goes** Atlantic 8066
A-6115 **Spring Can Really Hang You Up the Most** unissued
A-6116 **Medley: I Hear Music/Lullaby of Broadway** unissued
A-6117 **Mountain Greenery** (*note 1*) Atlantic 8066; Rhino Flashback R2 72886
A-6118 **untitled instrumental** unissued
A-6119 **Medley: Buddy Can You Spare a Dime/Love Me or Leave Me** unissued
A-6120 **How Are Things in Glocca Morra** unissued
A-6121 **Medley: A Foggy Day/A Nightingale Sang in Berkeley Square** Atlantic 8066, 80066
A-6122 **Early Autumn** Atlantic 8066, 80066
A-6123 **Blues** unissued
A-6124 **Don't Get Around Much Anymore** unissued
A-6125 **I'm Beginning to See the Light** Atlantic 8066
A-6126 **It Never Entered My Mind** unissued
A-6127 **Medley: Blue Moon/Polka Dots and Moonbeams** unissued
A-6128 **Bye Bye Blackbird** unissued
A-6129 **How About Me** unissued
A-6130 **Love for Sale** (*note 1*) Atlantic 8066.

Note 1: Tormé, also plays piano, omit Wisner.

Note 2: All the titles on Atlantic 8066 also on Atlantic SD8066, London HAK8021 and SHK8021, Collectors' Choice Music CCM0074-2. On CCM0074-2, a little of Tormé's spoken introductions to the tunes has been deleted without affecting any of the music.

Note 3: All the titles on Atlantic 80066 also on Atlantic SD80066.

SESSION 620325 (The Red Hill Club, Pennsauken, PA, 25th March 1962) MEL TORMÉ accompanied by the Jimmy Wisner Trio (Jimmy Wisner, piano; Ace Tesone, bass; Dave Levin, drums).

A-6131 **It's Delovely** (*note 1*) Atlantic 8066, 80066; Rhino R2 71589; Read RC7-012-1; Rhino Flashback R2 72886
A-6132 **Nevertheless** Atlantic 8066
A-6133 **You're Driving Me Crazy** unissued
A-6134 **Don't Take Your Love from Me** unissued
A-6135 **Anything Goes** unissued
A-6136 **Again** unissued
A-6137 **Shooting High** unissued
A-6138 **The One That Got Away** unissued

Note 1: Tormé, also plays piano, omit Wisner.
Note 2: The two titles on Atlantic 8066 also on Atlantic SD8066, London HAK8021 and SHK8021, Collectors' Choice Music CCM0074-2. On CCM0074-2, a little of Tormé's spoken introductions to the tunes has been deleted without affecting any of the music.
Note 3: The title on Atlantic 80066 also on Atlantic SD80066.

SESSION 620711 (Los Angeles, 11th July 1962) MEL TORMÉ with Orchestra arranged and conducted by Shorty Rogers. Joe Burnett, Oliver Mitchell, Al Porcino, Ray Triscari, trumpets; Milt Bernhart, Harry Betts, Ken Shroyer, trombones; John Kitzmiller, tuba; Buddy Collette, Bob Cooper, Bill Hood, Bud Shank, woodwinds;

Gene Estes, vibes; Mike Wofford, piano; Joe Mondragon, bass; Larry Bunker, drums. Shorty Rogers, leader and arrangements.

A-6360 **Hi-Fly** Atlantic 8069
A-6361 **On Green Dolphin Street** Atlantic 8069; Rhino R2 71589, R2 75481
A-6362 **Dat Dere** Atlantic 8069; Rhino R2 71589
A-6363 **Moanin'** Atlantic 8069.

Note 1: All four titles also on Atlantic SD8069, 590008, 30P2-2322; London HAK8065 and SHK8065.

SESSION 620713 (Los Angeles, 13th July 1962) MEL TORMÉ with Orchestra arranged and conducted by Shorty Rogers. Same or similar personnel as last. A flugelhorn, possibly played by Rogers, can be heard on A-6365 and A-6366. On A-6364, the accompaniment is by a smaller group, consisting of Joe Burnett, trumpet; Milt Bernhart, trombone; John Kitzmiller, tuba; Bob Cooper, Bud Shank, woodwinds; Gene Estes, vibes; Mike Wofford, piano; Joe Mondragon, bass; Larry Bunker, drums.

A-6364 **Walkin' Shoes** Rhino R2 71589
A-6365 **Walkin'** Atlantic 8069
A-6366 **Whisper Not** Atlantic 8069; Rhino R2 72473
A-6367 **Sidney's Soliloquy** Atlantic 8069.

Note 1: The three titles on Atlantic 8069 also on Atlantic SD8069, 590008, 30P2-2322; London HAK8065 and SHK8065.

SESSION 620716 (Los Angeles, 16th July 1962) MEL TORMÉ with Orchestra arranged and conducted by Shorty Rogers similar to the personnel for 620711.

A-6368 **The Lady's in Love with You** Atlantic 8069; Rhino R2 75481
A-6369 **Sing, You Sinners** Atlantic 8069
A-6370 **You Belong to Me** Atlantic 2202
A-6371 **Puttin' on the Ritz** Atlantic 8069; Rhino R2 75481; Rhino Flashback R2 72886.

Note 1: The three titles on Atlantic 8069 also on Atlantic SD8069, 590008, 30P2-2322; London HAK8065 and SHK8065.

SESSION 620913 (New York City, 13th September 1962) MEL TORMÉ with accompaniment arranged and conducted by Claus Ogermann. Instrumentation is brass, piano, organ and rhythm with a female trio vocal backing group called The Cookies.

A-6456 **Comin' Home Baby** Atlantic 2165; London REK1372; Rhino Flashback R2 72886
A-6457 **Right Now** Atlantic 2165.

Note 1: Both titles also on Atlantic 8069, SD8069, 590008, 30P2-2322; Rhino R2 71589; London HAK8065, SHK8065 and 45-HLK 9643 and Read RC7-012-1.

SESSION 630208 (Los Angeles, 8th February 1963) MEL TORMÉ with accompaniment arranged and conducted by Marty Paich. Victor Arno, Arnold Belnick, James Getzoff, Bernard Kundell, Alfred Lustgarten, Lou Raderman, Paul Shure, Marshall Sosson, Joseph Stepansky, Gerald Vinci, violins; Joseph DiFiore, Allan Dinkin, Virginia Majewski, violas; Paul Bergstrom, Armard Kaproff, cellos; Jimmy Wisner, piano; Laurindo Almeida, Al Hendrickson, guitars; Joe Mondragon, bass; Alvin Stoller, drums; Milt Holland, bongos; unknown vocal group.

A-6780 **Cast Your Fate to the Wind** Atlantic 2183; London REK1372; Rhino R2 71589; Rhino Flashback R2 72886
A-6781 **The Gift** Atlantic 2183; London REK1372
A-6782 **My Gal's Back in Town** Atlantic 2187
A-6783 **Gravy Waltz** Atlantic 2187; London REK1372.

SESSION 630513 (Los Angeles 13th May 1963) **MEL TORMÉ** with Shorty Rogers and His Giants. Shorty Rogers, trumpet, flugelhorn and arrangements; George Roberts or Ken Shroyer, bass trombone; Buddy Collette, Paul Horn, flutes, clarinets and alto-saxes; Bill Hood, bass-clarinet, bass-sax, tuba; Lou Levy, piano; Larry Bunker, vibes; Monte Budwig, bass; Shelly Manne, drums. Tormé also plays piano.

A Foggy Day Stash ST252, ST-CD-4
Porgy and Bess Medley: Summertime (*note 2*), **It Ain't Necessarily So**, **Bess You Is My Woman Now** (*note 2*) Stash ST252, ST-CD-4
Hello, Young Lovers Stash ST252, ST-CD-4
Marie (*note 3*) Stash ST252
The Surrey with the Fringe on Top Stash ST252, ST-CD-4
The Lady's in Love with You Stash ST252, ST-CD-4
Sugar Loaf (*note 3*) Stash ST252
Lulu's Back in Town Stash ST252
Hey, Look Me Over Stash ST252, ST-CD-4; Rhino R2 71589
'Round Midnight Stash ST252, ST-CD-4; Viper's Nest VN-165/6.

Note 1: These were recorded for a National Guard "Guard Session" program.
Note 2: Tormé, plays piano.
Note 3: Omit Tormé.
Note 4: The notes of Stash ST-CD-4 erroneously credit these tracks to a session on 9th September 1961 and the error is repeated on the reissue of "'Round Midnight" on Viper's Nest.
Note 5: Viper's Nest has a catalog number of VN-165 on the disc and VN-166 on the sleeve.

SESSION 630605 (Los Angeles, 5th June 1963) **MEL TORMÉ** with Orchestral accompaniment.

A-7049-11 **You Can't Love 'Em All** Atlantic 2202.

From June 1963 to February 1964, Mel Tormé was a musical associate on *The Judy Garland Show*, made for CBS Television and shown on Sunday nights at 9 PM EST from 12th August 1963 to 29th March 1964. His role was that of a writer of special musical material. This involved liaisons with Garland and her guests over the material that they would perform in the shows and then writing musical arrangements and additional lyrics that were needed. In addition, he appeared as a performer on four of the shows. Details of the shows on which he appeared as a performer are given below in the appropriate chronological position. A simple listing of the shows with the relevant dates and the names of the guests is given in Part 4 together with information about video releases of the material.

Extracts from the soundtracks were issued on Capitol W 2062 *Just for Openers* (LP album), Paragon 1001 (LP album), Broadcast Tributes BTRIB 0002 (LP album) and 32 Records *The Box* (2 CD set with 100-page book — no catalog number), Wiley Entertainments *Judy Duets / Judy at the Palace* (2 CD set with 24-page booklet & 4-page leaflet — no catalog number), LaserLight 12 467 (this is the whole of the Christmas Show apart from some of the non-vocal music and solo songs by Joey Luft and Mel Tormé). Extracts from the soundtracks of other shows also appeared on LaserLight CDs: 12 480 — *Come Rain or Come Shine*; 12 481 — *Over the Rainbow*; 12 482 — *The Man That Got Away*; 12 483 — *Stormy Weather*; 12 484 — *Fly Me to the Moon*. These were issued individually and also collectively in a 5-CD set, LaserLight 15 942 — *The Judy Garland Show*. The material on the individual CDs was also issued as cassettes with the catalog number 72 xxx in place of the 12 xxx e.g., 72 567 for 12 567. The 5-CD set was not issued in cassette format. The Broadcast Tributes album has no audible vocal contribution by Tormé. Release information from the

Wiley set and LaserLight 12 467 is given where appropriate in the session listing. I have not been able to hear the 32 Records set nor the remaining LaserLight issues and therefore cannot state whether there is any vocal performance by Tormé on any of them.

SESSION 630707 (recorded Hollywood, 7 July 1963; transmitted 10 November 1963) **THE JUDY GARLAND SHOW.** Show # 7. Judy Garland. Orchestra and chorus directed by Mort Lindsey on all items unless otherwise noted. Co-host and resident comedian: Jerry Van Dyke (JVD). Dance troop led by Peter Gennaro. Guests: Count Basie and his Orchestra (CBO) (*note 2*), Judy Henske (JH) and Mel Tormé (MT)

    1 **I Hear Music / The Sweetest Sounds / Strike Up the Band** JG w CBO Wiley "Judy Duets"
    2 **Banjo Sketch** JG w JVD & MT
    3 **Fascinatin' Rhythm** MT Stash ST-CD-4
    4 **Memories of You** JG w CB on organ
    5 **Electric Banjo Sketch** JG w JVD
    6 **Shiny Stockings** (instrumental) Dancers
    7 **God Bless the Child** JH
    8 **Peter, Paul and Irving Sketch** (including Walk Right In / Low-down Alligator / Lemon Tree/ Walk Right In) JH, MT & JVD
    9 **Count Basie Medley:** One O'clock Jump CBO; I Can't Stop Lovin' You CBO; I've Got My Love to Keep Me Warm JG w CBO; Don't Dream of Anybody But Me (*note 3*) MT w CBO Stash ST-CD-4; April in Paris JG w MT & CBO
    10 **One Note Samba** JVD & CBO
    11 **Soul Bossa Nova** (instrumental) JG w Dancers
    12 **Born in a Trunk sequence** JG.

Note 1: Wiley "Judy Duets" is one disc in a 2-CD set that has no catalog number.

Note 2: The personnel of the Count Basie Orchestra was: Don Rader, Sonny Cohn, Fip Ricard, Al Aarons, trumpets; Henry Coker, Grover Mitchell, Benny Powell, trombones; Marshal Royal, clarinet and alto-sax; Frank Wess, flute, alto- and tenor-saxes; Eric Dixon, flute and tenor-sax; Frank Foster, tenor-sax; Charlie Fowlkes, baritone-sax; Count Basie, piano; Freddie Green, guitar; Buddy Catlett, bass; Sonny Payne, drums. The notes of Stash ST-CD-4 also list Joe Newman, trumpet and Urbie Green, trombone but their presence is not confirmed.

*Note 3: Labeled on Stash as "**Li'l Darlin'**" which was, of course, the title of the original instrumental version of the tune.*

SESSION 630810 (Los Angeles, 10th August 1963) **MEL TORMÉ** with the Donn Trenner Octet; personnel may include Bob Enevoldsen, trombone.

    Swinging on the Moon LaserLight 12222
    I'm Gonna Miss You LaserLight 12222
    Don't Let the Moon Get Away LaserLight 12222; Stash ST-CD-4
    Portia Brown LaserLight 12223
    'Round Midnight LaserLight 12223
    All I Need Is the Girl LaserLight 12224; Stash ST-CD-4
    The Moon Was Yellow LaserLight 12224
    I'll Be Seeing You LaserLight 12224; Stash ST-CD-4.

Note 1: These tracks recorded for "The Navy Swings" programs.
Note 2: All 8 titles also on Hindsight HCD 253.

SESSION 630901 (San Francisco, 1963–64) **MEL TORMÉ** with the Benny Barth Trio: Gary Long, piano; Perry Lind, bass; Benny Barth, drums.

    Quiet Night of Quiet Stars (*note 1*) Stash ST-CD-4
    When Sunny Gets Blue (*note 2*) Stash ST-CD-4

Dat Dere Stash ST-CD-4
I've Got a World That Swings Stash ST-CD-4
Comin' Home Baby! Stash ST-CD-4
Sidney's Soliloquy Stash ST-CD-4.

Note 1: Tormé, also plays baritone ukulele.
Note 2: Tormé, also plays piano.

SESSION 631018 (recorded Hollywood, 18 October 1963; transmitted 5 January 1964) THE JUDY GARLAND SHOW. Show # 14. Judy Garland. Orchestra and chorus directed by Mort Lindsey on all items unless otherwise noted. Dance troop led by Peter Gennaro. Guests: Steve Allen (SA), Jayne Meadows (JM) and Mel Tormé (MT)
  1 **This Could Be the Start of Something Big** JG
  2 **Be My Guest** JG w SA & MT
  3 **Cheer for Old Hyde Park** SA & MT
  4 **We're from Old Metro** JG
  5 **Be My Guest** (reprise) JG
  6 **Here's That Rainy Day** JG
  7 **Comedy dialogue** JG w SA
  8 **Comedy sketch** SA then joined by JG
  9 **Sophie Medley**: I Love You Today JG w SA; When I'm in Love JG w SA; I'll Show Them All JG
  10 **Comin' Home Baby** MT
  11 **Comedy dialogue** JG w MT (seated on motorcycles)
  12 **The Party's Over** JG w MT
  13 **Tea for Two sequence** JG w JM
  14 **Comedy dialogue** JG w SA & MT
  15 **Songwriter medley**: Ain't Misbehavin' JG; Makin' Whoopee MT; The Glory of Love SA; Way Back Home JG; Wrap Your Trouble in Dreams MT; You Took Advantage of Me SA; Mean to Me JG; The Girl Friend SA & MT; Tip Toe Through the Tulips JG; Truckin' MT; The Gypsy in My Soul SA; Nice Work If You Can Get It JG; The Glory of Love SA & MT; My Heart Stood Still JG; Let's Do It JG w/SA & MT
  16 **Born in a Trunk sequence** JG.

For the Judy Garland Show broadcast on 10th November 1963 see 7th July 1963.

SESSION 631115 (Los Angeles, 15th November 1963) SUNDAY IN NEW YORK (Film soundtrack). MEL TORMÉ with accompaniment orchestrated and conducted by Peter Nero.
Sunday in New York Turner 7243 8 21963 2 7, 821 9632.

Note 1: This recording was used behind the credit titles of the film.

SESSION 631120 (Los Angeles, November 1963) SAMMY DAVIS JR. with orchestra arranged and conducted by Marty Paich.
2432 **California Suite** (*note 1*) Reprise R-/RS- 6126.

Note 1: Tormé is one of the many participants in the "Party Sequence." He is not audible as an individual.

SESSION 631202 (Los Angeles, 2nd December 1963) MEL TORMÉ with Orchestra arranged and conducted by Dick Hazard. Arnold Koblentz, oboe; Israel Baker, Harry Bluestone, James Getzoff, Marvin Limonick, Lou Raderman, Henry Roth, Paul Shure, Gerald Vinci, violins; Alvin Dinkin, Allan Harshman, violas; Margaret Aue, Edgar Lustgarten, cellos; Dorothy Remsen, harp; Jimmy Rowles, piano; Dave Barbour, guitar; Joe Mondragon, bass; Shelly Manne, drums; Dick Hazard, leader and arrangements.
A-7453 **Autumn in New York** Atlantic 8091, 80091
A-7454 **Manhattan** Atlantic 8091
A-7455 **Harlem Nocturne** Atlantic 8091
A-7456 **Forty Second Street** (*note 3*) Atlantic 8091, 2219; Rhino R2 71589; Read RC7-012-1

A-7457 **My Time of Day** Atlantic 8091.

Note 1: All the titles on Atlantic 8091 also on Atlantic SD8091, ATL5005, SAL5005 and 80 078-2.

Note 2: The title on Atlantic 80091 also on SD80091 and AET6005.

Note 3: This song also issued on City Songs — New York.

SESSION 631204 (Los Angeles, 4th December 1963) MEL TORMÉ with Orchestra arranged and conducted by Johnny Williams. Frank Beach, Al Porcino, Ray Triscari, Stu Williamson, trumpets; Lew McCreary, Dick Nash, Lloyd Ulyate, trombones; John Kitzmiller, tuba; Buddy Collette, Gene Cipriano, Paul Horn, Ronnie Lang, John Lowe, woodwinds; Jimmy Rowles, piano; Joe Mondragon, bass; Alvin Stoller, drums; Johnny Williams, leader and arrangements.

A-7458 **Let Me Off Uptown** Atlantic 8091

A-7459 **Sunday in New York** Atlantic 8091, 2219, 80091; Rhino R2 71589, R2 75481, Rhino Flashback R2 72886

A-7460 **Broadway** Atlantic 8091

A-7461 **Sidewalks of New York** Atlantic 8091, 80091.

Note 1: The titles on Atlantic 8091 also on Atlantic SD8091, ATL5005, SAL5005 and 80 078-2.

Note 2: The titles on Atlantic 80091 also on SD80091 and AET6005.

SESSION 631206 (recorded Hollywood, 6 December 1963; transmitted 22 December 1963) THE JUDY GARLAND SHOW. Show # 12 — The Christmas Show. Judy Garland. Orchestra and chorus directed by Mort Lindsey on all items unless otherwise noted. Dance troop led by Peter Gennaro. Guests: Tracy Everitt (TE), Jack Jones (JJ), Joey Luft (JL), Lorna Luft (LL), Liza Minnelli (LM) and Mel Tormé (MT).

1 **Have Yourself a Merry Little Christmas** JG
2 **Consider Yourself** JG w LL & JL
3 **Consider Yourself** (reprise) JG w LL, JL & LM
4 **Where Is Love?** JL
5 **Steam Heat** LM & TE
6 **Little Drops of Rain** JG
7 **Wouldn't It Be Loverly** JJ
8 **Lollipops and Roses** JJ
9 **Santa Claus Is Coming to Town** LL
10 **Alice Blue Gown** LM
11 **Holiday medley**: Jingle Bells JG w LM & JJ; Sleigh Ride JG w LM & JJ; It Happened in Sun Valley LM & JJ; Winter Wonderland JG; Rudolph the Red-nosed Reindeer (instrumental) Dancers; Jingle Bells (reprise) JG w LM & JJ
12 **Here We Come A-Caroling** MT & Chorus
13 **Take Five** (instrumental) Dancers
14 **The Christmas Song** JG & MT
15 **Traditional Carol Medley**: Caroling, Caroling* Chorus; What Child Is This? JG; God Rest Ye Merry, Gentlemen Chorus; Hark! the Herald Angles Sing JJ & MT; Good King Wenceslas Chorus; It Came Upon a Midnight Clear LM & TE; Silent Night LL, JL & Chorus; Deck the Halls JG w JJ, LM, TE, LL, JL & MT; Here We Come A-Caroling (reprise)* Chorus; Rudolph the Red-nosed Reindeer (instrumental)* JG & Dancers
16 **Over the Rainbow** JG w LL & JL.

Note 1: All items except 12, 13, and 15 issued on LaserLight 12 467 and 72 467.*

SESSION 631207 (Los Angeles, 7th December 1963) MEL TORMÉ with Orchestra arranged and conducted by Shorty Rogers. The orchestra is small but includes flute, vibes, piano, guitar, bass and drums. Shorty Rogers, leader and arrangements.

A-7462 **Lullaby of Birdland** Atlantic 8091; Rhino Flashback R2 72886

A-7463 **New York, New York** Atlantic 8091, 80091; Rhino Flashback R2 72886

A-7464 **There's a Broken Heart for Every Light on Broadway** Atlantic 8091

A-7465 **The Brooklyn Bridge** Atlantic 8091.

Note 1: The titles on Atlantic 8091 also on Atlantic SD8091, ATL5005, SAL5005 and 80 078-2.

Note 2: The title on Atlantic 80091 also on SD80091 and AET6005.

For the Judy Garland Show broadcast on 22nd December 1963 see 6th December 1963.

For the Judy Garland Show broadcast on 5th January 1964 see 18th October 1963.

SESSION 640131 (recorded Hollywood, 31 January 1964; transmitted 16 February 1964). THE JUDY GARLAND SHOW. Show # 20. Judy Garland. Orchestra and chorus directed by Mort Lindsey on all items unless otherwise noted. Dance troop led by Peter Gennaro. Guests: Diahann Carroll (DC) and Mel Tormé (MT).

1 **I Can't Give You Anything But Love/Just You, Just Me** (instrumental) orchestra

2 **Hey, Look Me Over** JG

3 **Smile** JG

4 **I Can't Give You Anything But Love** JG

5 **After You've Gone** JG

6 **Alone Together** JG

7 **Come Rain or Come Shine** JG

8 **Quiet Nights of Quiet Stars** DC

9 **Goody, Goody** DC

10 **A Stranger in Town** (a few bars only) JG

11 **Blues in the Night** MT (with the Dancers)

12 **The Trolley Song** JG w MT Wiley Judy Duets

13 **Richard Rodgers and Harold Arlen medley**: Let's Call the Whole Thing Off JG w DC; It's Only a Paper Moon JG; Dancing on the Ceiling DC; That Old Black Magic JG; The Gentleman Is a Dope DC; Ill Wind JG; It Might As Well Be Spring DC; Hit the Road to Dreamland JG; The Surrey with the Fringe on Top DC; It's a New World JG; Stormy Weather JG w DC; Let's Take the Long Way Home JG w DC; Bali Ha'i DC; Manhattan DC; The Sweetest Sounds DC; Anyplace I Hang My Hat Is Home JG w DC

14 **Born in a Trunk sequence** JG.

Note 1: Wiley "Judy Duets" is one disc in a 2-CD set that has no catalog number.

For the Judy Garland Show broadcast on 16th February 1964 see 31st January 1964.

SESSION 640309 MEL TORMÉ 4 titles with Robert Mersey. Given on Columbia CK 53779 as recorded on 9th March 1964; but see 9th March 1965.

SESSION 640310A (Hollywood, 10th March 1964) MEL TORMÉ with Orchestra arranged and conducted by Dick Hazard.

CO 81822 **I Know Your Heart** Columbia 4-43022, CK 53779, CK 65165; Signature CBS 53779; CBS AAG227

CO 81823 **You'd Better Love Me** Columbia 4-43022, CK 53779, CK 65165; Signature CBS 53779; CBS AAG227; Rhino R2 71589; Read RC7-012-1.

Note 1: See note 1 for the next session concerning the recording location of this session.

SESSION 640310B (Hollywood, 10th March 1964) MEL TORMÉ with Orchestral accompaniment arranged and conducted by Robert Mersey.

CO 82255 **I See It Now** Columbia 4-43087, CK 65165; CBS AAG212

CO 82256 **Once in a Lifetime** Columbia 4-43087, CK 65165; CBS AAG212.

Note 1: There is some doubt over the location at which this and the previous session was

recorded. In his book The Other Side of the Rainbow, *Tormé maintains that for legal reasons he did not leave Los Angeles from the date of the recording of Episode # 22 of The Judy Garland Show on 14th February 1964 until after the final episode (# 26) had been recorded on 13th March 1964. Even then, he went a few days later to perform at a club in San Jose, California for two weeks. It is therefore impossible that these sessions took place in New York as Columbia imply by showing the prefix CO for these masters in the booklet for CD "That's All" (CK 65165). The notes for the Rhino set, give the location as Hollywood for CO 81823.*

SESSION 641005 (New York City, 5th October 1964) **MEL TORMÉ** with Orchestra arranged and conducted by Robert Mersey.

CO 83819 **One Little Snowflake** Columbia 4-43167, CK 65165; CBS 201737

CO 83820 **Ev'ry Day's a Holiday** Columbia 4-43167, CK 53779, CK 65165; Signature CBS 53779; CBS 201737.

Note 1: The label of CBS 201737 erroneously credits 83820 to Mort Garson, possibly because Garson is co-composer.

Note 2: CO 83819 also reputed to have been issued on Columbia 4-45283

SESSION 641216 (Hollywood, 16th December 1964) **MEL TORMÉ** with Orchestra and vocal group arranged and conducted by Robert Mersey. Probably similar instrumentation and personnel to the next session.

HCO 72210 **The Nearness of You** Columbia CL2318; Read RC7-012-1

HCO 72211 **My Romance** Columbia CL2318, 4-43383

HCO 72212 **Do I Love You Because You're Beautiful?** Columbia CL2318, 4-43230

HCO 72213 **Isn't It a Pity?** Columbia CL2318.

Note 1: The titles on Columbia CL2318 also on Columbia CS9118, CK 53779 and CK 65165, Signature CBS 53779, Columbia Special Products EN13090, CBS BPG/SBPG 62250.

Note 2: In the booklet with Columbia CK 53779, master 72210 has a CO prefix indicating a New York City recording, while masters 72211-13 are given the prefix HCO indicating a Hollywood location. A possible but unlikely situation. See also Session 641219. The notes for CK 65165 give all the prefixes as HCO.

SESSION 641219 (Hollywood, 19th December 1964) **MEL TORMÉ** with Orchestra arranged and conducted by Robert Mersey. James Decker, Richard Perissi, French horns; Gene Capriano, Plas Johnson, woodwinds; Leonard Atkins, Jacques Gasselin, Benny Gill, Sarah Kreindler, Carl LaMagna, Lou Raderman, Mischa Russell, Paul Shure, Gerald Vinci, violins; Alvin Dinkin, Allan Harshman, violas; Armand Kaproff, cello; Dave Grusin, piano; Barney Kessel, guitar; Rollie Bundock, bass; Jack Spurling, drums; Louis Adrian, Dale Anderson, Sol Babitz, Jesse Ehrlich, Elizabeth Ershoff, John Gray, Louis Kievman and Gertrude Schrager, unknown instruments. (*Note 3*).

HCO 72214 **I've Got You Under My Skin** Columbia CL2318; Rhino R2 71589; Read RC7-012-1

HCO 72215 **That's All** Columbia CL2318, 4-43230

HCO 72216 **What Is There to Say?** Columbia CL2318

HCO 72217 **The Folks That Live on the Hill** Columbia CL2318; Rhino R2 71589; Read RC7-012-1.

Note 1: The titles on Columbia CL2318 are also on Columbia CS9118, CK 53779 and CK 65165, Signature CBS 53779, Columbia Special Products EN13090, CBS BPG/SBPG 62250.

Note 2: It sounds as if there are more than

just two woodwinds on most of these tracks and there is a significant amount of percussion on 72214. A harp and vibes are also audible on 72215. I cannot hear the previously reported 8 brass and 5 saxes on any of the tracks recorded for Columbia CL2318 (Sessions 641216, 641219 and 650309) except possibly on master 85638 (Session 650309).

Note 3: Prefixes for master numbers 72214 and 72216 are in the booklet for Columbia CK 53779 as CO. The idea that the recordings were made alternately in New York City and Hollywood on the same day is rather bizarre.

SESSION 650003 (New York City, 1965) **ALL THAT JAZZ** (Film soundtrack) MEL TORMÉ with Junior Mance, piano; Aaron Bell, bass; Herbie Lovelle, drums.

All That Jazz (3'03") Reprise R-/RS-6180; Rhino R2 75481

All That Jazz (1'45") Reprise R-/RS-6180.

Note 1: These tracks are from the soundtrack of the film A Man Called Adam, with compositions and arrangements by Benny Carter. Tormé, also appears in the film as himself.

SESSION 650309 (New York City, 9th March 1965 [note 2]) MEL TORMÉ with Orchestra (woodwinds, vibes, strings, piano, guitar, bass and drums) arranged and conducted by Robert Mersey.

CO 85637 **P.S. I Love You** Columbia CL2318, CK 53779; Signature CBS 53779; Read RC7-012-1.

CO 85638 **Ho-ba-la-la** Columbia CL2318, 4-43383

CO 85639 **Haven't We Met?** (note 3) Columbia CL2318, CK 53779; Signature CBS 53779; Rhino R2 71589

CO 85640 **The Second Time Around** Columbia CL2318, CK 53779; Signature CBS 53779; Read RC7-012-1.

Note 1: The titles on Columbia CL2318 are also on Columbia CS9118 and CK 65165, Columbia Special Products EN13090, CBS BPG/SBPG 62250.

Note 2: The date for this session has also been given as March 1964 but the master numbers fit the later date.

Note 3: Add brass section.

Note 4: In the booklet with CK 53779 the master number of Haven't We Met? is wrongly given as CO 85638.

SESSION 660128 (Los Angeles, 28th January 1966) MEL TORMÉ with Orchestra arranged and conducted by Shorty Rogers (SR) or Dave Grusin (DG).

HCO 87691 **Dominique's Discotheque** (SR) Columbia 4-43550, CK 65164; CBS 202065

HCO 87692 **The Power of Love** (DG) Columbia 4-43550, CK 65164; CBS 202065, SBPG/BPG 62809.

Note 1: Master HCO 87692 is credited to Shorty Rogers in the notes for CK 65164.

SESSION 660225 (Hollywood, 25th February 1966) MEL TORMÉ with Orchestra arranged and conducted by Mort Garson.

HCO 87727 **Hang on to Me** Columbia 4-43677, CK 65165

HCO 87728 **Seventeen** Columbia CK 65165

HCO 87729 **I Remember Suzanne** Columbia 4-44180, CK 65165; CBS 2857; Read RC7-012-1

HCO 87730 **Only the Very Young** Columbia CK 65165; Read RC7-012-1.

SESSION 660418 (Hollywood, 18th April 1966) MEL TORMÉ with orchestra arranged and conducted by Mort Garson.

HCO 87827 **Walk on By** Columbia CL2535, G3P-23

HCO 87828 **Time** Columbia CL2535, 4-43872

HCO 87829 **Homeward Bound** Columbia CL2535

HCO 87830 **All That Jazz** Columbia 4-43677, CK 65164, COL 487890 2.

Note 1: The titles on Columbia CL2535 are also on Columbia CS9335 and CK 65164 and on CBS BPG/SBPG 62809.

SESSION 660610 (Hollywood, 10th June 1966) **MEL TORMÉ** with Orchestra arranged and conducted by Mort Garson. Robert Barene, Arnold Belnick, Harry Bluestone, James Getzoff, Nathan Ross, Henry Roth, Sidney Sharp, Marshall Sosson, violins; Joseph DiFiore, Myron Sadler, violas; Armand Kaproff, Frederick Seykora, cellos; Michael Melvoin, piano; Howard Roberts, guitar; Al McKibbon, bass; Jim Gordon, drums; Gary Coleman, vibes.

HCO 87869 **Strangers in the Night** Columbia CL2535, CK 53779; Signature CBS 53779; CBS BPG/SBPG 62809; Rhino R2 71589; Read RC7-012-1; Capitol 72434-94749-0-1

HCO 87870 **Better Use Your Head** Columbia CL2535

HCO 87871 **You Don't Have to Say You Love Me** Columbia CK 65164.

Note 1: The titles on Columbia CL2535 are also on Columbia CS9335 and CK 65164 and on CBS BPG/SBPG 62809.
Note 2: The date for 87869 has also been given, wrongly, as 22nd August 1966.

SESSION 660611 (Hollywood, 11th June 1966) **MEL TORMÉ** with Orchestra arranged and conducted by Mort Garson.

HCO 87872 **If I Had a Hammer** Columbia CL2535; CBS WEP1136

HCO 87873 **Comin' Home Baby** Columbia CL2535

HCO 87942 **Pretty Flamingo** Columbia CL2535

HCO 87943 **My Little Red Book** Columbia CL2535

HCO 87944 **Red Rubber Ball** Columbia CL2535; CBS 202488

HCO 87945 **Secret Agent Man** Columbia CL2535.

Note 1: The titles on Columbia CL2535 are also on Columbia CS9335 and CK 65164 and on CBS BPG/SBPG 62809.

SESSION 661001 (New York City, 1st October 1966) **MEL TORMÉ** with Orchestra arranged and conducted by Pat Williams.

CO 90316 **Paris Smiles** Columbia 4-43872, CK 65165; CBS 202488; Read RC7-012-1

CO 90317 **The Christmas Song** Columbia 4-45283, CK 53779, CK 65165; Signature CBS 53779; Read RC7-012-1.

SESSION 661029 (Basin Street East, New York City, 29th October 1966) **MEL TORMÉ** with Woody Herman and the Swingin' Herd. Marvin Stamm, Bill Chase, Lyn Biviano, Bill Byrne, trumpets; Jerry Collins, Carl Fontana, Henry Southall, trombones; Woody Herman, clarinet and alto-sax; Bob Pierson, Louis Orenstein, Sal Nistico, tenor-saxes; Tom Anastos, baritone-sax; Nat Pierce, piano; Tony Leonardi, bass; Ronnie Zito, drums (*note 1*).

Four Brothers (*note 2*) Stash ST-CD-4
Lonely Girl Stash ST-CD-4
Bluesette Stash ST-CD-4.

Note 1: This personnel is for July 1966 and may not be entirely accurate for the October date.
Note 2: No vocal, Tormé plays drums.

SESSION 670427 (Hollywood, 27th April 1967) **MEL TORMÉ** with Orchestra arranged and conducted by Ernie Freeman.

HCO 94782 **Lover's Roulette** Columbia 4-44180, CK 65164; CBS 2857; Read RC7-012-1

HCO 94783 **Ciao Baby** Columbia CK 65164

HCO 94784 **Molly Marlene** Columbia CK 65164

HCO 94785 **The King** Columbia CK 65164.

SESSION 671117 (Hollywood, 17th

November 1967) **MEL TORMÉ** with Orchestra arranged and conducted by Arnold Goland.

HCO 95359 **Lima Lady** Columbia 4-44399, CK 65164

HCO 95360 **Wait Until Dark** Columbia 4-44399, CK 65164

HCO 95361 **Only When I'm Lonely** Columbia CK 65164.

1968–1982: LIBERTY, CAPITOL, LONDON, ATLANTIC, CENTURY, GRYPHON, FINESSE AND FLAIR

SESSION 680201 (Los Angeles, 1st February 1968 [*note 2*]) **MEL TORMÉ** with Orchestra arranged by Lincoln Mayorga. Lincoln Mayorga, leader and arranger; Eugene Dinovi, piano and organ; Michael Deasy, Herb Ellis, Barney Kessel, guitars; Ray Pohlman, bass; John Cyr, drums; Buddy Childers, John Audino, trumpets; Frank Rosolino, trombone; George Auld, Dave Pell, Bill Green, saxes.

LB-2527 **A Day in the Life of Bonny and Clyde** Liberty 56022, LST7560; Rhino R2 71589

LB-2528 **Brother, Can You Spare a Dime?** Liberty 56022, LST7560.

Note 1: Both titles also on Liberty LPR 3560, LBL-/LBS-83119E and LBF15064.
Note 2: the horns were overdubbed in Los Angeles on 5th February 1968.

SESSION 680202 (Los Angeles, February 1968) **MEL TORMÉ** with Orchestra arranged by Lincoln Mayorga probably a similar personnel to the previous session.

Button Up Your Overcoat Liberty LST7560

Annie Doesn't Live Here Any More Liberty LST7560

I Found a Million Dollar Baby Liberty LST7560

I Concentrate on You Liberty LST7560

The Music Goes Round and Round Liberty LST7560

We're in the Money Liberty LST7560
Little White Lies Liberty LST7560
With Plenty of Money and You Liberty LST7560

You're the Cream in My Coffee Liberty LST7560
Cab Driver Liberty LST7560.

Note 1: All titles also on Liberty LPR 3560, LBL-/LBS-83119E.

SESSION 680301 (Los Angeles, early 1968) **MEL TORMÉ** with Orchestra arranged by Shorty Rogers.

LB-2625 **Five-Four** Liberty 56066
LB-2626 **Didn't We** Liberty 56066.

SESSION 680401 (Los Angeles, ca 1968) **MEL TORMÉ** with unidentified studio orchestra.

That Face (interpolating *Look at That Face*) Stash ST-CD-4.

SESSION 690602 (Los Angeles, 2nd June 1969) **MEL TORMÉ** with Orchestra arranged and conducted by Jimmy Jones or (JH) Jay Hill.

72544-A3 **Games People Play** Capitol ST-313, P-2613, ST21585

72545 **Midnight Swinger** Capitol ST-313

72546 **Windmills of Your Mind** (JH) Capitol ST-313, ST21585; Curb D2-77618; Ranwood 8270-2; Read RC7-012-1

72547 **Happy Together** Capitol ST-313, ST21585; Curb D2-77618.

SESSION 690603 (Los Angeles, 3rd June 1969) **MEL TORMÉ** with Orchestra arranged and conducted by Jimmy Jones or (BB) Bob Bain.

72548 **A Time for Us** Capitol ST-313, ST21585; Curb D2-77618; Read RC7-012-1

72549 **Yesterday, When I Was Young** (BB) Capitol ST-313; Curb D2-77618; Rhino R2 71589; Read RC7-012-1
72550 **The Right to Love** Capitol unissued
72551 **She's Leaving Home** Capitol ST-313, ST21585.

SESSION 690718 (Los Angeles, 18th July 1969) MEL TORMÉ with Orchestra arranged and conducted by Jimmy Jones.
72843-A3 **Willie & Laura Mae Jones** Capitol ST-313, P-2613
72844 **If** Capitol unissued
72845 **Hurry on Down** Capitol ST-313
72846 **A Bucket Full of Tears** Capitol ST-313.

SESSION 691201 (Los Angeles, 1st December 1969) MEL TORMÉ with Orchestra arranged and conducted by Jimmy Jones.
73207 **Requiem: 820 Latham** Capitol ST-430, ST21585, 2743
73208 **Something** Capitol unissued
73209 **Wanderin' Star** Capitol unissued
73210 **Take a Letter Maria** Capitol ST-430, ST21585.

SESSION 691211 (Los Angeles, 11th December 1969)
73699 **Catch a Robber by the Toe** Capitol ST-430
73700 **Hung Up Being Free** Capitol ST-430, ST21585
73701 **You've Made Me So Very Happy** Capitol ST-430, ST21585; Curb D2-77618; Read RC7-012-1
73702 **Into Something** Capitol ST-430, ST21585.

SESSION 691223 (Los Angeles, 23rd December 1969)
73735 **Spinning Wheel** Capitol ST-430, ST21585, 2743; Curb D2-77618; Read RC7-012-1
73736 **Sunshine Superman** Capitol ST-430, ST21585, CDP 7243 8 55161 2 2

73737 **Traces** Capitol ST-430, ST21585; Curb D2-77618; Read RC7-012-1
73738 **Raindrops Keep Fallin' on My Head** Capitol ST-430, ST21585; Curb D2-77618; Ranwood 8270-2; Read RC7-012-1.

SESSION 710101 (unknown location, 1971) MEL TORMÉ with unknown orchestra including brass, reeds and strings. A trumpet is featured.
Whose Garden Was This London 45-171, HLU10355
Morning Star London 45-171
ZCL7960 **A Phone Call to the Past** London 45-180, HLU10355
ZCL7961 **I Cried for You** London 45-180.

Note 1: According to the label of the USA issues, these recordings were made by Flamingo Records, while the UK issue gives the original recording company as Fancibird.

SESSION 740901 (The Maisonette, St. Regis Hotel, New York City, September 1974) MEL TORMÉ featuring AL PORCINO AND HIS ORCHESTRA. Personnel unknown but instrumentation is 4 trumpets, 3 trombones, 5 saxes and rhythm.
30207 **Introduction** Atlantic SD18129, K50135
30208 **Jet Set** Atlantic SD18129, K50135
30209 **What Are You Doing the Rest of Your Life?** Atlantic SD18129, K50135; Rhino R2 71589
30210 **Mountain Greenery** Atlantic SD18129, K50135
30211 **It Takes Too Long to Learn to Live Alone** Atlantic SD18129, K50135
30212 **(Get Your Kicks) on Route 66** Atlantic SD18129, K50135; Rhino Flashback R2 72886
30213 **Gershwin Medley** Atlantic SD18129, K50135; Rhino R2 71589:
a. **I Got Rhythm**; b. **Mine**; c. **Do-Do-Do**; d. **'S Wonderful**; e. **Embraceable**

You; f. **Love Walked In**; g. **Love Is Here to Stay**; h. **Oh, Lady Be Good**; i. **A Foggy Day**; j. **How Long Has This Been Going On?** (*note 2*); k. **Oh Bess, O Where's My Bess?** (*note 3*); l. **Who Cares?**; m. **Love Is Sweeping the Country**; n. **Of Thee I Sing**; o. **Swanee**; p. **Strike Up the Band**; q. **I'll Build a Stairway to Paradise**

30214 **Superstition** Atlantic SD18129, K50135

30215 **The Party's Over** Atlantic SD18129, K50135.

Note 1: All the items on Atlantic SD18129 also on Collectors' Choice Music CCM0074-2. On CCM0074-2, a little of Tormé's spoken introductions to the tunes has been deleted without affecting any of the music.
Note 2: Tormé plays his own piano accompaniment.
Note 3: These recordings were made privately and sold to Atlantic Records.

SESSION 770601 (London, June 1977) MEL TORMÉ with the Chris Gunning Orchestra. Orchestrations and arrangements by Chris Gunning except for *Send in the Clowns* which is arranged by Tormé. Personnel includes Phil Woods, alto-sax; Gordon Beck, Barry Miles, keyboards; Vic Juris, guitar; Brian Hodges, electric bass; Terry Silverlight, drums and percussion. Unknown strings.

All in Love Is Fair Gryphon G-916
The First Time Ever I Saw Your Face Gryphon G-916
New York State of Mind Gryphon G-916
Stars Gryphon G-916
Send in the Clowns Gryphon G-916
Ordinary Fool Gryphon G-916
Medley: When the World Was Young/ Yesterday When I Was Young Gryphon G-916
Bye Bye Blackbird Gryphon G-916
It's Too Late Paddle Wheel KICJ 128
Never Look Back Paddle Wheel KICJ 128
Charade Paddle Wheel KICJ 128
Like a Lover Paddle Wheel KICJ 128
What's This? Paddle Wheel KICJ 128

Note 1: The titles on Gryphon G-916 may also have been issued as Gryphon G-796.
Note 2: The titles on Gryphon G-916 also issued on, Phoenix 20 P20 627, Rhapsody RH CD 3, Sandstone SAN 5005, CD33083 and Paddle Wheel KICJ 128.

SESSION 780101 (New York City, January 1978) MEL TORMÉ AND BUDDY RICH with the Buddy Rich Band. Chuck Schmidt, Dean Pratt, John Marshall, Dave Kennedy, trumpets; John Mosca, Dale Kirkland, Dave Boyle, trombone; Tony Price, tuba; Chick Wilson, Alan Vu Gauvin, Steve Marcus, Gary Pribeck, Greg Smith, saxes; Hank Jones, piano; Tom Warrington, bass; Buddy Rich, drums and leader.

When I Found You Century CRDD-1100; Phoenix 20 P20 627
Here's That Rainy Day Century CRDD-1100
Blues in the Night Century CRDD-1100
Bluesette Century CRDD-1100
You Are the Sunshine of My Life Century CRDD-1100
I Won't Last a Day Without You Century CRDD-1100
Lady Be Good Century CRDD-1100.

Note 1: Century CRDD-1100 is a direct-to-disc recording.
Note 2: The titles on Century CRDD-1100 also on Gryphon G-784, RCA Victor PL25178 and BBC CJCD833 and ZCJC 833.
Note 3: The titles on Century CRDD-1100 also on Hindsight HCD-272 which also includes two instrumental tracks without Tormé recorded at a different session.

SESSION 800612 (Marty's, New York City, 12th and 13th June 1980) MEL TORMÉ

accompanied by Mike Renzi, piano; Rufus Reid, bass; Donny Osborne, drums.
Let's Take a Walk Around the Block Finesse W2X 37484
New York State of Mind Finesse W2X 37484
Silly Habits (*note 2*) Finesse W2X 37484
Mountain Greenery (*note 3*) Finesse W2X 37484
Medley: Watch What Happens, Fly Me to the Moon, You and the Night and the Music, Shaking the Blues Away Finesse W2X 37484
The Folks Who Live on the Hill Finesse W2X 37484
Chase Me Charlie Finesse W2X 37484
The Best Is Yet to Come (*note 4*) Finesse W2X 37484; Rhino R2 71589
Isn't It a Pity? Finesse W2X 37484.

Note 1: The titles on Finesse W2X 37484 also on Finesse 30JD-20/21 and DCC 631.
Note 2: Add Janis Ian, vocal.
Note 3: Tormé replaces Renzi on piano.
Note 4: Cy Coleman, piano and vocal replaces Renzi.

SESSION 810826 (Marty's, New York City, 26th and 27th August 1981) MEL TORMÉ same as last except Jay Leonhart, bass; replaces Reid.
When the World Was Young Finesse W2X 37484
Pick Yourself Up Finesse W2X 37484; Rhino R2 71589
Cottage for Sale Finesse W2X 37484
Take a Letter Miss Jones Finesse W2X 37484
Real Thing (*note 2*) Finesse W2X 37484
Medley (*note 2*): **Line for Lyons, Venus de Milo, Walking Shoes** Finesse W2X 37484
Isn't It Romantic Finesse W2X 37484
Porgy and Bess Medley (*note 3*): **Summertime, They Pass by Singin', I Got Plenty o' Nuttin', It Takes a Long Pull to Get There, It Ain't Necessarily So, Strawberry Woman, Oh Bess, Oh Where's My Bess, Bess You Is My Woman** Finesse W2X 37484
Wave Finesse W2X 37484
I Guess I'll Have to Change My Plan (*note 4*) Finesse W2X 37484
Love for Sale Finesse W2X 37484.

Note 1: The titles on Finesse W2X 37484 also on Finesse 30JD-20/21 and DCC 631.
Note 2: Add Gerry Mulligan, baritone sax.
Note 3: Tormé replaces Renzi on piano.
Note 4: Add Jonathan Schwartz, vocal.

SESSION 820327 (Marty's, New York City 27th March 1982) MEL TORMÉ accompanied by Mike Renzi, piano; Jay Leonhart, bass; Donny Osborne, drums.
Lulu's Back in Town Flair PG 8200
Looking at You Flair PG 8200
That Face Flair PG 8200
I'm Gonna Miss You Flair PG 8200
Medley — A Tribute to Fred Astaire Flair PG 8200
What Are You Doing the Rest of Your Life? Flair PG 8200
Too Close for Comfort Paddle Wheel KIJC 129
Sophisticated Lady Flair PG 8200
Stormy Weather Flair PG 8200
When the Sun Comes Out Flair PG 8200
Autumn Leaves (*note 2*) Flair PG 8200
The Folks Who Live on the Hill Paddle Wheel KIJC 129
Pieces of Dreams Flair PG 8200
I Like to Recognize the Tune Flair PG 8200
Day In, Day Out Flair PG 8200
Watch What Happens Flair PG 8200.

Note 1: All the tracks on Flair PG 8200 except "Pieces of Dreams" are also on Paddle Wheel KIJC 129 (a CD). The CD also includes more of Tormé's narrative between the songs than is heard on the Flair LP. All the tracks on Paddle Wheel KIJC 129 also on Jazz Heritage 512965T.

Note 2: Autumn Leaves on Paddle Wheel (a CD) includes an introduction that was edited from the Flair issue.

1982–1996 CONCORD JAZZ AND TELARC

SESSION 820401 (Miami Beach or Detroit, 1982) **WAS (NOT WAS) with MEL TORMÉ**. Orchestra arranged and conducted by Mike Renzi. Marin Alsop, Carol Poole-Cross, violins; Jill B Jaffe, viola; Beverly Lauidsen, cello; Mike Renzi, piano; Luis Resto, emulator; Don Was, Oberheim bells; Jay Leonhart, bass.

Zaz Turned Blue Geffen GHS-4016; Rhino R2 71589.

Note 1: In the notes to Rhino R2 71589, Don Was describes the session as being in Miami Beach but the discography gives Detroit.

SESSION 820415 (Concert, Peacock Court, Hotel Mark Hopkins, San Francisco, 15th April 1982) **GEORGE SHEARING & MEL TORMÉ**. George Shearing, piano; Mel Tormé, vocal; Brian Torff, bass.

All God's Chillun Got Rhythm Concord Jazz CJ-190

Born to Be Blue Concord Jazz CJ-190, CCD-4811-2

Give Me the Simple Life Concord Jazz CJ-190

Good Morning Heartache (*note 2*) Concord Jazz CJ-190

Manhattan Hoedown (*note 2*) Concord Jazz CJ-190

You'd Be So Nice to Come Home to Concord Jazz CJ-190

A Nightingale Sang in Berkeley Square Concord Jazz CJ-190

Love Concord Jazz CJ-190

It Might as Well Be Spring Concord Jazz CJ-190

Lullaby of Birdland Concord Jazz CJ-190.

Note 1: The titles on CJ-190 are also on CCD-4190, CJC-190 and CJ-190-C.
Note 2: Omit Tormé.

SESSION 830120 (New York City; instrumental recordings made 17–19th January 1983; vocal over dubbing 20th January 1983) **THE GLENN MILLER ORCHESTRA**: Larry O'Brien, leader; Marvin Stamm, Markie Markowitz, Jimmy Maxwell, John Frosk, trumpets; Sonny Rosso, Wayne Andre, George Masson, Paul Faulise, trombones; Walt Levinsky, lead clarinet and saxes; Phil Bodner, Bill Saplin, Morty Lewis, Sol Schlinger, saxes; Bernie Leighton, piano; Bucky Pizzarelli, guitar; Jay Leonhart, bass; Ronnie Zito, drums. Vocal group: Julius LaRosa, Mel Tormé, Marlene Ver Planck, Marty Nelson, Michael Mark.

Chattanooga Choo Choo (*note 2*) GRP GRP-A-1002

Kalamazoo GRP GRP-A-1002

Pennsylvania 6-5000 (*note 3*) GRP GRP-A-1002.

Note 1: The titles on GRP-A-1002 are also on GRPC-1002, GRPD-9502 and GRD 2004.
Note 2: Tormé also takes the whistling solo.
Note 3: Add Christopher LaRosa, vocal. The GRP sleeve notes are ambiguous about the vocal group on this. It sounds like just the members of the band chanting "Pennsylvania 6-5000" but the notes imply that Christopher LaRosa joined in having come to watch his father (Julius) recording the group vocals. Personally, I do not think that the vocal group contributed to this track and therefore, Tormé is not present.

SESSION 830301 (San Francisco, March 1983) **GEORGE SHEARING — MEL TORMÉ**. George Shearing, piano; Mel Tormé, vocal; Don Thompson, bass.

Shine on Your Shoes Concord Jazz CJ-219

How Do You Say Auf Wiedersehen?
(*note 2*) Concord Jazz CJ-219, CCD-4790-2
 Oleo (*note 3*) Concord Jazz CJ-219
 Stardust Concord Jazz CJ-219
 Hi Fly Concord Jazz CJ-219, CCD-4811-2
 Smoke Gets in Your Eyes Concord Jazz CJ-219
 What's This? Concord Jazz CJ-219
 Away in a Manger (*note 3*) Concord Jazz CJ-219
 Here's to My Lady (*note 2*) Concord Jazz CJ-219, CCD-4790-2.

Note 1: The titles on CJ-219 are also on CCD-4219, CJC-219 and CJ-219-C.
Note 2: Omit Thompson.
Note 3: Omit Tormé.

SESSION 831001 (Washington, D.C., October 1983, in concert, Charlie's, Georgetown) **MEL TORMÉ — GEORGE SHEARING.** Mel Tormé, vocal; George Shearing, piano; Don Thompson, bass; Donny Osborne, drums.
 Medley Concord Jazz CJ-248
 Just One of Those Things Concord Jazz CJ-248
 On Green Dolphin Street Concord Jazz CJ-248
 Dream Dancing Concord Jazz CJ-248
 I'm Hip Concord Jazz CJ-248
 Then I'll Be Tired of You Concord Jazz CJ-248
 Medley: Caught in the Middle of My Years, Welcome to the Club Concord Jazz CJ-248
 Nica's Dream (*note 2*) Concord Jazz CJ-248
 Chase Me Charlie Concord Jazz CJ-248
 Love Is Just Around the Corner Concord Jazz CJ-248.

Note 1: The titles on CJ-248 are also on CCD-4248, CJC-248 and CJ-248-C.
Note 2: omit Tormé and Osborne.

SESSION 840101 (Los Angeles, mid 1984) **BARRY MANILOW.** Barry Manilow, piano and vocal; Bill Mays, piano and rhodes keyboard, Mundell Lowe, guitar; George Duvivier, bass; Shelly Manne, drums; Mel Tormé, vocal.
 Big City Blues Arista AL-8-8254; Rhino R2 71589.

Note 1: This track also on Arista 206 496, 406 496 and 07822-18945-2.
*Note 2: This track is on the album **2:00 AM Paradise Cafe**. The rehearsals for this album were filmed and released as a video. The UK issue of this is Video Collection VC 4008.*

SESSION 850501 (San Francisco, May 1985) **GEORGE SHEARING — MEL TORMÉ.** George Shearing, piano; Mel Tormé, vocal.
 I'll Be Seeing You Concord Jazz CJ-294, CCD-4790-2, CCD-4811-2
 Moon Medley: Love and the Moon, Oh, You Crazy Moon, No Moon at All Concord Jazz CJ-294
 After the Waltz Is Over Concord Jazz CJ-294, CCD-4790-2
 This Time the Dream's on Me Concord Jazz CJ-294
 Last Night, When We Were Young Concord Jazz CJ-294
 You Changed My Life Concord Jazz CJ-294
 Dream Medley: I Had the Craziest Dream, Darn That Dream Concord Jazz CJ-294
 Brigg Fair Concord Jazz CJ-294
 My Foolish Heart Concord Jazz CJ-294, CCD-4790-2
 You're Driving Me Crazy Concord Jazz CJ-294.

Note 1: The titles on CJ-294 are also on CCD-4294, CJC-294 and CJ-294-C.

SESSION 850919 (Broadcast. New York City, 19th September 1985) **MEL TORMÉ.** Mike Renzi, piano; Jay Leonhart,

bass; Donny Osborne, drums. From a broadcast on the WNEW radio program "New York Tonight."
Theme from Arthur (The Best That You Can Do) Rhino R2 71589.

SESSION 860500 (Toronto, Canada, May 1986 [recording started on 16th May]) MEL TORMÉ— ROB McCONNELL AND THE BOSS BRASS. Arnie Chycoski, Erich Traugott, Guido Basso, Dave Woods, John MacLeod, trumpets and flugelhorns; Rob McConnell, trombone, arrangements and conductor; Ian McDougall, Bob Livingston, Dave McMurdo, trombones; Ron Hughes, bass trombone; George Stimpson, James MacDonald, French horns; Moe Koffman, clarinet, soprano- and alto-saxes, flute; Jerry Toth, alto-sax, clarinet and flute; Eugene Amaro, tenor-sax and flute; Rick Wilkins, tenor-sax and clarinet; Robert Leonard, baritone-sax, bass-clarinet and flute; Jim Dale, acoustic and electric pianos; Ed Bickert, guitar; Steve Wallace, bass; Jerry Fuller, drums; Brian Leonard, percussion.
Just Friends Concord Jazz CJ-306, CCD-4811-2
September Song Concord Jazz CJ-306
Don' Cha Go 'Way Mad Concord Jazz CJ-306
A House Is Not a Home Concord Jazz CJ-306, CCD-4790-2
The Song Is You Concord Jazz CJ-306
Cow Cow Boogie (*note 2*) Concord Jazz CJ-306
A Handful of Stars/Stars Fell on Alabama Concord Jazz CJ-306
Duke Ellington Medley: It Don't Mean a Thing (If It Ain't Got That Swing), Do Nothing Till You Hear from Me, Mood Indigo, Take the "A" Train; Sophisticated Lady, Satin Doll Concord Jazz CJ-306.

Note 1: The titles on CJ-306 are also on CCD-4306, CJC-306 and CJ-306-C.

Note 2: On this track, Guido Bass also plays harmonica and Dave Woods also plays violin.

SESSION 870100 (Hollywood, January 1987) DAFFY DUCK'S QUACKBUSTERS: Night of the Living Duck (Film soundtrack). MEL TORMÉ (as Daffy Duck) with Mike Renzi, piano.
Monsters Lead Such Interesting Lives Rhino R2 7548.

SESSION 870800 (Paul Masson Mountain Winery, Saratoga, CA, August 1987) MEL TORMÉ— GEORGE SHEARING. Mel Tormé, vocal; George Shearing, piano; John Leitham, bass; Donny Osborne, drums.
Whisper Not/Love Me or Leave Me Concord Jazz CJ-341
Out of This World Concord Jazz CJ-341
Someday I'll Find You Concord Jazz CJ-341
The Midnight Sun Concord Jazz CJ-341
New York, New York Medley: Me and My Girl, Mack the Knife, Birth of the Blues, Send a Little Love My Way, How High the Moon, New York, New York Concord Jazz CJ-341, CCD-4811-2
Folks Who Live on the Hill Concord Jazz CJ-341
Bitter Sweet Concord Jazz CJ-341
Since I Fell for You Concord Jazz CJ-341
The Way You Look Tonight Concord Jazz CJ-341
Anyone Can Whistle/A Tune for Humming Concord Jazz CJ-341
When Sunny Gets Blue Concord Jazz CJ-341
Little Man You've Had a Busy Day Concord Jazz CJ-341.

Note 1: The titles on CJ-341 are also on CCD-4341, CJC-341 and CJ-341-C.

SESSION 880000 MEL TORMÉ with Orchestra: A Christmas Album was recorded for Concord in 1988 but never released.

SESSION 880800 (Hollywood, August 1988) MEL TORMÉ and the MARTY PAICH DEK-TETTE; Warren Luening, Jack Sheldon, trumpets; Bob Enevoldsen, valve trombone; Lou McGarity, trombone; Jim Self, tuba; Gary Foster, alto-sax; Ken Peplowski, tenor-sax; Bob Efford, baritone-sax; Pete Jolly, piano; Chuck Berghofer, bass; Jeff Hamilton, drums; Joe Porcaro, Efrain Toro, percussion; Marty Paich, arranger and conductor.

Sweet Georgia Brown Concord Jazz CJ 360
Walk Between Raindrops Concord Jazz CJ 360
When You Wish Upon a Star/I'm Wishing Concord Jazz CJ 360
Bossa Nova Potpourri: The Gift, One Note Samba, How Insensitive Concord Jazz CJ 360
The Trolley Song/Get Me to the Church on Time Concord Jazz CJ 360
More Than You Know Concord Jazz CJ 360, CCD-4790-2
The Goodbye Look Concord Jazz CJ 360
The Blues Concord Jazz CJ 360
For Whom the Bell Tolls/Spain (I Can Recall) Concord Jazz CJ 360.

Note 1: The titles on CJ-360 are also on CCD-4360 and CJ-360-C.

SESSION 881200 (Fujitsu-Concord Jazz Concert, Kan-i Hoken Hall, Tokyo, Japan, December 1988) MEL TORMÉ and the MARTY PAICH DEK-TETTE. Warren Luening, Jack Sheldon, trumpets; Bob Enevoldsen, valve trombone; Dan Barrett, trombone; Jim Self, tuba; Gary Foster, alto-sax; Ken Peplowski, tenor-sax and clarinet; Bob Efford, baritone-sax; Allen Farnham, piano; Chuck Berghofer, bass; John Von Ohlen, drums; Marty Paich, DX-7, arranger and conductor.

It Don't Mean a Thing (If It Ain't Got That Swing) (*note 2*) Concord Jazz CJ-382
Sweet Georgia Brown Concord Jazz CJ-382, CCD-4811-2
Just in Time Concord Jazz CJ-382
When the Sun Comes Out Concord Jazz CJ-382
The Carioca Concord Jazz CJ-382
More Than You Know Concord Jazz CJ-382
Too Close for Comfort Concord Jazz CJ-382, CCD-4811-2
The City Concord Jazz CJ-382
Bossa Nova Potpourri: The Gift, One Note Samba, How Insensitive Concord Jazz CJ-382
On the Street Where You Live Concord Jazz CJ-382
Cotton Tail (*note 3*) Concord Jazz CJ-382
The Christmas Song (*note 4*) Concord Jazz CJ-382
It Don't Mean a Thing (If It Ain't Got That Swing) (*note 2*) Concord Jazz CJ-382.

Note 1: The titles on CJ-382 are also on CCD-4382 and CJ-382-C.
Note 2: Omit Tormé.
Note 3: This is an instrumental on which Tormé plays drums and Ken Peplowski plays clarinet.
Note 4: Also on Concord CCD-4720. Tormé is accompanied only by Sheldon, Paich, Farnham, Berghofer and Von Ohlen.

SESSION 890000 (Hollywood, 1989) DICK TRACY (Film soundtrack) MEL TORMÉ with a studio orchestra.
Live Alone and Like It Rhino R2 75481.

Note 1: Tormé sings this song "off screen" for this animated cartoon.

SESSION 900801A (22nd Concord Jazz Festival, Concord, CA, August 1990)

MEL TORMÉ accompanied by John Campbell, piano; Bob Maize, bass; Donny Osborne, drums.

Sing for Your Supper/Sing, Sing, Sing/Sing (Sing a Song) Concord Jazz CCD-4433

You Make Me Feel So Young Concord Jazz CCD-4433

Early Autumn Concord Jazz CCD-4433

Guys and Dolls Medley: Guys and Dolls, Fugue for Tinhorns, The Oldest Established, If I Were a Bell, My Time of Day, I've Never Been in Love Before, Sit Down, You're Rocking the Boat, Luck Be a Lady Concord Jazz CCD-4433

Medley: I Could Have Told You; Losing My Mind; Deep in a Dream; Goin' Out of My Head Concord Jazz CCD-4433

Too Darn Hot Concord Jazz CCD-4433

Day in Day Out Concord Jazz CCD-4433.

Note 1: The titles on CCD-4433 are also on CJ-433-C.

SESSION 900801B (22nd Concord Jazz Festival, Concord, CA, August 1990) MEL TORMÉ with the FRANK WESS — HARRY EDISON ORCHESTRA. Harry Edison, Ray Brown, Pete Minger, Joe Newman, trumpets; Al Grey, Grover Mitchell, Benny Powell, trombones; Curtis Peagler, Marshal Royal, alto-saxes; Frank Wess, Billy Mitchell, tenor-saxes; Bill Ramsey, baritone-sax; John Campbell, piano; Ted Dunbar, guitar; Bob Maize, bass; Donny Osborne, drums.

Down for Double Concord Jazz CCD-4433

You're Driving Me Crazy (What Did I Do) Concord Jazz CCD-4433, CCD-4811-2

Sent for You Yesterday and Here You Come Today Concord Jazz CCD-4433.

Note 1: The titles on CCD-4433 are also on CJ-433-C.

SESSION 900902 (Paul Masson Mountain Winery, Saratoga, CA, 2nd & 3rd September 1990) MEL TORMÉ / GEORGE SHEARING. Mel Tormé, vocal; George Shearing, piano; Neil Swainson, bass; Donny Osborne, drums.

Lili Marlene Concord Jazz CCD-4471

(It Seems to Me) I've Heard That Song Before Concord Jazz CCD-4471

I Know Why and So Do You Concord Jazz CCD-4471

Love Concord Jazz CCD-4471

Aren't You Glad You're You Concord Jazz CCD-4471

Ellington Medley: Cotton Tail; I Didn't Know About You; Don't Get Around Much Anymore; I'm Beginning to See the Light Concord Jazz CCD-4471

Walk Medley: I Don't Want to Walk Without You; I'll Walk Alone Concord Jazz CCD-4471

I Could Write a Book Concord Jazz CCD-4471

(This Is) a Lovely Way to Spend an Evening Concord Jazz CCD-4471

On the Swing Shift/The Five O'clock Whistle Concord Jazz CCD-4471

Ac-cent-tchu-ate the Positive Concord Jazz CCD-4471

This Is the Army Mister Jones Concord Jazz CCD-4471

We Mustn't Say Goodbye Concord Jazz CCD-4471.

Note 1: The titles on CCD-4471 are also on CJ-471-C.

SESSION 901111A (5th Fujitsu-Concord Jazz Festival, Kan-i Hoken Hall, Tokyo, Japan, 11th November 1990) MEL TORMÉ accompanied by John Campbell, piano; Bob Maize, bass; Donny Osborne, drums.

Shine on Your Shoes Concord Jazz CCD-4481

Medley: Looking at You; Look at That Face Concord Jazz CCD-4481

A Nightingale Sang in Berkeley Square Concord Jazz CCD-4481
Wave Concord Jazz CCD-4481
Star Dust (*note 2*) Concord Jazz CCD-4481, CCD-4811-2
Medley: Don't 'Cha Go 'Way Mad; Come to Baby Do Concord Jazz CCD-4481
Medley: The Christmas Song; Autumn Leaves Concord Jazz CCD-4481.

Note 1: The titles on CCD-4481 are also on CJ-481-C.
Note 2: Add Frank Wess, tenor saxophone.

SESSION 901111B (5th Fujitsu-Concord Jazz Festival, Kan-i Hoken Hall, Tokyo, Japan, 11th November 1990) **MEL TORMÉ with the FRANK WESS ORCHESTRA.** Snooky Young, Ron Tooley, Pete Minger, Joe Newman, trumpets; Art Baron, Grover Mitchell, Dennis Wilson, Doug Purviance, trombones; Curtis Peagler, Bill Ramsey, alto-saxes; Frank Wess, Billy Mitchell, tenor-saxes; Arthur Clarke, baritone-sax; John Campbell, piano; Ted Dunbar, guitar; Bob Maize, bass; Donny Osborne, drums.

Medley: You're Driving Me Crazy (What Did I Do); Moten Swing Concord Jazz CCD 4481
Sent for You Yesterday and Here You Come Today Concord Jazz CCD 4481
Swingin' the Blues (*note 2*) Concord Jazz CCD 4481
New York State of Mind Concord Jazz CCD 4481.

Note 1: The titles on CCD-4481 are also on CJ-481-C.
Note 2: Tormé, plays drums.

SESSION 910312 (Hollywood, 12th & 13th March 1991) **MEL TORMÉ — CLEO LAINE.** Mel Tormé, vocal; Cleo Laine, vocal; John Dankworth, musical director, soprano- and alto-saxophones and clarinet; Guy Barker, trumpet and flugelhorn; Chris Smith, trombone; Ray Swinfield, alto-sax and clarinet; David Roach, tenor-sax and flute; Jamie Talbot, baritone-sax, bass-clarinet and clarinet; Ray Colianni, piano; Larry Koonse, guitar; John Leitham, bass; Donny Osborne, drums; Martyn David, Latin percussion. Arrangements by John Dankworth except the songs indicated in notes 2 and 3.

I'm Nothing Without You (You're Nothing Without Me) Concord Jazz CCD 4515; Life, Times and Music — Jazz Duets
I Thought About You (*note 2*) Concord Jazz CCD 4515, CCD-4811-2
Where or When Concord Jazz CCD 4515
I Wish I Were in Love Again Concord Jazz CCD 4515
Girl Talk Concord Jazz CCD 4515
After You've Gone Concord Jazz CCD 4515
Medley (*note 3*): **Brazil**; **Baia** Concord Jazz CCD 4515
Birdsong Concord Jazz CCD 4515
Isn't It a Pity (*note 2*) Concord Jazz CCD 4515
Love You Madly Concord Jazz CCD 4515
Angel Eyes (*note 2*) Concord Jazz CCD 4515, CCD-4790-2
Two Tune Medley (*note 2*): Two Tune Verse; Sweet Sue; Honeysuckle Rose; I May Be Wrong (But I Think You're Wonderful); The Nearness of You; There's No You; Blue Moon; Heart and Soul; Watch What Happens; Exactly Like You; Take the "A" Train; I Found a Million Dollar Baby; On the Alamo; Fly Me to the Moon; Autumn Leaves; Yesterday When I Was Young; You and the Night and the Music; Sing (Sing a Song); Guilty; Feelin' Groovy (The 59th Street Bridge Song) Concord Jazz CCD 4515
I Don't Think I'll Fall in Love Today Concord Jazz CCD 4515
Ev'ry Time We Say Goodbye Concord Jazz CCD 4515.

Note 1: The titles on CCD-4515 are also on CJ-515-C.
Note 2: Arranged by Mel Tormé.
Note 3: Scores by John Dankworth based on ideas by Mel Tormé.
Note 4: Life, Times and Music — Jazz Duets is a package of a CD and book. The ISBN is 1 56799 360 5.

SESSION 920129 (New York City 29th to 31st January 1992) **GERRY MULLIGAN ORCHESTRA.** Wallace Roney, trumpet; Dave Bargeron, trombone; John Clark, French-horn; Bill Barber, tuba; Phil Woods, alto-sax; Gerry Mulligan, baritone-sax; John Lewis, piano; Dean Johnson, bass; Ron Vincent, drums; Mel Tormé, vocal.
Darn That Dream GRP GRP967921.

SESSION 920405 (Music Hall, Cincinnati, Ohio, 5th & 6th April 1992) **MEL TORMÉ** with the Cincinnati Symphonietta, conducted by Keith Lockhart. Plus John Colianni, piano; John Leitham, bass; Donny Osborne, drums.
Christmas Medley: Jingle Bells; Santa Claus Is Coming to Town; Winter Weather; Winter Wonderland Telarc Jazz CD-83315
Christmastime Is Here Telarc Jazz CD-83315
Good King Wenceslas Telarc Jazz CD-83315
What Child Is This? (*note 2*) Telarc Jazz CD-83315
God Rest Ye Merry Gentlemen (*note 2*) Telarc Jazz CD-83315.

Note 1: All titles on CD-83315 also on TEL-83315.
Note 2: Omit Tormé.

SESSION 920619 (The same as the last. Orchestra recorded Music Hall, Cincinnati, Ohio, 5th and 6th April 1992 with personnel as above. Vocals recorded Cleveland, Ohio, 19th to 21st June 1992) **MEL TORMÉ.**
Sleigh Ride Telarc Jazz CD-83315
The Christmas Song Telarc Jazz CD-83315
Glow Worm Telarc Jazz CD-83315
The Christmas Feeling Telarc Jazz CD-83315
It Happened in Sun Valley Telarc Jazz CD-83315
Silver Bells Telarc Jazz CD-83315
Christmas Was Made for Children Telarc Jazz CD-83315
The Christmas Waltz Telarc Jazz CD-83315
Medley: Just Look Around; Have Yourself a Merry Little Christmas Telarc Jazz CD-83315
Medley: Happy Holiday; Let's Start the New Year Right; What Are You Doing New Year's Eve? Telarc Jazz CD-83315
White Christmas Telarc Jazz CD-83315.

Note 1: All titles on CD-83315 also on TEL-83315.

SESSION 921007 (Live, Michael's Pub, New York City, 7th & 8th October 1992) **MEL TORMÉ with the GREAT AMERICAN SONGBOOK ORCHESTRA.** Bob Milikan, Ross Konikoff, John Walsh, Frank London, trumpets; Tom Artin, Timothy Newman, trombones; Rich Willey, valve trombone; Jack Stuckley, alto-sax, flute and clarinet; Adam Brenner, alto-sax and clarinet; Jerry Weldon, tenor-sax and clarinet; Jeff Rupert, tenor-sax and clarinet; Dave Schmacher, baritone-sax and bass-clarinet; John Colianni, leader and piano; John Leitham, bass; Donny Osborne, drums. Arrangements by Mel Tormé, except songs indicated in notes 2, 3, 4 and 5.
You Gotta Try (*note 2*) Telarc Jazz CD-83328
Medley: Ridin' High; I'm Shooting High Telarc Jazz TEL-83328, CD-83328

You Make Me Feel So Young Telarc Jazz TEL-83328, CD-83328
Stardust (*note 3*) Telarc Jazz TEL-83328, CD-83328
I'm Gonna Go Fishin' (*note 4*) Telarc Jazz TEL-83328, CD-83328
Medley: Don't Get Around Much Anymore; I Let a Song Go Out of My Heart (*note 4*) Telarc Jazz TEL-83328, CD-83328
Medley: Sophisticated Lady; I Didn't Know About You Telarc Jazz TEL-83328, CD-83328
Rockin' in Rhythm (*notes 1 & 5*) Telarc Jazz TEL-83328, CD-83328
It Don't Mean a Thing If It Ain't Got That Swing Telarc Jazz CD-83328
A Lovely Way to Spend an Evening Telarc Jazz TEL-83328, CD-83328
Medley: I'll Remember April; I Concentrate on You Telarc Jazz CD-83328
Autumn in New York Telarc Jazz TEL-83328, CD-83328
Medley: Just One of Those Things; Green Dolphin Street Telarc Jazz CD-83328
All God's Chillun' Got Rhythm Telarc Jazz TEL-83328, CD-83328
The Party's Over Telarc Jazz CD-83328.

Note 1: Tormé, plays drums.
Note 2: Arranged by Sam Nestico.
Note 3: Arranged by Bob Alberti.
Note 4: Arranged by Johnny Mandel.
Note 5: Arranged by Bill Berry.

SESSION 921114 (Fujitsu-Concord Jazz Festival, Kan-i Hoken Hall, Tokyo, Japan, 14th November 1992) **MEL TORMÉ and his ALL-STAR QUINTET.** Ken Peplowski, clarinet; Peter Appleyard, vibraharp; John Colianni, piano; John Leitham, bass; Donny Osborne, drums. Arrangements by Mel Tormé.
Lulu's Back in Town Concord Jazz CCD 4542
Memories of You Concord Jazz CCD 4542
It's All Right with Me/Love Concord Jazz CCD 4542
These Foolish Things Concord Jazz CCD 4542
"All" Medley: All the Things You Are; All of You; All of Me Concord Jazz CCD 4542
Tribute to Benny Goodman (Medley): Stompin' at the Savoy; Don't Be That Way; And the Angels Sing; Gotta Be This or That; Jersey Bounce; Why Don't You Do Right; Air Mail Special; Avalon; Sing, Sing, Sing (*note 2*) Concord Jazz CCD 4542
Get Happy Concord Jazz CCD 4542
Three Little Words Concord Jazz CCD 4542
Guess I'll Hang My Tears Out to Dry Concord Jazz CCD-4552, CCD-4811-2
Lover, Come Back to Me Concord Jazz CCD-4552, CCD-4811-2
Ev'ry Time We Say Goodbye Concord Jazz CCD-4552.

Note 1: The titles on CCD 4552 are also on Concord Jazz CJ-542-C.
Note 2: Tormé plays drums.

SESSION 940512 (Hollywood, 12th, 13th, 16th & 17th May 1994) **MEL TORMÉ** with orchestra conducted by Alan Broadbent. Alan Broadbent, conductor; Randy Sandke, trumpet and flugelhorn; Ken Peplowski, clarinet and tenor-sax; Howard Alden, guitar; John Colianni, piano; John Leitham, bass; Donny Osborne, drums; Murray Adler, Israel Baker, Robert Brosseau, Bobby Bruce, Ross Cantor, Maurice Dicterow, Bonnie Douglas, James Getzoff, Endre Granat, Gina Kronstadt, Paul Shure, John Wittenberg, Tibor Zelig, violins; Carole Mukogawa, Marilyn Baker, Jorge Moraga, Helaine Wittenberg, violas; Fred Seykora, Jodi Burnett, Paula Hochhalter, Ray Kramer, cellos.
This Is My Night to Dream/It Must

Be True (*note 2*) Concord Jazz CCD 4614, CCD-4790-2
   Moonlight Becomes You (*note 3*) Concord Jazz CCD 4614, CCD-4790-2
   I Can't Escape from You (*note 3*) Concord Jazz CCD 4614
   With Every Breath I Take (*note 4*) Concord Jazz CCD 4614
   A Man and His Dreams (*note 3*) Concord Jazz CCD 4614
   Without a Word of Warning (*note 5*) Concord Jazz CCD 4614
   May I ? (*note 5*) Concord Jazz CCD 4614
   Please (*note 5*) Concord Jazz CCD 4614
   Thanks (*note 3*) Concord Jazz CCD 4614
   Don't Let That Moon Get Away (*note 3*) Concord Jazz CCD 4614
   Soon (*note 5*) Concord Jazz CCD 4614
   It's Easy to Remember/Adios (*note 5*) Concord Jazz CCD 4614, CCD-4811-2
   Love in Bloom (*note 4*) Concord Jazz CCD 4614
   The Day You Came Along (*note 4*) Concord Jazz CCD 4614
   Pennies from Heaven (*note 5*) Concord Jazz CCD 4614
   Learn to Croon (*note 5*) Concord Jazz CCD 4614.

Note 1: The titles on CCD 4614 are also on Concord Jazz CJ-614-C.
Note 2: Arranged by Mel Tormé.
Note 3: Arranged by Bob Krogstad.
Note 4: Arranged by Angela Morley.
Note 5: Arranged by Alan Broadbent.

SESSION 940600 (Instruments recorded in Philadelphia, 1994; Tormé, recorded in Hollywood, 1994) **PETER NERO.** Peter Nero, piano; Michael Barrett, bass; Steve Pemberton, drums; Mel Tormé, vocal.
   Long Ago and Far Away Intersound CDS 3505.

SESSION 950505 (Toronto, Canada, 5th and 6th May 1995) **MEL TORMÉ with ROB McCONNELL AND THE BOSS BRASS.** Arnie Chycoski, Steve McDade, Guido Basso, Kevin Turcott, John MacLeod, trumpets and flugelhorns; Rob McConnell, valve trombone, arrangements and conductor; Alastair Kay, Bob Livingston, Jerry Johnson, trombones; Ernie Pattison, bass trombone; Gary Pattison, James MacDonald, French horns; Moe Koffman, clarinet, soprano- and alto-saxes, flute; John Johnson, soprano- and alto-sax, clarinet and flute; Alex Dean, tenor-sax, clarinet and flute; Rick Wilkins, tenor-sax and clarinet; Robert Leonard, clarinet, baritone-sax, bass-clarinet and flute; David Restivo, piano; Reg Schwager, guitar; Jim Vivian, bass; Ted Warren, drums; Brian Leonard, percussion.
   Nobody Else But Me Concord Jazz CCD 4667
   Liza (All the Clouds'll Roll Away) Concord Jazz CCD 4667
   If You Could See Me Now Concord Jazz CCD 4667, CCD-4790-2
   I Get a Kick Out of You Concord Jazz CCD 4667, CCD-4811-2
   Have You Met Miss Jones? Concord Jazz CCD 4667
   Love Walked In Concord Jazz CCD 4667
   Autumn Serenade Concord Jazz CCD 4667
   My Sweetie Went Away Concord Jazz CCD 4667
   I'll Be Around Concord Jazz CCD 4667, CCD-4790-2
   On the Swing Shift Concord Jazz CCD 4667
   High and Low Concord Jazz CCD 4667
   In the Still of the Night Concord Jazz CCD 4667
   I'm Glad There Is You Concord Jazz CCD 4667.

Note 1: The titles on CCD 4667 are also on Concord Jazz CJ-667-C.

SESSION 950801 (Hollywood, August 1995) **RAY ANTHONY and HIS ORCHESTRA.** Mel Tormé, vocal; Rick Baptist, Frank Szabo, George Graham, Gary Halopoff, Bill Armstrong, trumpets; Alan Caplan, Lloyd Ulyate, Bill Tole, Andy Martin, Morris Repass, trombones; Ralph Lapolla, clarinet; Sal Lozano, Leo Anthony, alto-saxes; Roger Neumann, Bob Efford, tenor-saxes; Carol Anderson, piano; Doug MacDonald, guitar; Kirk Smith, bass; Gregg Field, drums; arrangements by Don Simpson.

My Christmas Dream Aero Space RACD 1039

I'll Be Home for Christmas Aero Space RACD 1039.

Note 1: Tormé's vocals were overdubbed on the instrumental recordings.

SESSION 960723 (Disney Institute, Florida 23rd July 1996) **MEL TORMÉ** accompanied by Mike Renzi, piano; John Leitham, bass; Donny Osborne, drums.

Just One of Those Things/On Green Dolphin Street Concord Jazz CCD-4736

You Make Me Feel So Young Concord Jazz CCD-4736

A Nightingale Sang in Berkeley Square Concord Jazz CCD-4736

Pick Yourself Up Concord Jazz CCD-4736

Stardust Concord Jazz CCD-4736

Love for Sale Concord Jazz CCD-4736

Since I Fell for You Concord Jazz CCD-4736

Three Little Words / Slipped Disc / Smooth One / Rachel's Dream Concord Jazz CCD-4736

I Remember You / It's Easy to Remember Concord Jazz CCD-4736

Lover Come Back to Me Concord Jazz CCD-4736

Stairway to the Stars Concord Jazz CCD-4736

Oh, Lady Be Good Concord Jazz CCD-4736

Ev'ry Time We Say Goodbye Concord Jazz CCD-4736, CCD-4811-2.

Note 1: A video of this performance is available in the A & E Biography series.

PART 3

RECORD ISSUES

Singles 78 and 45 rpm

Unless otherwise indicated, the artist credit is Mel Tormé (including, if relevant, "and The Mel-Tones") or similar. Other artists are indicated by initials with an expansion at the end of the listing of each label. Labels are US unless otherwise stated.

ATLANTIC
(45 rpm only)

2165
   Comin' Home, Baby
   Right Now
2183
   Cast Your Fate to the Wind (A-6780-Z1)
   The Gift (A-6781-Z1)
(a second copy has stampers A-6780-4 and A-6781-3)
2187
   Gravy Waltz (A-6383-3)
   My Gal's Back in Town (A-6782-4)
2202
   You Belong to Me (A-6370-11)
   You Can't Love 'Em All (A-7049-11)
2219
   Forty-Second Street (A-7456-11)
   Sunday in New York (A-7459-11)
3278
   Mountain Greenery
   It Takes Too Long to Learn to Live Alone

BRUNSWICK (UK)
(78 rpm only)
03831
   A Stranger in Town (L 3686 A)
   You've Laughed at Me for the Last Time (L 3687 A)
03731
   BC Day by Day (L3965 A)
   BC Prove It by the Things You Do (L 3966 A)

BC: Bing Crosby

BETHLEHEM
(45 rpm and possibly 78 rpm)
45-11008
   Lulu's Back in Town (B-45-11008-A-2)
   Keeping Myself for You (B-45-11008-B-2)

CAPITOL (1948–1952)

There is a good deal of confusion over the numerical prefixes of the Capitol 78 rpm series. I am listing what I have seen myself or had reported reliably to me. Most singles in the 1948–1952 period were issued both on 78 rpm and 45 rpm. Some of the 57- series of 78s have a prefix of 54- for the equivalent 45 rpm issues. Once the 57- prefix was discontinued, the 45 rpm issue has the same number as the 78 rpm issue but with a F- prefix. Only 57-591 does not seem to have been issued on 45 rpm but the same two titles are on 54-583. Some issues (particularly those in the 1700 series) are listed in the Capitol log as having a 5- prefix but the discs themselves do not show this prefix. The significance of the prefix is not known but it has been suggested that it is a book keeping indicator by Capitol that the record was issued on 78 and 45 rpm. This 5- prefix has shown up in other discographies presumably because the information was taken from the Capitol log rather than from the discs themselves.

10-inch 78 rpm

163
    EMM   The Patty Cake Man
    Morse without Tormé
164
    JM   Sam's Got Him
    Mercer without Tormé
176
    EMM   Hello Suzanne
    Morse without Tormé
EMM: Ella Mae Morse
JM: Johnny Mercer

10-inch 78 rpm & 7-inch 45 rpm. Master numbers are from 78 rpm discs unless otherwise stated.

54- 583
    You're Getting to Be a Habit with Me
    There Isn't Any Special Reason

57- 591
    There Isn't Any Special Reason (3869-4D)
    You're Getting to Be a Habit with Me (3872-5D)
57-/54- 671
    The Four Winds and the Seven Seas (4476-3D)
    It's Too Late Now (4477-2D)
57-/54- 743
    The Meadows of Heaven (4916-5D)
    (see note at the end of Capitol 78s)
    Sonny Boy (4917-4D)
57-/54- 751
    Oh, You Beautiful Doll (4918-8D)
    There's a Broken Heart for Every Light on Broadway (4919-4D)
57-/54- 775
    The Blossoms on the Bough (5176-6D)
    Don't Do Something to Someone Else (5177-6D)
791
    Bless You (5217-4D)
    The Old Master Painter (5218-3D)
    (both with Peggy Lee)
825
    The Queen of Hearts Is Missing (5325-6D)
    There's an "X" in the Middle of Texas (5328-4D)
880
    I Hadn't Anyone Till You (5324-7D)
    Cross Your Heart (5327-7D)
1000
    The Piccolino (5709-5D)
    Bewitched (5710-2D)
1177
    Do-Do-Do
    Recipe for Romance
1237
    I Owe a Kiss to a Girl in Iowa (6365-5D)
    Say No More (6495-5D)
1291
    Skylark (5707-D1)
    Lullaby of the Leaves (5708-D1
1383

Around the World (6977-D1)
The Sidewalk Shufflers (6978-N3)
1402
You're Getting to Be a Habit with Me
Sailing Away on the Henry Clay
(a 45 rpm copy has masters 3872-N4 and 6980-N4)
1524
(I'm Sending You a) Bundle of Love (6292-N2 and -D2)
The World Is Your Balloon (6293-N2 and D1)
1598
Who Sends You Orchids? (6291-D1)
You Locked My Heart (6294-D1)
(a 45 rpm copy has masters 45-6291-D1 and 45-6294-D1)
1662
Blue Moon
Bewitched
(a 45 rpm copy has masters 3411-D1 and 5710-D4)
1712
The One for Me (7272-N2)
Love Is Such a Cheat (7273-N2)
1738
Don't Fan the Flame (7294-N2)
Telling Me Yes, Telling Me No (7295-N1)
both with Peggy Lee
(a second copy has masters 7294-N2 and 7295-N2)
1761
My Buddy (7274-D2)
Take My Heart (7275-D2)
1864
You're a Heavenly Thing (7735-N1)
Foolish Little Rumors (7750-N2)
2131
Black Moonlight (10176-D3)
Don't Leave Me (10109-D2)
2263
Anywhere I Wander (20046-N1)
Casually (20048-N2)
(a 45 rpm copy has masters 20046-N2 and 20048-N2)

2529
A Stranger in Town (10108-N1)
It Made You Happy When You Made Me Cry (10175-N1)
(a 45 rpm copy has masters 45-10108-N1 and 45-10175-N1)
15379
She's a Home Girl (3868-2D)
Careless Hands (3870-2D)
15428
Blue Moon (3411-4D)
Again (3412-5D)

Note: Capitol issued a promotional disc that coupled:

57-743: Mel Tormé: The Meadows of Heaven (4916-5D-7)
with 57-710: Jo Stafford: The Last Mile Home (4658-4D-2)

12-inch 78 rpm

California Suite Parts 1 to 8:
8-28004 (5463-1D-1 / 5470-1D-1)
8-28005 (5464 / 5469)
8-28006 (5465-1D-1 / 5468-1D-4)
8-28007 (5466-1D-1 / 5467-1D-1)
 These were issued only in an Album: EDD 200 (auto-coupled).

7-inch 45 rpm

6F-28004 to 6F-28006 California Suite Parts 1 to 6.
These were issued only in an Album: KCF 200 (auto-coupled).

CAPITOL (1969-70)
(45 rpm only)

2613
Games People Play (S-45-72544-A3),
Willie and Laura Mae Jones (S-45-72843-A3)
2743
Requiem : 820 Latham
Spinning Wheel

CAPITOL (UK)
(78 rpm only)

CL13094
  Careless Hands (3870-2E)
  Again (3412-5E)
CL13123
  You're Getting to Be a Habit with Me (3872-5E)
  Blue Moon (3411-4E)
CL13131
  She's a Home Girl (3868-2E)
  It's Too Late Now (4477-2E)
CL13148
  There Isn't Any Special Reason (3869-4E)
  The Four Winds and the Seven Seas (4476-3E)
CL13232
  The Meadows of Heaven (4916-5E)
  Sonny Boy (4917-E)
CL13241
  Bless You (5217-4D-10)
  The Old Master Painter (5218-3D-10) (both with Peggy Lee)
CL13244
  The Blossoms on the Bough (5176)
  Don't Do Something to Someone Else (5177)
CL13291
  I Hadn't Anyone Till You (5324-7D-1)
  The Piccolino (5709)
CL13292
  Oh, You Beautiful Doll (4918-8D-2)
  There's a Broken Heart for Every Light on Broadway (4919-4D-1)
CL13322
  The Queen of Hearts Is Missing (5325)
  Bewitched (5710-2D-7)
CL13448
  Do-Do-Do (3866-4D-1)
  Recipe for Romance (6378-6D-1)
CL13495
  Around the World (6977-D1 #3)
  The Sidewalk Shufflers (6978-N1)
CL13591
  You Locked My Heart
  Love Is Such a Cheat
CL13609
  Don't Fan the Flame (with Peggy Lee), *Peggy Lee without Tormé*
CL13675
  Lullaby of the Leaves (5708-N1)
  You're a Heavenly Thing (DCAP 7735)
CL13837
  Anywhere I Wander
  Casually
CL13851
  Skylark (DCAP 10176)
  Black Moonlight (DCAP 5707)

CBS (UK)
(45 rpm only)

AAG 212
  Once in a Lifetime (AAG 212 1F)
  I See It Now (AAG 212 2F)
AAG 227
  I Know Your Heart (AAG 227 1F)
  You'd Better Love Me (AAG 227 2F)
201737
  One Little Snowflake (A 5027-1)
  Ev'ry Day's a Holiday (A-5026-1)
202065
  Dominique's Discotheque (A-5349-1)
  The Power of Love (A-5348-1)
202488
  Paris Smiles (5645)
  Red Rubber Ball (5644)
2857
  I Remember Suzanne (7001-2)
  Lover's Roulette (7000-2)

COLUMBIA
(45 rpm only, all have 4- prefix)

43022
  I Know Your Heart (J ZSP-77226-1E)
  You'd Better Love Me (J ZSP-77227-1F)
43087
  See It Now (JZSP-78078-1F)
  Once in a Lifetime (JZSP-78079-1F)

43167
  Ev'ry Day's a Holiday (ZSP-79138-1D)
  One Little Snowflake (JZSP-79137-1E)
43230
  Do I Love You Because You're Beautiful? (RZSP-72212-1H)
  That's All (RZSP-72215-1H)
(another copy has JRZSP-72212-1F and (JRZEP-72215-1E)
43383
  Ho-Ba-La-La
  My Romance
43550
  The Power of Love (JZSP113134-2C)
  Dominique's Discotheque (JZSP113133-2C)
43677
  All That Jazz (ZSP-114434 1B)
  Hang on to Me (ZSP-114433 1B)
43872
  Time (ZSP116384-1E)
  Paris Smiles (J ZSP-78078-1F)
44180
  Lover's Roulette (ZS116385-1F)
  I Remember Suzanne (ZSP118996-1A)
44399
  Lima Lady (ZSP118608-1F),
  Wait Until Dark (ZSP118609-1F)
45283
  The Christmas Song (Chestnuts Roasting on an Open Fire) (ZSP154371-1A)
(same on both sides; probably only issued to DJs)

CORAL
(78 rpm and also on 45 rpm with a 9- prefix) master numbers are from 78 rpm discs unless otherwise stated
60071
  A Stranger in Town (L 3636A)
  You've Laughed at Me for the Last Time (L3637AA)
61089
  Blue Skies (WL 85294 A 1)
  Oo-Ya-Ya (WL 85295A 1)

61136
  Just One More Chance (W85292T3A)
  Anything Can Happen Mambo (W85293T1A)
(a 45 rpm copy has masters 85292 2 and 85293 2)
61263
  Tutti Frutti
  I's a Muggin'
61294
  All of You
  Spellbound
(a 45 rpm copy has masters 7775 4 and 7776 2)
61452
  Rose O'Day
  It Don't Mean a Thing
61507
  Goody Goody
  Jeepers Creepers
61588
  How
  My Rose Marie
61709
  Mountain Greenery
  Bernie's Tune
(a 45 rpm copy has masters 87600-2 and 87605-2)

DECCA
(78 rpm only)
7
  Night Must Fall (L3758A)
  I'm Down to My Last Dream (L3818AA)
18653
  A Stranger in Town (L3636A)
  You've Laughed at Me for the Last Time (L3637A)
18707
  EB Am I Blue (L3817A)
  EB I Fall in Love Too Easily (L3818AA)
18746
  BC Day by Day (L3965A)
  BC Prove It by the Things You Do (L3966A)

EB: Eugenie Baird
BC: Bing Crosby

DECCA (UK)
(78 rpm and 45 rpm with a 45- prefix)

F10800
    Walkin' Shoes (DRX-22457-T1-1)
    The Cuckoo in the Clock (DRX-22458-T1-1)
    (a 45 rpm copy has masters DRF-22457-T1-1C and DRF-22458-T1-1C)
F10809
    Waltz for Young Lovers
    I Don't Want to Walk Without You
    (a 45 rpm copy has masters DRF-22461-T1-1C and DRF-22462-T1-1C)

HIS MASTER'S VOICE (UK)
(45 rpm only)

45-POP 859
    Moon Song (7XEA 20019-1N)
    Blue Moon (7XEA 20018-1N)

JEWEL
(78 rpm only)

G-4000
    White Christmas
    Where or When
S-3001
    LE Who'll Be the Fool
untraced

LE: Leon Edgar

LIBERTY
(45 rpm only)

56022
    Brother Can You Spare a Dime? (LB-2525)
    A Day in the Life of Bonnie and Clyde (LB-2527)

56066
    Didn't We? (LB-2626)
    Five-Four (LB-2625)

LIBERTY (UK)
(45 rpm only)

LBF 15064
    Brother Can You Spare a Dime (LBF 15064 B 1)
    A Day in the Life of Bonnie and Clyde (LBF 15064 A 1)

LONDON
(45 rpm only)

45-171
    Morning Star
    Whose Garden Was This?
45-180
    A Phone Call to the Past (ZCL 7960)
    I Cried for You (Now It's Your Turn to Cry Over Me) (ZCL 7961)

(45 rpm and possibly 78 rpm)

1699
    Walkin' Shoes
    The Cuckoo in the Clock
1700
    Shenandoah Valley
    Hooray for Love
1701
    Waltz for Young Lovers
    I Don't Want to Walk Without You

LONDON (UK)
(78 rpm and also on 45 rpm with 45- prefix)

HLN 8305
    The Lady Is a Tramp (MSB-1348-1)
    Lulu's Back in Town (MSB-1347-1)
HLN 8322
    Lullaby of Birdland
    I Love to Watch the Moonlight

(45 rpm only)
HLU 10355
   Whose Garden Was This (MSP-8368-1C)
   Phone Call to the Past (MSP-8369-1C)

LONDON ATLANTIC (UK)
(78 rpm and 45 rpm with 45- prefix)
HLK 9643
   Comin' Home Baby
   Right Now
(a 45 rpm copy has masters 45-MSM-6161-1C and 45-MSM-6162-1C)

M-G-M
(78 rpm and 45 rpm) 1946-47. Master numbers are from 78 rpm copies. K prefix denotes 45 rpm
10584
   A Cottage for Sale (10584B)
   Gone with the Wind (10584A)
10612
   AS   What Is This Thing Called Love?
   Shaw without Tormé
10730
   AS   I Got the Sun in the Morning
   There's No Business Like Show Business
The second side is credited on the label to Artie Shaw but is actually by Mel Tormé without Shaw
10730 also reported with "Along with Me" in place of "There's No Business Like Show Business"
10844
   Making Whoopee (5980-3D2)
   Dream Awhile (5802-4)
10874
   Until the Real Thing Comes Along
   A Foggy Day
K30243
   AS   What Is This Thing Called Love?
   Shaw without Tormé
K30244 & K30245 are by Shaw without Tormé
K30246
   AS   Love for Sale
   Shaw without Tormé
K 30243/4/5/6 (these are 45 rpm) issued in album K 54— Artie Shaw Plays Cole Porter
K30354
   I Cover the Waterfront (K30354A)
   County Fair (K 30354B)
K30355
   A Cottage for Sale (K30355B)
   Little White Lies (K30355A)
K30356
   A Little Kiss Each Morning (K30356A)
   Love You Funny Thing! (K30356B)
K30357
   I Can't Give You Anything But Love (K30357B)
   The Best Things in Life Are Free (K30357A)
K30354/5/6/7 (these are 45 rpm) issued in Album K79— Mel Tormé Sings

M-G-M (UK)
(78 rpm and also on 45 rpm with a 45-prefix)
MGM-922
   There's No Business Like Show Business
   I Can't Give You Anything but Love Baby
(a 45 rpm copy has masters 7XSM 1274-1N and 7XSM 1289-1N)

(45 rpm only)
MGM-1144
   The Christmas Song (Chestnuts Roasting on an Open Fire) (7XSM 1375-1N)
   A Shine on Your Shoes (7XSM 1376-1N)

MUSICRAFT
(78 rpm only)
363
   There's No One But You (5427B)

Willow Road (5428A)
365
    AS   I Got the Sun in the Morning (5474-4)
    AS   Along with Me (5473-4)
381
    South America, Take It Away (2 OM 5509 C)
    Try A Little Tenderness (2 OM 5510 B)
389*
    AS   Get Out of Town (3 OM 5542 A)
    Shaw without Tormé
390*
    AS   What Is This Thing Called Love? (L5548)
    Shaw without Tormé
397
    It Happened in Monterey (1 OM 5512 A)
    Born to Be Blue (5511-3R1-A)
(a second copy has 5511 and 5512)
412
    AS   For You, for Me, for Evermore (5629)
    AS   Changing My Tune (5635)
428
    AS   Guilty (2 OM 5048)
    Shaw without Tormé
441
    AS   They Can't Convince Me (2 OM 5447)
    AS   And So to Bed (2 OM 5650)
445
    AS   Don't You Believe It Dear (5701-2)
    Shaw without Tormé
492
    AS   It's the Same Old Dream (5702-1)
    AS   I Believe (5743-7)
495
    Willow Road
    Try a Little Tenderness
512
    AS   When You're Around
    Shaw without Tormé
528#
    I Can't Give You Anything But Love (5886-3D3)
    Three Little Words (5887-4-3D)
529#
    I'll Always Be in Love with You (5890)
    Love You Funny Thing (5892)
530#
    The Day You Came Along (5893-2D4)
    Fine and Dandy (5900-D3)
534
    Making Whoopee (5980-3D3)
    Do It Again (5982-3D4)
538
    But Beautiful (5971-5D3)
    Night and Day (5983-4-D4)
558
    Gone with the Wind (MU 5975-3D4)
    Little White Lies (MU 5981-4D4)
573
    If I Had a Girl Like You (5899-3D3)
    A Cottage for Sale (5972-5D2)
589
    My Baby Just Cares for Me (MU 5889-1)
    A Foggy Day (MU 5979)
(both sides of 589 also have CC 8-17-48 in the run-off area — a mastering date?)
595
    County Fair
    You're Driving Me Crazy

AS: Artie Shaw
* *discs 389/390/391/392 are in Musicraft 78 rpm album S-2, Artie Shaw plays Cole Porter*
\# *discs 528/529/530 are in Musicraft 78 rpm album S-8, The Velvet Fog*

15099
    Dream Awhile
    There's No Business Like Show Business
15102
    It's Dreamtime (5805-3)
    You're Driving Me Crazy (5806-5)
15104
    Who Cares What People Say (5807-3)
    I'm Yours (5808-1)
15107
    One for My Baby (5800-2A)
    A Little Kiss Each Morning (5801-113)

15109
   Kokomo, Indiana (5879-4D9)
   How Long Has This Been Going On (5880-2D11)
15111
   That's Where I Came In (5429-1)
   There's No Business Like Show Business (5803-6-B)
15114
   Boulevard of Memories (5881-2D10)
   ....and Mimi (5888-2D3)
15116
   Ballerina (5896-D1)
   What Are You Doing New Year's Eve (5888-2D3)
15118
   The Best Things in Life Are Free (5894-D3)
   Magic Town (5898-D3)

12"

5009
   I Cover the Waterfront (5977-5D4)
   County Fair (5978-3D3)

PARLOPHONE (UK)
(78 rpm only)

R3032
   AS   What Is This Thing Called Love? (5548-1)
   Shaw without Tormé
R3042
   AS   Guilty
   Shaw without Tormé
R3054
   AS   And So to Bed (5650-2A)
   AS   I Believe (5703-3)
R3067
   AS   They Can't Convince Me (5647-3B)
   AS   It's The Same Old Dream (5702-7)
R3074
   AS   Get Out of Town
   Shaw without Tormé
R3080
   AS   Don't You Believe It Dear (5701-2A)
   Shaw without Tormé
R3094
   It's Dreamtime (5805-3)
   I'm Yours (5808-1)
R3100
   AS   Changing My Tune (5635)
   Shaw without Tormé
R3131
   Little White Lies (5981-2)
   Night and Day (5983-1)
R3138
   Makin' Whoopee (5980-1)
   Please Do It Again (5982-1)
R3152
   A Cottage for Sale (5972-1)
   Gone with the Wind (5975-1)

It is reported that R3074 was limited to a few copies only and was withdrawn soon after being released.
AS: Artie Shaw

PHILIPS (UK)
(78 rpm and 45 rpm)

PB.728
   Ev'ry Which Way
   Time Was
PB.1045
   The White Cliffs of Dover
   I've Got a Lovely Bunch of Coconuts
(a 45 rpm copy has masters AA 326417 1 F and AA 326417 2 F)

POLYDOR (GERMANY ?)
(78 rpm only)

580087
   both sides without Tormé
580088
   How High the Moon
   without Tormé
580089
   Honeysuckle Rose
   without Tormé

VERVE
(45 rpm only)

10174
   The Crossroads
   Frenesi

10211
   Walk Like a Dragon
   Wayfaring Stranger

10230
   Hey, Look Me Over
   What's New at the Zoo

(both with Margaret Whiting)

10232
   Her Face
   Yes, Indeed

VERVE (UK)
(45 rpm only)

VS 505
   Her Face (45-V-10232-B-N1)
   Yes, Indeed (45-V-10232-A-N1)

VOGUE CORAL (UK)
(78 rpm and 45 rpm with 45- prefix)

Q 72150
   Jeepers Creepers
   Mountain Greenery

Q 72159
   Blue Moon
   That Old Black Magic

Q 72185
   Love Is Here to Stay
   Goody Goody

(a 45 rpm copy has masters 45-VC-87596-1C and 45-VC-87595-1C)

Q 72202
   It Don't Mean a Thing
   All of You

Q 72217
   How (VCL-8911-1A)
   My Rosemarie (VCL-8912-1A)

(a 45 rpm copy has masters 45-VCL-8911-1C and 45-VCL-8912-1C)

VOX (USA)
(78 rpm only)

16027
   both sides without Tormé

16028
   How High the Moon
   without Tormé

16029
   Honeysuckle Rose
   without Tormé

16027/8/9 issued in Vox set VSP-303 Saturday Night Swing Session — Volume 1

EPs and MPs

This section covers 7-inch microgroove issues either at 45 rpm (EP) or 33⅓ rpm (MP). All those listed are mono unless otherwise stated.

A.R.C. (UK)

ARC 67 (MP)

ARTIE SHAW and his Orchestra. Mel Tormé is only present on two tracks, as indicated.
   1. Love for Sale; Guilty (MT)
   2. When You're Around; Get Out of Town (MT)

ATLANTIC (UK)

AET 6005
Sunday in New York/ Autumn in New York/ New York, New York

BOMAR (USA)

RD 104 (MP)

MEL TORMÉ
   1. I'm Getting Sentimental Over You

I Can't Believe That You're in Love with Me
Between the Devil & the Deep Blue Sea
2. I Surrender Dear
I've Got the World on a String
I Can't Give You Anything but Love

Stereo. No dialogue between the tracks.

CONCERT HALL (UK)
SEE POP PARADE

DECCA (UK)

DFE 6384 (EP)
MEL TORMÉ.
1. Walkin' Shoes; Shenandoah Valley
2. The Cuckoo in the Clock; Hooray for Love

HIS MASTER'S VOICE — VERVE SERIES (UK)

7EG 8721
Do Re Mi (EP)
MEL TORMÉ and MARGARET WHITING.
1. Fireworks; What's New at the Zoo; All You Need Is a Quarter
2. Cry Like the Wind; Make Someone Happy

LONDON (UK)
EZ-N 19027 Part 1
Mel Tormé Sings Fred Astaire,
Nice Work If You Can Get It/ A Foggy Day/ A Fine Romance/ The Way You Look Tonight
EZ-N 19028 Part 2
Mel Tormé Sings Fred Astaire
Something's Gotta Give/ Let's Call the Whole Thing Off/ They Can't Take That Away from Me/ Cheek to Cheek
EZ-N 19039 *details required*

LONDON ATLANTIC (UK)

RE-K 1372
The Magic of MEL (EP) MEL TORME.
1. Cast Your Fate to the Wind; Comin' Home Baby
2. Gravy Waltz; The Gift

M-G-M (USA)

X1042 (EP)
ARTIE SHAW plays COLE PORTER Artie Shaw and His Orchestra.
1. What Is This Thing Called Love; In the Still of the Night
2. Get Out of Town; You Do Something to Me

M-G-M (UK)

MGM-EP-562 (EP)
Voice in Velvet MEL TORME.
1. I'm Yours; (It Will Have to Do) Until the Real Thing Comes Along
2. Dream Awhile; Love, You Funny Thing!
MGM-EP-591 (EP)
Voice in Velvet (No. 2) MEL TORME.
1. Little White Lies; A Little Kiss Each Morning
2. Makin' Whoopee; The Best Things in Life Are Free
MGM-EPC-3 (EP)
ARTIE SHAW plays COLE PORTER Artie Shaw and His Orchestra. reissue of M-G-M X1042

PARLOPHONE (UK)

GEP 8773 (EP)
Isn't It Romantic.
Isn't It Romantic/I Know Why/You Leave Me Breathless/Stay As Sweet As You Are

GEP 8790 (EP)
For Swingers MEL TORMÉ.
1. Lulu's Back in Town; The Carioca

2. The Lady Is a Tramp; I Like to Recognize the Tune
GEP 8830 (EP)
Mel Tormé Sings while Marty Paich Swings.
　Nice Work If You Can Get It/Something's Gotta Give/The Way You Look Tonight/The Piccolino/Let's Face the Music and Dance

PHILIPS (UK)

BBE 12181 (EP)
Tormé Meets the British.
　Limehouse Blues/A Nightingale Sang in Berkeley Square/White Cliffs of Dover/London Pride

P.R.I. (USA)

SPL 9 (MP)
The Touch of Your Lips MEL TORME.
　1. Something to Live For; I'm Gettin' Sentimental Over You; I Let a Song Go Out of My Heart; One Morning in May
　2. I Surrender Dear; Between the Devil and the Deep Blue Sea; I Can't Believe That You're in Love with Me; I've Got the World on a String
Stereo. No dialogue between tracks

POP PARADE (CONCERT HALL) (UK)

BPC-721 (MP)
MEL TORME SINGS MEL TORME.
　1. Limehouse Blues; Danny Boy; Try a Little Tenderness
　2. My One and Only Highland Fling; Let There Be Love; A Nightingale Sang in Berkeley Square

ROYALE (USA)

EP246 (EP)
MEL TORME SINGS MEL TORME.
　1. Love You Funny Thing; If I Had a Girl Like You
　2. I Can't Give You Anything but Love; Do It Again

18151 (EP). label details wanted. Includes four tracks by Artie Shaw of which two have vocals by Mel Tormé.
　What Is This Thing Called Love?/Get Out of Town

VOGUE CORAL (UK)

FEP 2026 (EP)
Mel Tormé Sings at the Crescendo No. 1.
　That Old Black Magic/Get Out of Town/Goody Goody/Love Is Here to Stay

FEP 2027 (EP)
Mel Tormé Sings at the Crescendo No. 2.
　Old Devil Moon/Get Happy/Mountain Greenery/You're Driving Me Crazy/Bernie's Tune

FEP 2028 (EP)
Mel Tormé Sings at the Crescendo No. 3.
　The County Fair/Christmas Song/Jeepers Creepers

LPs (albums)

　This section covers long-playing records, or "albums" as they are usually known in the USA. All those listed are 12-inch and mono unless otherwise stated.

AFFINITY (UK)
AFF85
　Mel Tormé: Lulu's Back in Town.
　(Reissue of Bethlehem BCP-52)

AFF(D) 100 (Double Album)
　Mel Tormé: Live at the Crescendo.
　(Reissue of Bethlehem BCP6020 and BX4015. Sides 1/2 correspond to

BCP6020 and Sides 3/4 correspond to BX4015.)

AFF 107
Mel Tormé Sings Fred Astaire.
(Reissue of Bethlehem BCP6013)

AFF 138
It's a Blue World.
(Reissue of Bethlehem BCP-34)

ALLEGRO (UK)

ALL 748
Mel Tormé: I've Got the World on a String!
- 1.1 I Don't Stand a Ghost of a Chance with You
- 1.2 I'm Getting Sentimental Over You
- 1.3 I Can't Believe That You're in Love with Me
- 1.4 Prelude to a Kiss
- 1.5 I've Got the World on a String
- 2.1 Between the Devil and the Deep Blue Sea
- 2.2 I Surrender Dear
- 2.3 Don't Worry About Me
- 2.4 One Morning in May
- 2.5 I Can't Give You Anything But Love Baby

No dialogue between tracks.

ALLEGRO / ALLEGRO ELITE / ALLEGRO ROYALE (USA)

1400 series are 12-inch, 4000 series are 10-inch. The 10-inch issues usually carry the label name "Allegro Elite" with Allegro at 12 o'clock and Elite at 6 o'clock. The 12-inch issues usually carry the name "Allegro Royale" with Allegro at 12 o'clock and Royale at 6 o'clock but some issues have just Allegro as the label name — still at 12 o'clock — while at 6 o'clock the legend is "Ultraphonic High Fidelity."

1405
Artie Shaw
Title sequence and division of tracks between the two sides required. Twelve tracks by Artie Shaw with vocals by Mel Tormé on Get Out of Town, Changing My Tune, They Can't Convince Me, Guilty, I Believe, and possibly, For Me, for You, for Evermore.

1408
Details wanted
Compilation including one title by Artie Shaw with vocal by Mel Tormé: For You, for Me, for Evermore.

1466
Artie Shaw
Title sequence and division of tracks between the two sides required. Twelve tracks by Artie Shaw with vocals by Mel Tormé on Along with Me, What Is This Thing Called Love?, And So to Bed, Don't You Believe It, It's the Same Old Dream, I Believe.

4023
Artie Shaw. Artie Shaw Plays
Title sequence and division of tracks between the two sides required. Eight tracks by Artie Shaw and his Orchestra with Mel Tormé vocals as indicated: The Hornet, How Deep Is the Ocean?, I Don't Stand a Ghost of a Chance with You, Begin the Beguine, What Is This Thing Called Love? (MT), Get Out of Town (MT), You Do Something to Me, Love for Sale.

4030
Artie Shaw. Artie Shaw and His Orchestra
Title sequence and division of tracks between the two sides required. Eight tracks by Artie Shaw and his Orchestra, two with vocals by Mel Tormé as indicated: The Glider, Night and Day, My Heart Belongs to Daddy, Guilty (MT), I've Got You Under My Skin, Love of My Life, In the Still of the Night, Along with Me (MT).

4107

Artie Shaw Plays Cole Porter
   Title sequence and division of tracks between the two sides required. Eight tracks by Artie Shaw and his Orchestra, two with vocals by Mel Tormé as indicated: Night and Day, Get Out of Town (MT), In the Still of the Night, What Is This Thing Called Love? (MT), Love for Sale, You Do Something to Me, I've Got You Under My Skin, My Heart Belongs to Daddy.

4117

Mel Tormé Sings
   1.1 If I Had a Girl Like You
   1.2 A Cottage for Sale
   1.3 Little White Lies
   1.4 I Cover the Waterfront
   2.1 Makin' Whoopie
   2.2 I Can't Give You Anything but Love
   2.3 Do It Again
   2.4 Three Little Words

APEX (UK)

AX5

The Great Song Stylists. Volume 2 Mel Tormé
   1.1 Limehouse Blues
   1.2 A Nightingale Sang in Berkeley Square
   1.3 I've Got a Lovely Bunch of Coconuts
   1.4 These Foolish Things
   1.5 Geordie
   1.6 My One and Only Highland Fling
   1.7 The White Cliffs of Dover
   2.1 Danny Boy
   2.2 Let There Be Love
   2.3 Greensleeves
   2.4 Try a Little Tenderness
   2.5 London Pride
   2.6 Time Was
   2.7 (You've Got Me Goin') Ev'ry Which Way

ARCHIVE OF JAZZ (USA)
See Everest

ARISTA (USA)

AL-8-8254

Barry Manilow 2.00 am — Paradise Cafe
   All tracks are by Barry Manilow. Mel Tormé is present on one track in a duet with Manilow. 2.3 Big City Blues.
Stereo.

ARISTA (GERMANY)

206 496

Barry Manilow 2.00 am — Paradise Cafe
   European version of Arista AL-8-8254. Distributed in the UK.

ATLANTIC (USA)

8066

Mel Tormé at the Red Hill
   1.1 Shakin' the Blues Away
   1.2 I'm Beginning to See the Light
   1.3 In Other Words
   1.4 Medley: (a) A Foggy Day, (b) A Nightingale Sang in Berkeley Square
   1.5 Love for Sale
   1.6 It's Delovely
   2.1 Mountain Greenery
   2.2 Nevertheless
   2.3 Early Autumn
   2.4 Anything Goes
   2.5 (Ah, the Apple Trees) When the World Was Young
   2.6 Love Is Just Around the Corner

8069

Mel Tormé "Comin' Home Baby!"
   1.1 Comin' Home Baby
   1.2 Dat Dere
   1.3 The Lady's in Love with You
   1.4 Hi-Fly
   1.5 Puttin' on the Ritz
   1.6 Walkin'
   2.1 Moanin'
   2.2 Sing You Sinners
   2.3 Whisper Not

2.4 On Green Dolphin Street
2.5 Sidney's Soliloquy
2.6 Right Now

8091

Mel Tormé: Sunday in New York & Other Songs About New York
1.1 Sunday in New York
1.2 Autumn in New York
1.3 Lullaby of Broadway
1.4 Broadway
1.5 The Brooklyn Bridge
1.6 Let Me Off Up Town Broadway
2.1 Forty Second Street
2.2 Sidewalks of New York
2.3 Harlem Nocturne
2.4 New York, New York
2.5 There's a Broken Heart for Every Light On
2.6 Manhattan
2.7 My Kind of Day

SD 8066

Mel Tormé at the Red Hill
(Stereo version of 8066.)

SD 8069

Mel Tormé: "Comin' Home Baby!"
(Stereo version of 8069.)

SD 8091

Mel Tormé: Sunday in New York & Other Songs About New York
(Stereo version of 8091.)

SD-18129

Mel Tormé: Live at the Maisonette
1.1 Introduction
1.2 Jet Set
1.3 What Are You Doing the Rest of Your Life?
1.4 Mountain Greenery
1.5 It Takes Too Long to Live Alone
1.6 (Get Your Kicks On) Route 66
2.1 Gershwin Medley (a. I Got Rhythm, b. Mine, c. Do-Do-Do, d. 'S Wonderful, e. Embraceable You, f. Love Walked In, g. Love Is Here to Stay, h. Oh, Lady Be Good, i. A Foggy Day, j. How Long Has This Been Going On?, k. Oh Bess, O Where's My Bess? l. Who Cares?, m. Love Is Sweeping the Country, n. Of Thee I Sing, o. Swanee, p. Strike Up the Band, q. I'll Build a Stairway to Paradise)
2.2 Superstition
2.3 The Party's Over.

Stereo.

ATLANTIC (UK)

590 008 *Right Now*
1.1 Right Now
1.2 Dat Dere
1.3 The Lady's in Love with You
1.4 Hi-Fly
1.5 Puttin' on the Ritz
1.6 Walkin'
2.1 Moanin'
2.2 Sing You Sinners
2.3 Whisper Not
2.4 On Green Dolphin Street
2.5 Sidney's Soliloquy
2.6 Comin' Home Baby

Reissue of Atlantic 8069 with a different album title and revised track sequence.

ATL 5005

Mel Tormé: Sunday in New York & Other Songs About New York
(Reissue of Atlantic 8091.)

K50135

Mel Tormé: Live at the Maisonette
(Reissue of Atlantic SD 18129.)
Stereo.

SAL5005

Mel Tormé: Sunday in New York & Other Songs About New York.
(Reissue of Atlantic SD 8091.)
Stereo.

AUDIOPHILE (USA)

AP-67

Mel Tormé Sings About Love
1.1 Where Are You?
1.2 It's Easy to Remember (And So Hard to Forget)

1.3 The Christmas Song
1.4 I Could Have Told You
1.5 All in Fun
1.6 Too Late Now
1.7 You Took Advantage of Me
2.1 I Concentrate on You
2.2 In Love in Vain
2.3 Long Ago and Far Away
2.4 Star Eyes
2.5 The Night We Called It a Day
2.6 Isn't It Romantic?
2.7 Day In, Day Out

BETHLEHEM (USA)

There are three periods of Bethlehem issues. The original label which shows addresses on the sleeve as New York, N.Y. and Hollywood, Calif. The second period is when Bethlehem was associated with King Records and the sleeves of these show an address of Cincinnati 7. The final period is when Bethlehem was issued by International Jazz Emporium — A Cayre Industries Company of 240 Madison Avenue, New York. The albums in this last period often had redesigned sleeves. Some of the labels do not carry the label name "Bethlehem," on these there is no label name at all.

BCP-34
Mel Tormé: It's a Blue World
1.1 I Got It Bad and That Ain't Good
1.2 Till the Clouds Roll By
1.3 Isn't It Romantic?
1.4 I Know Why
1.5 All This and Heaven Too
1.6 How Long Has This Been Going On
2.1 Polka Dots and Moonbeams
2.2 You Leave Me Breathless
2.3 I Found a Million Dollar Baby
2.4 Wonderful One
2.5 It's a Blue World
2.6 Stay as Sweet as You Are

The Cayre reissue of this album has no Bethlehem name on the label.

BCP-52
Mel Tormé and the Marty Paich Dek-Tette
1.1 Lulu's Back in Town
1.2 When the Sun Comes Out
1.3 I Love to Watch the Moonlight
1.4 Fascinating Rhythm
1.5 The Blues
1.6 The Carioca
2.1 The Lady Is a Tramp
2.2 I Like to Recognize the Tune
2.3 Keeping Myself for You
2.4 Lullaby of Birdland
2.5 When April Comes Again
2.6 Sing for Your Supper

BCP-6009
Highlights from George Gershwin's Porgy and Bess
(This is a Cayre issue.) Tormé only appears on the indicated tracks.
1.1 Overture
1.2 Summertime
1.3 A Woman Is a Sometime Thing
1.4 The Wake, Gone, Gone, Gone/Overflow (MT)
1.5 Porgy's Prayer (see note below)
1.6 I Got Plenty of Nuthin' (MT)
1.7 Law Scene (MT)
2.1 Bess, You Is My Woman (MT)
2.2 It Ain't Necessarily So
2.3 What You Want with Bess
2.4 I Loves You, Porgy (MT)
2.5 Clara, Clara
2.6 There's a Boat That Leaving Soon for New York
2.7 Oh, Where's My Bess (MT)
2.8 I'm on My Way (MT).

This album contains the same material as Bethlehem BCP-6040. The track labeled as "Porgy's Prayer" and credited to Mel Tormé is actually "My Man's Gone Now" by Frances Faye.

BCP-6013
Mel Tormé Sings Fred Astaire
1.1 Nice Work If You Can Get It
1.2 Something's Gotta Give

1.3 A Foggy Day
1.4 A Fine Romance
1.5 Let's Call the Whole Thing Off
1.6 Top Hat, White Tie and Tails
2.1 The Way You Look Tonight
2.2 The Piccolino
2.3 They Can't Take That Away from Me
2.4 Cheek to Cheek
2.5 Let's Face the Music and Dance
2.6 They All Laughed

BCP-6016
Mel Tormé's California Suite
(Same content as BX-4016. Label details of BCP-6016 are required.)

BCP-6020
Gene Norman Presents Mel Tormé at the Crescendo
1.1 It's Only a Paper Moon
1.2 What Is This Thing Called Love
1.3 One for My Baby (One for the Road)
1.4 Love Is Just a Bug
1.5 A Nightingale Sang in Berkeley Square
2.1 Autumn Leaves
2.2 Just One of Those Things
2.3 The Boy Next Door
2.4 Lover Come Back to Me
2.5 Looking at You
2.6 (Love Is) the Tender Trap
2.7 I'm Beginning to See the Light

BCP-6022
Mel Tormé Loves Fred Astaire
(This is a Cayre reissue.)
(Reissue of BCP-6013.)

BCP-6031
Songs for Any Taste Mel Tormé
(First version with front cover picture of shelves of cheese, sausages, fruit etc.)
1.1 It's All Right with Me
1.2 Manhattan
1.3 Taking a Chance on Love
1.4 Home by the Sea
1.5 I Got Plenty o' Nuttin'
2.1 It's D'lovely
2.2 Tenderly
2.3 I Wish I Were in Love Again
2.4 Autumn Leaves
2.5 Nobody's Heart

BCP-6031
Songs for Any Taste: Mel Tormé
(Second version with front cover picture of a selection of sweetmeats, a jar of sweets and a glass.)
1.1 It's All Right with Me
1.2 Manhattan
1.3 Taking a Chance on Love
1.4 Home by the Sea
1.5 I Got Plenty O' Nuttin'
2.1 De Lovely
2.2 Tenderly
2.3 I Wish I Were in Love Again
2.4 Autumn Leaves
2.5 Nobody's Heart

Track 1.3 as "Here I Go Again" on the front cover.

BCP-6040
A Jazz Version of Highlights from the Opera Porgy and Bess.
This album contains a selection of tracks taken from the complete work on EXLP-1. Mel Tormé is present only on the tracks indicated.
1.1 Overture
1.2 Summertime
1.3 A Woman Is a Sometime Thing
1.4 The Wake: Gone, Gone, Gone/OverfloPorgy's Prayer (MT)
1.5 My Man's Gone Now
1.6 I Got Plenty of Nothin' (MT)
1.7 Law Scene (MT)
2.1 Bess, You Is My Woman Now (MT)
2.2 It Ain't Necessarily So
2.3 What You Want with Bess
2.4 I Loves You, Porgy
2.5 Clara, Clara
2.6 There's a Boat That Leaving Soon for New York
2.7 Oh, Where's My Bess (MT)
2.8 I'm on My Way (MT)

BCP-6042
The Tormé Touch

(Title sequence and division of tracks between the two sides required. Reissue of BCP-52.)

BX-4015
The Golden Voice of Mel Tormé
(This is a Cincinnati reissue.)
(Reissue of Bethlehem BCP 6031 [second version] with the tracks in a different order.)
1.1 Autumn Leaves
1.2 Tenderly
1.3 I Wish I Were in Love Again
1.4 It's De Lovely
1.5 It's All Right with Me
2.1 Manhattan
2.2 Taking a Chance on Love
2.3 Home by the Sea
2.4 I Got Plenty o' Nuttier
2.5 Nobody's Heart

Track 2.2 as "Here I Go Again" on the front cover.

BX-4016
Mel Tormé's California Suite
(This is a Cincinnati reissue.)
1.1 California Suite
2.1 California Suite
(Reissue of Bethlehem BCP-6016.)

EXLP-1
Porgy and Bess (3 LP box set)

This is a complete version of the opera. The musical items are linked by a narrator (Al Collins) and some incidental music. The cast includes Mel Tormé (as Porgy), Frances Faye (Bess), Betty Roche (Clara), George Kirby (Sportin' Life), Johnny Hartman (Crown), Sallie Blair (Serena) and Frank Rosolino (Jake). Other voices are Loulie Jean Norman, Joe Derise and Bob Dorough. Music by Russ Garcia and the Bethlehem Orchestra and Chorus, Duke Ellington and his Orchestra, the Australian Jazz Quartet, the Stan Levey Group, the Howard McGhee Group and the Pat Moran Quartet (vocal harmony group). The records are not banded and the sides are labeled "Porgy and Bess, Side 1" to "…Side 6." These are the musical items.

Record 1:
1.1 Introduction (BO)
1.2 Summertime (DEO from Bethlehem BCP6005)
1.3 Summertime (BR HMG)
1.4 A Woman Is a Sometime Thing (FR SLG)
1.5 The Honey Man (JD AJQ)
1.6 They Pass by Singing (MT BO & C)
1.7 Crap Game Fugue (BO)
1.8 Crown and Robbins Fight (BO)
2.1 Gone, Gone, Gone (SB & BO & C)
2.2 Overflow (MT BO & C)
2.3 I Can't Puzzle This Thing Out (MT BO & C)
2.4 My Man Is Gone Now (SB BO and C)
2.5 Train Song (Leavin' for the Promised Land (BO & C)

Record 2:
1.1 It Takes a Long Pull to Get There (FR SLG)
1.2 I Got Plenty of Nuthin' (MT Chorus & HMG)
1.3 The Buzzard Song (MT BO & C)
1.4 Bess You Is My Woman Now (MT, FF BO & C)
1.5 I Got Plenty of Nuthin' (reprise)
2.1 It Ain't Necessarily So (BR BO)
2.2 It Ain't Necessarily So (GK STG)
2.3 Why Do You Want Bess? (FF, JH BO & C)
2.4 It Takes a Long Pull to Get There (reprise)
2.5 Doctor Jesus (SB BO & C)
2.6 Street Cries, The Honey Man (JD AJQ), Strawberry Woman (LJN unaccompanied), Crab Man (BD AJQ)

Record 3:
1.1 I Love You Porgy (FF, MT BO & C)
1.2 Storm Music (BO & C)
1.3 Summertime (reprise; BR, Chorus & HMG)
1.4 Somebody Knockin' (BO & C)

1.5 If Got Wants to Kill Me (JH BO & C)
1.6 A Red Headed Woman (JH, Chorus & HMG)
1.7 Doctor Jesus (BO & C)
2.1 Clara, Don't Be Downhearted (BO & C)
2.2 Summertime (reprise; BR, Chorus & HMG)
2.3 There's a Boat Data Leavin' (Soon for New York) (GK BO & C)
2.4 Good Mornin' (BO & C)
2.5 Oh, Where's My Bess? (MT, LJN BO & C)
2.6 I'm on My Way (MT BO & C)
EXLP-1-SP (10-inch)
Highlights from "Porgy and Bess"
Mel Tormé appears only on the track marked with an asterisk [*].
1.1 Bess You Is My Woman Now*
1.2 It Ain't Necessarily So
1.3 Summertime
2.1 Woman Is a Sometime Thing
2.2 My Man's Gone Now
2.3 If God Want to Kill Me
3BP-1
Porgy and Bess (3 LP box set) (This is a Cayre reissue).
Sides A to F: Porgy and Bess (no individual tunes are listed on the labels).
(Reissue of Bethlehem EXLP-1.)

BIAC (BELGIUM)
BRAD 10528-529
Nat King Cole, Vic Damone, Mel Tormé at His Rarest of All Rare Performances. This is a double album of which Record 1 (BRAD 10.528) is entirely by Nat King Cole.
Record 2 (BRAD 10.529):
1.1 Juanita
1.2 Straighten and Fly Right
1.3 St. Louis Blues
1.4 On the Atchison Topeka and Santa Fe
1.5 East Side, West Side

Side 2 is entirely by Vic Damone.

BOULEVARD (UK)
4025
(Reissue of Society SOC-982.)

BROADCAST TRIBUTES (USA)
BTRIB 0002
The Greatest Duets Judy Garland...
This record is taken from the soundtracks of the "Judy Garland Show" CBS television series (1963–64) and although it contains performances of material arranged or created by Mel Tormé it contains no examples of him singing. The artists that can be heard are: Judy Garland with Bobby Darin, Steve Allen, June Allyson, Peggy Lee, Mickey Rooney, Van Johnson, Jane Powell, Ray Bolger, Ethel Merman, Martha Raye and Donald O'Connor.

BULLDOG (UK)
BDL 1017
Mel Tormé: Sings
(Reissue of Strand SL 1076.)

CALLIOPE (USA)
CAL 3026
Sessions, Live. Charlie Barnet. Mel Tormé
Mel Tormé is present on only two tracks. The remainder of the tracks on side 1 are by Charlie Barnet. The tracks on side 2 are by Bev Kelly and Pat Moran.
1.3 Cross My Heart
1.4 Looking at You

CAMAY (USA)
CA-3034
Boy Meets Girl: Mel Tormé Meets June Valli

1.1 Trouble Is a Girl
1.2 You're Driving Me Crazy
1.3 April Showers
1.4 You Ought to Be in Pictures
1.5 Blue Room.

Side 2 is by June Valli without Tormé. The labels carry a catalog number of CA-3034-S.

CA-3034-S
Boy Meets Girl: Mel Tormé Meets June Valli
(The sleeve claims this to be a [pseudo] stereo version of CA-3034 but it is actually mono and identical to CA-3034.)

CAPITOL (USA)

P-200
Mel Tormé Sings His Own California Suite
1.1 Mel Tormé's CALIFORNIA SUITE Part 1
2.1 Mel Tormé's CALIFORNIA SUITE Part 2

ST-313
A Time for Us (Love Theme from Romeo & Juliet). Mel Tormé
1.1 Games People Play
1.2 Yesterday, When I Was Young
1.3 Happy Together
1.4 Windmills of Your Mind
1.5 Midnight Swinger
2.1 Willie & Laura Mae Jones
2.2 A Time for Us (Love Theme from Romeo & Juliet)
2.3 She's Leaving Home
2.4 Hurry on Down
2.5 A Bucket of Tears

Stereo
ST-430
Raindrops Keep Fallin' on My Head. Mel Tormé
1.1 Take a Letter Maria
1.2 Traces
1.3 Sunshine Superman
1.4 Hung Up Being Free
1.5 Spinning Wheel
2.1 Catch a Robber by the Toe
2.2 Requiem: 820 Latham
2.3 Into Something
2.4 Raindrops Keep Fallin' on My Head
2.5 You've Made Me So Very Happy

Stereo
ST 23869 Details required
ST 24585 Details required

CAPITOL (UK)

LCT 6004
California Suite. Mel Tormé
1.1 California Suite, Part 1 Intro.: Mountain-Desert Theme, We Think the West Coast Is the Best Coast in the Land, Coney Island, The Miami Waltz, They Go to San Diego
2.1 California Suite, Part 2 Intro.: Sunday Night in San Fernando, Got the Gate on the Golden Gate, Prelude to "Poor Little Extra Girl," Poor Little Extra Girl, We Think the West Coast Is the Best Coast in the Land, Mountain-Desert Theme

ST 21585
Raindrops Keep Fallin' on My Head. Mel Tormé
1.1 Games People Play
1.2 Take a Letter Maria
1.3 Traces
1.4 Sunshine Superman
1.5 Hung Up Being Free
1.6 Spinning Wheel
1.7 She's Leaving Home
2.1 Happy Together
2.2 The Windmills of Your Mind
2.3 Requiem: 820 Latham
2.4 Into Something
2.5 Raindrops Keep Fallin' on My Head
2.6 You've Made Me So Very Happy
2.7 A Time for Us (Love Theme from Romeo & Juliet)

RECORD ISSUES: LPs (ALBUMS) • 97

Stereo

EST 23368 Details required.

CBS (USA)
   None of these has been checked.

P 18337B
   William B. Williams Make Believe Ballroom Volume 12
   Mel Tormé is present on only one track: What Is There to Say?
SL 9298 A
   William B. Williams Make Believe Ballroom Volume 13
   Mel Tormé is present on only one track: Hurry on Down
SL 9299 A
   William B. Williams Make Believe Ballroom Volume 13
   Mel Tormé is present on only one track: A Time for Us
SL 9299 B
   William B. Williams Make Believe Ballroom Volume 13
   Mel Tormé is present on only one track: Yesterday When I Was Young
P 18761 A
   William B. Williams Make Believe Ballroom Volume 14
   Mel Tormé is present on only one track: Haven't We Met?
SL 9351 A
   William B. Williams Make Believe Ballroom Volume 15
   Mel Tormé is present on only one track: Again
ML 7001 B
   William B. Williams Make Believe Ballroom Volume 24
   Mel Tormé is present on only one track: I've Got the World on a String
ML 7002 B
   William B. Williams Make Believe Ballroom Volume 24
   Mel Tormé is present on only one track: Prelude to a Kiss
ML 7003 B
   William B. Williams Make Believe Ballroom Volume 24
   Mel Tormé is present on only one track: Ghost of a Chance
ML 7004 B
   William B. Williams Make Believe Ballroom Volume 24
   Mel Tormé is present on only one track: I Surrender Dear

CBS (UK)
BPG 62550
   That's All. Mel Tormé
   (Reissue of Columbia CL 2318.)
BPG 62809
   Mel Tormé. Right Now!
   1.1 Comin' Home Baby
   1.2 Homeward Bound
   1.3 My Little Red Book
   1.4 Walk on By
   1.5 If I Had a Hammer
   1.6 Strangers in the Night
   2.1 Better Use Your Head
   2.2 Time
   2.3 Secret Agent Man
   2.4 Pretty Flamingo
   2.5 Red Rubber Ball
   2.6 (You Got) the Power of Love
SBPG 62550
   That's All. Mel Tormé
   Stereo version of CBS BPG 62550
SBPG 62809
   Mel Tormé. Right Now!
   Stereo version of CBS BPG 62809

CENTURY (USA)
CRDD-1100
   Together Again — For the First Time. Mel Tormé and Buddy Rich
   1.1 When I Found You
   1.2 Here's That Rainy Day
   1.3 Blues in the Night
   2.1 Bluesette
   2.2 You Are the Sunshine of My Life

2.3 I Won't Last a Day Without You
2.4 Lady Be Good

Stereo. Recorded direct to disc

CITY SONGS (USA)

This is a series of CDs devoted to cities and is intended as much for promotional purposes for the cities concerned as for conventional retail sale. These compilations are also issued in cassette format.

NEW YORK: *With Fondest Memories*
This compilation includes one track by Mel Tormé,
track 14: 42nd Street

SAN FRANCISCO: *With Fondest Memories*
This compilation includes one track by Mel Tormé, track 6: Got the Gate on the Golden Gate

SOUTHERN CALIFORNIA: *With Fondest Memories*
This compilation includes one track by Mel Tormé, track 15: They Go to San Diego

COLUMBIA (USA)

CL 2318
That's All Mel Tormé
1.1 I've Got You Under My Skin
1.2 That's All
1.3 What Is There to Say?
1.4 Do I Love You Because You're Beautiful?
1.5 The Folks That Live on the Hill
1.6 Isn't It a Pity?
2.1 Ho-Ba-La-La
2.2 P.S. I Love You
2.3 The Nearness of You
2.4 My Romance
2.5 The Second Time Around
2.6 Haven't We Met?

CL 2535
Mel Tormé Right Now!
1.1 Comin' Home Baby
1.2 Homeward Bound
1.3 My Little Red Book
1.4 Walk on By
1.5 If I Had a Hammer
1.6 Strangers in the Night
2.1 Better Use Your Head
2.2 Time
2.3 Secret Agent Man
2.4 Pretty Flamingo
2.5 Red Rubber Ball

CS 9118
That's All Mel Tormé
Stereo version of CL 2318

CL 9335
Mel Tormé Right Now!
Stereo version of CL 2535

CONCORD JAZZ (USA)

Records with the same catalog numbers and contents as the American albums were pressed and released in Germany for distribution throughout Europe. Although it is known that all the LPs have the same content as the corresponding CDs, I have given a designation of "not checked" for the LPs that I have not seen. This is in order to indicate simply that although I know the titles, I do not know how they were divided between the two sides of the LP. All Concord issues are in stereo

CJ-190
An Evening with George Shearing & Mel Tormé
1.1 All God's Chillun Got Rhythm
1.2 Born to Be Blue
1.3 Give Me the Simple Life
1.4 Good Morning Heartache
1.5 Manhattan Hoedown
2.1 You'd Be So Nice to Come Home To
2.2 A Nightingale Sang in Berkeley Square
2.3 Love
2.4 It Might as Well Be Spring
2.5 Lullaby of Birdland

CJ-219
Top Drawer George Shearing Mel Tormé
1.1 Shine on Your Shoes
1.2 How Do You Say Auf Wiedersehen?
1.3 Oleo
1.4 Stardust
2.1 Hi Fly
2.2 Smoke Gets in Your Eyes
2.3 What's This?
2.4 Away in a Manger
2.5 Here's to My Lady

CJ-248
Mel Tormé, George Shearing: An Evening at Charlie's
1.1 Medley: Just One of Those Things / On Green Dolphin Street
1.2 Dream Dancing
1.3 I'm Hip
1.4 Then I'll Be Tired of You
2.1 Medley: Caught in the Middle of My Years / Welcome to the Club
2.2 Nica's Dream
2.3 Chase Me Charlie
2.4 Love Is Just Around the Corner

CJ-294
An Elegant Evening: George Shearing and Mel Tormé
1.1 I'll Be Seeing You
1.2 Moon Medley: Love and the Moon / Oh, You Crazy Moon / No Moon At All
1.3 After the Waltz Is Over
1.4 This Time the Dream's on Me
1.5 Last Night, When We Were Young
2.1 You Changed My Life
2.2 Dream Medley: I Had the Craziest Dream / Darn That Dream
2.3 Brigg Fair
2.4 My Foolish Heart
2.5 You're Driving Me Crazy

CJ-306
Mel Tormé, Rob McConnell and the Boss Brass
1.1 Just Friends
1.2 September Song
1.3 Don'cha Go 'Way Mad
1.4 A House Is Not a Home
1.5 The Song Is You
2.1 Cow Cow Boogie
2.2 A Handful of Stars/Stars Fell on Alabama
2.3 Duke Ellington Medley: It Don't Mean a Thing (If It Ain't Got That Swing) / Do Nothing Till You Hear from Me / Mood Indigo / Take the "A" Train / Sophisticated Lady / Satin Doll

CJ-341
Mel Tormé, George Shearing a Vintage Year
Whisper Not/Love Me or Leave Me
Out of This World
Someday I'll Find You
The Midnight Sun
New York, New York Medley: Me and My Girl/Mack the Knife/Birth of the Blues/Send a Little Love My Way/How High the Moon?/New York, New York
Folks Who Live on the Hill
Bitter Sweet
Since I Fell for You
The Way You Look Tonight
Anyone Can Whistle/A Tune for Humming
When Sunny Gets Blue
Little Man You've Had a Busy Day

Not checked

CJ-360
Mel Tormé and the Marty Paich Dek-Tette Reunion
1.1 Sweet Georgia Brown
1.2 When You Wish Upon a Star/I'm Wishing
1.3 Between Raindrops
1.4 The Blues
1.5 Bossa Nova Potpourri: The Gift/One Note Samba/How Insensitive
2.1 The Trolley Song/Get Me to the Church on Time
2.2 More Than You Know

2.3 The Goodbye Look
2.4 For Whom the Bell Tolls/Spain (I Can Recall)

CJ-382

> *Mel Tormé and the Marty Paich Dek-Tette in Concert, Tokyo Fujitsu-Concord Jazz Festival in Japan '88*
> It Don't Mean a Thing (If It Ain't Got That Swing)
> Sweet Georgia Brown
> Just in Time
> When the Sun Comes Out
> The Carioca
> More Than You Know
> Too Close for Comfort
> The City
> Bossa Nova Potpourri: The Gift, One Note Samba, How Insensitive
> On the Street Where You Live
> Cotton Tail
> The Christmas Song
> It Don't Mean a Thing (If It Ain't Got That Swing)

Not checked.

All later releases of Concord Jazz albums were issued only on CD and cassette.

CORAL (USA)

CRL 57012

> *gene norman presents: mel tormé actually recorded at the crescendo, Dec. 15, 1954*
> 1.1 From This Moment On
> 1.2 That Old Black Magic
> 1.3 Get Out of Town
> 1.4 Goody Goody
> 1.5 Love Is Here to Stay
> 1.6 Blue Moon
> 1.7 Old Devil Moon
> 2.1 Get Happy
> 2.2 Mountain Greenery
> 2.3 County Fair
> 2.4 The Christmas Song (Merry Christmas to You)
> 2.5 Jeepers Creepers

2.6 You're Driving Me Crazy
2.7 Bernie's Tune

CRL 57044

> *Mel Tormé. "Musical Sounds Are the Best Songs"*
> 1.1 The Flat Foot Floogee
> 1.2 The Hut-Sut Song (A Swedish Rhapsody)
> 1.3 All of You
> 1.4 Just One More Chance
> 1.5 It Don't Mean a Thing (If It Ain't Got That Swing)
> 1.6 Tutti Frutti
> 2.1 Cement Mixer (Put-ti, Put-ti)
> 2.2 Hold Tight (Want Some Sea Food Mama)
> 2.3 Blue Skies
> 2.4 Rose O'Day
> 2.5 Spellbound
> 2.6 I'se A-Muggin'

CORAL (UK)

CP 40

> *Mel Tormé at the Crescendo*
> (Reissue of MCA Coral MCL 1683.)

CROWN (USA)

CLP-5347

> *Mel Tormé: Mel Tormé, Robert Alda and Cesar Romero*
> 1.1 I Can't Give You Anything But Love
> 1.2 Don't Worry 'Bout Me
> 2.1 I Surrender Dear
> 2.2 I Don't Stand a Ghost of a Chance

No dialogue between tracks. Tormé is not on the remaining tracks of this record.

CSP (COLUMBIA SPECIAL PRODUCTS) (USA)

EN 13090

> *That's All Mel Tormé*
> Stereo.
> Reissue of Columbia CS 9118.

COUNTERPOINT (USA)

CPT 549 Details required

DÉJÀ VU (ITALY)

DVLP 2046
> *The Mel Tormé Collection: 20 Golden Greats*
> 1.1 That Ol' Black Magic*
> 1.2 Blue Moon*
> 1.3 Get Out of Town*
> 1.4 Jeepers Creepers*
> 1.5 From This Moment On*
> 1.6 Love Is Here to Stay*
> 1.7 Mountain Greenery*
> 1.8 Bernie's Tune*
> 1.9 Old Devil Moon*
> 1.10 Get Happy*
> 2.1 Don't You Believe It
> 2.2 Along with Me
> 2.3 Changing My Tune
> 2.4 They Can't Convince Me
> 2.5 Guilty
> 2.6 For You, for Me, Forever More
> 2.7 You're Driving Me Crazy*
> 2.8 Goody Goody*
> 2.9 The Christmas Song*
> 2.10 I Believe

This record is listed only because it has been claimed to contain recordings of Italian concert performances but it is actually, in part, recordings from Coral CRL 57012 (The Crescendo live album); these are marked (*) and the remainder are from Musicraft.

DISCOVERY (USA)

DS-910
> *Mel Tormé Sings His California Suite*
> 1.1 Introduction (Mountain-Desert Theme)
> 1.2 We Think the West Coast Is the Best Coast in the Land
> 1.3 Coney Island
> 1.4 The Miami Waltz
> 1.5 They Go to San Diego
> 2.1 Sunday Night in San Fernando
> 2.2 Got the Gate on the Golden Gate
> 2.3 Prelude to "Poor Little Extra Girl"
> 2.4 Poor Little Extra Girl
> 2.5 Reprise: We Think the West Coast Is the Best Coast in the Land
> 2.6 Finale (Mountain-Desert Theme)

This is from the Capitol version.

EASTON PRESS (USA)

EP4 17885
> *The Great Singers*
> County Fair
> Body and Soul
> This Can't Be Love
> They Can't Take That Away from Me
> Blues in the Night
> Once in a Lifetime
> My Romance
> Blue Moon
> Again
> My Funny Valentine
> Love Me Or Leave Me
> I've Got You Under My Skin
> The Christmas Song
> What Is There to Say?
> Moonlight in Vermont
> The Second Time Around

Title sequence and division of tracks between the two sides required.

EGMONT (UK)

EGM 8119
> *Mel Torme*
> (Reissue of Sutton SU-208 / Viking VK-006.)

EMBER (UK)

CEL 900
> *Porgy and Bess*
> (Reissue of Bethlehem BCP 6040.)

EMB 3328
> *"The King of Swing" Artie Shaw and His Orchestra*
> All titles are by Artie Shaw and his Orchestra with vocals by Mel Tormé as indicated.
> 1.1 The Hornet
> 1.2 My Heart Belongs to Daddy
> 1.3 The Glider
> 1.4 I've Got You Under My Skin
> 1.5 How Deep Is the Ocean?
> 2.1 I Don't Stand a Ghost of a Chance
> 2.2 Anniversary Song
> 2.3 Guilty (MT)
> 2.4 What Is This Thing Called Love? (MT)
> 2.5 You Do Something to Me

EMB 3335
> *Tribute to the Grand Order of Water Rats*
> Includes Artie Shaw's "What Is This Thing Called Love?" with vocal by Mel Tormé

FA 2015
> *"The King of Swing" Artie Shaw and His Orchestra*
> (Reissue of Ember EMB 3328.)

SE 8000 Details required

ESOTERIC (USA)

ESJ 2 Details required.

EVEREST (USA)

> The label also carries a sub-title "Archive of Jazz Series"

FS 231
> *1947 WNEW Saturday Night Swing Session*
> 1.1 Lover
> 1.2 Honeysuckle Rose
> 1.3 How High the Moon
> 1.4 Flip and Jazz
> 2.1 High on an Open Mike
> 2.2 Sweet Georgia Brown

FS-248
> *Artie Shaw Guest Artists Mel Tormé, Kitty Kallen, Hal Stevens and Teddy Walters*
> All titles are by Artie Shaw and his Orchestra. Only 1.2 has a vocal by Mel Tormé.
> 1.1 Let's Walk
> 1.2 What Is This Thing Called Love? (alt take)
> 1.3 I've Got You Under My Skin
> 1.4 How Deep Is the Ocean
> 1.5 Begin the Beguine
> 2.1 Night and Day
> 2.2 You Do Something to Me
> 2.3 Love of My Life
> 2.4 My Heart Belongs to Daddy
> 2.5 In the Still of the Night

FS 324
> *Mel Tormé with the Meltones and Artie Shaw*
> All titles are by Artie Shaw and his Orchestra with vocals by Mel Tormé.
> 1.1 For You, for Me, Forever More
> 1.2 Changing My Tune
> 1.3 They Can't Convince Me
> 1.4 Guilty
> 1.5 And So to Bed
> 2.1 I Believe
> 2.2 Don't You Believe It
> 2.3 I've Got the Sun in the Morning
> 2.4 Along with Me
> 2.5 Get Out of Town

FINESSE (USA)

W2X 37484 (Double)
> *Mel Tormé and Friends. Recorded Live at Marty's New York City*
> Record 1 (Set 1):
> 1.1 Let's Take a Walk Around the Block
> 1.2 New York State of Mind

1.3 When the World Was Young
1.4 Pick Yourself Up
1.5 Silly Habits
2.1 Mountain Greenery
2.2 Cottage for Sale
2.3 Take a Letter Miss Jones
2.4 Real Thing
2.5 Medley: Line for Lyons / Venus De Milo / Walking Shoes

Record 2 (Set 2):
1.1 Medley: Watch What Happens / Fly Me to the Moon / You and the Night and the Music / Shaking the Blues Away
1.2 Isn't It Romantic
1.3 Porgy and Bess Medley
1.4 The Folks Who Live on the Hill
1.5 Chase Me Charlie
2.1 The Best Is Yet to Come
2.2 Isn't It a Pity
2.3 Wave
2.4 I Guess I'll Have to Change My Plan
2.5 Love for Sale

Stereo

FIND 5661 (Double)
Mel Tormé and Friends
(Reissue of W2X 37484.)

FIRST HEARD (UK)

FHR-1974-8
Superb Performances Mostly Never Before Available by Boyd Raeburn and His Musicians 1943–1948 (All tracks are by Boyd Raeburn.) These tracks have vocals by Mel Tormé and the Mel-Tones:
2.1 Old Man River
2.2 That's Where I Came In

FLAIR (USA)

PG8200
Tormé Encore at Marty's New York (Exactly as it happened) March 27, 1982

1.1 Lulu's Back in Town
1.2 Looking at You
1.3 That Face
1.4 I'm Gonna Miss You
1.5 Medley — A Tribute to Fred Astaire
1.6 What Are You Doing the Rest of Your Life?
2.1 Sophisticated Lady
2.2 Stormy Weather
2.3 When the Sun Comes Out
2.4 Autumn Leaves
2.5 Pieces of Dreams
2.6 I Like to Recognize the Tune
2.7 Watch What Happens

Stereo.

FONTANA (UK)

6438 022
This Is ... Mel Tormé
1.1 Ghost of a Chance
1.2 I'm Getting Sentimental Over You
1.3 I Can't Believe That You're in Love with Me
1.4 Prelude to a Kiss
1.5 I've Got the World on a String
2.1 Between the Devil and the Deep Blue Sea
2.2 I Surrender Dear
2.3 Don't Worry 'Bout Me
2.4 One Morning in May
2.5 I Can't Give You Anything But Love

Stereo. No dialogue between tracks.

FRANKLIN MINT (USA)

FM 005, 006, 007 & 008 (box set of 4 LPs)
Institute of Jazz Studies Official Archive Collection. The Greatest Jazz Recordings of All Time: The Jazz Singers. This set includes one Mel Tormé item: Record No. 2 (FM 006) Side B
2.6 Oh What a Night for Love.

Stereo.

GALA (UK)

GLP 301
> *Mel Tormé Prelude to a Kiss*
> (Reissue of Tops L1615 with dialogue between the tracks.)

GALAXY (USA)

4852
> Details wanted. Eleven or twelve tracks by Artie Shaw including two with vocals by Mel Tormé. What Is This Thing Called Love? / Guilty

GLENDALE (USA)

GL 6007
> *Mel Tormé*
> 1.1 Isn't It a Lovely Day?
> 1.2 I Can't Get Started
> 1.3 Stranger in Town
> 1.4 When It's Sleepy Time Down South
> 1.5 I Cover the Waterfront
> 1.6 Country Boy
> 2.1 How Are Things in Glocca Morra?
> 2.2 The Blues
> 2.3 April in Paris
> 2.4 Long Has This Been Going On?
> 2.5 Cottage for Sale
> 2.6 Gone with the Wind

GL 6018
> *Mel Tormé. Easy to Remember*
> 1.1 It's Easy to Remember
> 1.2 They Didn't Believe Me
> 1.3 My Funny Valentine
> 1.4 County Fair
> 1.5 Love Me or Leave Me
> 1.6 September Song
> 2.1 The Best Things in Life Are Free
> 2.2 They Can't Take That Away from Me
> 2.3 April Showers
> 2.4 Don't Take Your Love from Me
> 2.5 Blues in the Night
> 2.6 This Can't Be Love

GOLDEN TONE (USA)

GT-4098
> 10-inch. Label details wanted. Thought to be the same as Tops 975. Eight tracks by Artie Shaw including one with vocal by Mel Tormé—Guilty

GRP (USA)

GRP-A-1002
> *The Glenn Miller Orchestra "In the Digital Mood"*
> All tracks are by the Glenn Miller Orchestra. Mel Tormé is present as part of the vocal group on
> 1.2 Chattanooga Choo-Choo
> 2.1 Kalamazoo
> and possibly on 2.4 Pennsylvania 6-5000

Stereo.

GRYPHON (USA)

G-916
> *Mel Tormé: Tormé a New Album*
> 1.1 All in Love Is Fair
> 1.2 The First Time Ever I Saw Your Face
> 1.3 New York State of Mind
> 1.4 Stars
> 2.1 Send in the Clowns
> 2.2 Ordinary Fool
> 2.3 Medley: When the World Was Young / Yesterday When I Was Young
> 2.4 Bye Bye Blackbird

Stereo.

HALL OF FAME (USA)

GP 701
> *Mel Tormé "Prime Time"*
> 1.1 Things to Live For
> 1.2 I'm Getting Sentimental Over You

1.3 A Ghost of a Chance
1.4 I Can't Believe That You're in Love with Me
1.5 Prelude to a Kiss
2.1 Between the Devil and the Deep Blue Sea
2.2 I Surrender Dear
2.3 Out of My Heart
2.4 Don't Worry About Me
2.5 One Morning in May

Stereo. No dialogue between tracks.

GP 705
Great Singers of the Fifties
Details required.

HALO (USA)

50243
Mel Tormé: Mel Tormé Sings
1.1 A Cottage for Sale
1.2 I Cover the Waterfront
1.3 Makin' Whoopie
1.4 If I Had a Girl Like You
1.5 Little White Lies
2.1 Do It Again
2.2 But Beautiful
2.3 Night and Day
2.4 I Can't Give You Anything but Love
2.5 Three Little Words

HIS MASTER'S VOICE, VERVE SERIES (UK)

CLP 1238
Mel Tormé Tormé
(Reissue of Verve MGV 2105.)

CLP 1315
Mel Tormé South of the Border
(Reissue of Verve MGV 2117.)

CLP 1328
Mel Tormé Back in Town
(Reissue of Verve MGV 2120.)

CLP 1405
Mel Tormé: Tormé Swings Shubert Alley

1.1 Too Close for Comfort
1.2 Once in Love with Amy
1.3 Sleeping Bee
1.4 On the Street Where You Live
1.5 Just in Time
2.1 Hello Young Lovers
2.2 The Surrey with the Fringe on Top
2.3 Old Devil Moon
2.4 Whatever Lola Wants
2.5 Too Darn Hot
2.6 Lonely Town

CLP 1445
Mel Tormé Swingin' on the Moon
(Reissue of Verve MGV 2144.)

CLP 1584
Mel Tormé. My Kind of Music
(Reissue of Verve V-8440.)

CSD 1330
Mel Tormé: Tormé Swings Shubert Alley
Stereo version of CLP 1405

CSD 1349
Mel Tormé Swingin' on the Moon
Stereo version of CLP 1445

CSD 1442
Mel Tormé. My Kind of Music
Stereo version of CLP 1584

HOLLYWOOD SOUNDSTAGE (USA)

HS 411
Higher and Higher
1.1 Main Title / It's a Most Important Affair
1.2 I'm a Debutante an Evening (reprise)
1.3 I Couldn't Sleep a Wink Last Night
1.4 The Music Stopped
1.5 I Saw You First
1.6 A Lovely Way to Spend an Evening
2.1 Incidental Music / A Lovely Way to Spend an Evening
2.2 You're on Your Own
2.3 You're on Your Own (reprise)

2.4 I Couldn't Sleep a Wink Last Night (reprise)
2.5 Minuet in Boogie
2.6 Finale (I Saw You First / A Lovely Way to Spend an Evening / The Music Stopped)

HURRAH (USA)

H- 1004
Mel Tormé Marty Paich Songs of Love
1.1 I Don't Stand a Ghost of a Chance with You
1.2 I'm Getting Sentimental Over You
1.3 I Can't Believe That You're in Love with Me
1.4 Prelude to a Kiss
1.5 I've Got the World on a String
2.1 Between the Devil and the Deep Blue Sea
2.2 I Surrender Dear
2.3 Don't Worry About Me
2.4 One Morning in May
2.5 I Can't Give You Anything but Love

No dialogue between the tracks.

HS- 1004
Mel Tormé Marty Paich Songs of Love
Stereo version of H-1004.

No dialogue between the tracks.

JASMINE (UK)

JASM 1004
Mel Tormé "Musical Sounds Are the Best Songs"
(Reissue of Coral CRL 57044.)
JASM 2529
Mel Tormé Live
(Reissue of Sounds Great SG 5012.)

JAZZ GREATS (USA)
SEE HALL OF FAME

JJA (USA)

1982-2
Words and Music
Details required.

JOYCE

5010
Boyd Raeburns Jubilee
Label gives catalog number as LP-5010. All tracks are by Boyd Raeburn but there are vocals by Mel Tormé and the Mel-Tones only on
1.2 Old Man River
1.5 That's Where I Came In

LIBERTY (USA)

LRP-3560
A Day in the Life of Bonnie and Clyde. Mel Tormé
1.1 We're in the Money
1.2 Annie Doesn't Live Here Anymore
1.3 Button Up Your Overcoat
1.4 You're the Cream in My Coffee
1.5 With Plenty of Money of You (Oh! Baby What I Couldn't Do)
1.6 A Day in the Life of Bonnie and Clyde
2.1 The Music Goes Round and Round
2.2 Cab Driver
2.3 I Found a Million Dollar Baby
2.4 Brother, Can You Spare a Dime?
2.5 I Concentrate on You
2.6 Little White Lies.
The titles are listed on the sleeve are in the wrong sequence.
LST-7560
A Day in the Life of Bonnie and Clyde. Mel Tormé
Stereo version of LRP-3560.

LIBERTY (UK)

LBL 83119E
The Music Goes Round. Mel Tormé
(Reissue of Liberty LRP-3560 with a different album title. The titles on the sleeve are in the correct sequence.)
LBS 83119E
The Music Goes Round. Mel Tormé
Stereo version of LBL 83119E.

LION (USA)

L-70058
Artie Shaw Plays Cole Porter and Irving Berlin
All tracks are by Artie Shaw and his orchestra except 2.5 which is by Mel Tormé and his Mel-Tones despite being labeled as by Artie Shaw.
Those with vocals by Mel Tormé are marked (MT).
1.1 What Is This Thing Called Love? (MT) (orig. version)
1.2 In the Still of the Night
1.3 Get Out of Town (MT)
1.4 You Do Something to Me
1.5 Night and Day
2.1 My Heart Belongs to Daddy
2.2 I've Got You Under My Skin
2.3 Love for Sale
2.4 I've Got the Sun in the Morning (MT)
2.5 There's No Business Like Show Business

LONDON (UK)

HA-N.2016
It's a Blue World. Mel Tormé with Orchestra conducted by Al Pellegrini
(Reissue of Bethlehem BPC-34.)
LTZ-N 15009
Mel Tormé with Marty Paich Dek-Tette
(Reissue of Bethlehem BCP-52.)
LTZ-N 15076
Mel Tormé Sings Fred Astaire
(Reissue of Bethlehem BCP-6013.)

LONDON ATLANTIC (UK)

HA-K 8021
Mel Tormé at the Red Hill
(Reissue of Atlantic 8066.)
HA-K 8065
Comin' Home Baby!
(Reissue of Atlantic 8069.)

SH-K 8021
Mel Tormé at the Red Hill
Stereo version of HA-K 8021

MAYFAIR (USA)

9615S
Mel Tormé Prelude to a Kiss
Stereo version of Tops L1615 with dialogue between the tracks

MCA (UK)

MCFM 2775
Bing & Co.
All the tracks are by Bing Crosby. Mel Tormé and the Mel-Tones are present on one track:
2.5 Prove It by the Things You Do
MCL 1683
Mel Tormé at the Crescendo Recorded Live
1.1 From This Moment On
1.2 That Old Black Magic
1.3 Get Out of Town
1.4 Goody Goody
1.5 Love Is Here to Stay
1.6 Blue Moon
1.7 Old Devil Moon
2.1 Get Happy
2.2 Mountain Greenery
2.3 County Fair
2.4 Jeepers Creepers
2.5 You're Driving Me Crazy
2.6 Bernie's Tune

MCA CORAL (UK)

CDL-8016
Details required

METRO (USA)

M532
Mel Tormé I Wished on the Moon
1.1 I Wished on the Moon

1.2 Don't Dream of Anybody But Me
1.3 It Happened in Monterey
1.4 Hit the Road to Dreamland
1.5 Blue Moon
2.1 Moon Song
2.2 In the Evening
2.3 Truckin'
2.4 County Fair
2.5 Some Like It Hot

MS532
Mel Tormé I Wished on the Moon
Stereo version of M532

M-G-M (USA)

E-517 (10-inch)
Artie Shaw Plays Cole Porter
Title sequence and division between the two sides required. It is reported that some pressings have two further titles but this is not confirmed.
Get Out of Town (MT)
You Do Something to Me
In the Still of the Night
What Is This Thing Called Love? (MT)
I've Got You Under My Skin
Night and Day
My Heart Belongs to Daddy
Love for Sale

E-552 (10-inch)
Mel Tormé Sings
1.1 Love, You Funny Thing!
1.2 A Little Kiss Each Morning
1.3 A Cottage for Sale
1.4 I Cover the Waterfront
2.1 The Best Things in Life Are Free
2.2 I Can't Give You Anything But Love
2.3 Little White Lies
2.4 County Fair

E-4219
Details wanted. This compilation includes one track by Artie Shaw with a vocal by Mel Tormé:
What Is This Thing Called Love?

E-4238
The Very Best of Rodgers & Hart: An All Star Tribute
This compilation contains one track by Mel Tormé:
1.6 Blue Moon

E-4240
The Very Best of Irving Berlin: An All Star Tribute
This compilation has one track by Artie Shaw with Mel Tormé and the Mel-tones: I Got the Sun in the Morning (Not checked.)

PM-14 *Joan of Arc presents MGM's Music to Your Taste Volume 1* This compilation contains one track by Mel Tormé:
1.4 Blue Moon

Joan of Arc is a supplier of canned foods especially kidney beans.

SE-4219
Stereo version of E-4219

SE-4238
The Very Best of Rodgers & Hart: An All Star Tribute
Stereo version of E-4238

SE-4240
The Very Best of Irving Berlin: An All Star Tribute
Stereo version of E-4240

M-G-M (UK)

MGM-C-990
The Very Best of the Big Bands. One track is by Artie Shaw with Mel Tormé:
What Is This Thing Called Love? (Not checked.)

MGM-C-991
The Very Best of Rodgers and Hart
One track is by Mel Tormé:
Blue Moon (Not checked.)

Probably the same compilation as MGM (USA) E-4238

MGM-C-1000

The Very Best of Irving Berlin.
  One track is by Artie Shaw with Mel Tormé and the Mel-tones:
  I Got the Sun in the Morning
Probably the same compilation as MGM (USA) E-4240

MURRAY HILL (USA)

931 680 (4 LP box set)
  The Marx Brothers
   Details required

MUSIC FOR PLEASURE (UK)

MFP 1112
  The Velvet Voice of Mel Tormé
  1.1 Oh You Beautiful Doll
  1.2 Blue Moon
  1.3 You're Getting to Be a Habit with Me
  1.4 I Hadn't Anyone Till You
  1.5 You're a Heavenly Thing
  1.6 Again
  2.1 Do-do-do
  2.2 Skylark
  2.3 Lullaby of the Leaves
  2.4 The Piccolino
  2.5 Black Moonlight
  2.6 The Four Winds and the Seven Seas

MUSICRAFT (USA)

MVS-503
  Artie Shaw, Volume 1 Clarinet Magic with the Big Band and Strings.
  All titles are by Artie Shaw and his orchestra. Mel Tormé is only present where indicated.
  1.1 Let's Walk
  1.2 Love of My Life
  1.3 Ghost of a Chance
  1.4 How Deep Is the Ocean?
  1.5 The Glider
  1.6 They Can't Convince Me (alt take) (MT)
  2.1 I Got the Sun in the Morning (MT)
  2.2 Along with Me (MT)
  2.3 You Do Something to Me
  2.4 In the Still of the Night
  2.5 My Heart Belongs to Daddy
  2.6 Night and Day
MVS-507
  Vol. 2 Artie Shaw and His Orchestra with Strings Featuring Mel Tormé and His Mel-Tones.
  All titles are by Artie Shaw and his orchestra. Mel Tormé is only present where indicated.
  1.1 What Is This Thing Called Love? (orig. version) (MT)
  1.2 For You, for Me, Forever More
  1.3 Changing My Tune (MT)
  1.4 I Believe (MT)
  1.5 Connecticut
  1.6 They Can't Convince Me (orig. take) (MT)
  1.7 Love for Sale
  2.1 I've Got You Under My Skin
  2.2 Guilty (MT)
  2.3 Get Out of Town (MT)
  2.4 And So to Bed (MT)
  2.5 It's the Same Old Dream (MT)
  2.6 Don't You Believe It Dear (MT)
  2.7 When You're Around
MVS-508
  Vol. 1 Mel Tormé
  1.1 A Foggy Day
  1.2 I Cover the Waterfront
  1.3 Do It Again
  1.4 But Beautiful
  1.5 County Fair
  1.6 Boulevard of Memories
  2.1 Until the Real Thing Comes Along
  2.2 Makin' Whoopee
  2.3 Three Little Words
  2.4 It's Dreamtime
  2.5 With You
  2.6 Kokomo, Indiana
MVS-510
  Mel Tormé and the Mel-Tones, "It Happened in Monterey"

    1.1 There's No Business Like Show Business
    1.2 Dream Awhile
    1.3 It Happened in Monterey
    1.4 Born to Be Blue
    1.5 That's Where I Came In
    1.6 Night and Day
    2.1 Willow Road
    2.2 America Take It Away
    2.3 Fine and Dandy
    2.4 There's No One But You
    2.5 Try a Little Tenderness

MVS-2000
    Vol. 2 Mel Tormé "I Can't Give You Anything But Love"
    1.1 I Can't Give You Anything but Love
    1.2 I'm Yours
    1.3 Little White Lies
    1.4 Love, You Funny Thing
    1.5 Cottage for Sale
    2.1 Love Is the Sweetest Thing
    2.2 You're Driving Me Crazy
    2.3 Who Cares What People Say?
    2.4 My Baby Just Cares for Me
    2.5 If I Had a Girl Like You

MVS-2005
    Mel Tormé Vol. 3 "Gone with the Wind"
    1.1 It's Easy to Remember
    1.2 How Long Has This Been Going On?
    1.3 A Little Kiss Each Morning
    1.4 When Is Sometime?
    1.5 Gone with the Wind
    1.6 What Are You Doing New Years Eve?
    2.1 The Day You Came Along
    2.2 And Mimi
    2.3 The Best Things in Life Are Free
    2.4 Magic Town
    2.5 I'll Always Be in Love with You
    2.6 Ballerina

PARLOPHONE (UK)

PMC 1096
    Gene Norman Presents Mel Tormé at the Crescendo
    (Reissue of Bethlehem BCP-6020.)

PMC 1114
    Songs for Any Taste Mel Tormé
    (Reissue of Bethlehem BCP-6031 [first version].)

PMC 1137
    Mel Tormé's California Suite
    1.1 California Suite
    2.1 California Suite
    (Reissue of Bethlehem BCP-6016.)

PHILIPS (UK)

BBL 7205
    Tormé Meets the British
    1.1 Limehouse Blues
    1.2 A Nightingale Sang in Berkeley Square
    1.3 I've Got a Lovely Bunch of Coconuts
    1.4 These Foolish Things
    1.5 Geordie
    1.6 My One and Only Highland Fling
    2.1 The White Cliffs of Dover
    2.2 Danny Boy
    2.3 Let There Be Love
    2.4 Greensleeves
    2.5 Try a Little Tenderness
    2.6 London Pride
    The export number of this record is *B 10729 L.*

PHOENIX 20 (UK)

P20 627
    20 Hits Lena Horne Mel Tormé
    Side 1 (10 titles) is by Lena Horne.
    Side 2 is by Mel Tormé.
    2.1 All in Love Is Fair
    2.2 The First Time I Saw Your Face
    2.3 New York State of Mind
    2.4 Stars
    2.5 Send in the Clowns
    2.6 Ordinary Fool
    2.7 When the World Was Young/Yesterday When I Was Young
    2.8 Bye Bye Blackbird
    2.9 When I Found You

POLYDOR (UK)

545 110
  Mel Tormé: Lulu's Back in Town
    (Reissue of Bethlehem BCP-52.)
    Pseudo-stereo

2317 076
  The Special Magic of Mel Tormé
  Shine on Your Shoes
  Blue Moon
  Just A-Sittin' and A-Rockin'
  How High the Moon
  Surrey with the Fringe on Top
  By Myself
  Lonely Town
  Just in Time
  Oh! What a Night for Love
  Light in Vermont
  Once in Love with Amy
  Christmas Song
  I Guess I'll Have to Change My Plan
  All I Need Is the Girl
Not checked.

PRESTO (UK)

PRE 681
  Artie Shaw and His Orchestra Also Featuring Mel Tormé and the Meltones.
    All the tracks are by Artie Shaw and his orchestra and Mel Tormé is on the six indicated tracks.
  1.1 Begin the Beguine
  1.2 I Believe (MT)
  1.3 For You, for Me, for Evermore (MT)
  1.4 Don't You Believe It Dear (MT)
  1.5 Guilty (MT)
  2.1 Let's Walk
  2.2 Get Out of Town (MT)
  2.3 Love for Sale
  2.4 Changing My Tune (MT)
  2.5 Night and Day

PRE 685
  Artie Shaw.
    This LP is reported as containing some tracks by Artie Shaw with Mel Tormé but its existence is not confirmed. The reported tracks are:
  Along with Me
  They Can't Convince Me
  It's the Same Old Dream

RCA (UK)

PL 25178
  Mel Tormé and Buddy Rich. Together Again — For the First Time
    (Reissue of Century CRDD-1100.)
    Stereo but not direct to disc.

REPRISE (USA)

R-6126
  Sammy Davis Jr. Sings Mel Tormé's California Suite.
    All the tracks are by Sammy Davis, Jr. Mel Tormé is only present on side 1. Side 2 consists of Mel Tormé compositions.
  1.1 California Suite
  2.1 A Stranger in Town
  2.2 A Stranger Called the Blues
  2.3 Welcome to the Club
  2.4 Willow Road
  2.5 Born to Be Blue
  2.6 The Christmas Song

R-6180
  Original Motion Picture Soundtrack: A Man Called Adam
    The tracks are by various artists including Sammy Davis, Jr., and Louis Armstrong. Mel Tormé is only on tracks 2.1 and 2.7.
  1.1 Main Title: All That Jazz
  1.2 I Want to Be Wanted
  1.3 Go Now
  1.4 Someday Sweetheart
  1.5 Ain't I?
  1.6 Soft Touch
  1.7 Claudia
  2.1 All That Jazz
  2.2 Back of Town Blues

2.3 Night Walk
2.4 Whisper to One
2.5 Claudia
2.6 Crack Up
2.7 All That Jazz
RS-6126
Sammy Davis Jr. Sings Mel Tormé's California Suite
Stereo version of R-6126
RS-6180
Original Motion Picture Soundtrack: A Man Called Adam
Stereo version of R-6180

RHAPSODY (UK)

RHAP 3
Tormé.
Stereo.
(Reissue of Gryphon G-916.)

RHINO (USA)

None of these has been checked

71505
Great American Song Writers.
Mel Tormé is only present on one track:
Mountain Greenery
71507
Great American Song Writers.
Mel Tormé is only present on one track:
Take the "A" Train
81907
Atlantic 40th Anniversary.
This compilation has one Mel Tormé track:
Comin' Home Baby

RONDOLETTE (USA)

A-852
Artie Shaw
Details required. Includes these Artie Shaw tracks with vocals by Mel Tormé:
Get Out of Town
For You, for Me, for Evermore
They Can't Convince Me
Guilty
I Believe
and possibly What Is This Thing Called Love?
L-1755
Same content as World Record Club R-23. Label details wanted.

ROYALE (USA)

1466
The existence of this disc is reported but not confirmed. It is said to include one track by Artie Shaw with vocal by Mel Tormé:
Get Out of Town. (Maybe a misreporting of Allegro Royale 1466)
18151
Reported variously as a 10-inch LP and as an EP. Details are in the EP section

SIGNATURE CBS (USA)

53779
Mel Tormé 16 Most Requested Songs
Strangers in the Night
What Is There to Say?
You'd Better Love Me
Everyday's a Holiday
That's All
I've Got You Under My Skin
I Know Your Heart
Isn't It a Pity?
Do I Love You Because You're Beautiful?
Haven't We Met?
The Second Time Around
The Christmas Song
The Folks Who Live on the Hill
My Romance
P.S. I Love You
The Nearness of You
Not checked.

SOCIETY (UK)

SOC 982

Duke Ellington, Fletcher Henderson and Artie Shaw and Their Orchestras.
This compilation includes four tracks by Artie Shaw and his orchestra, three of which have Mel Tormé.
2.2 Night and Day (no Tormé)
2.3 Along with Me
2.4 For You, for Me, for Evermore
2.5 I Believe

SOC 983

Artie Shaw and His Orchestra Featuring Mel Tormé and the Meltones
All tracks are by Artie Shaw and his Orchestra.
1.1 Love for Sale
1.2 Guilty (MT)
1.3 When You're Around
1.4 Get Out of Town (MT)
1.5 Changing My Tune (MT)
2.1 I've Got You Under My Skin
2.2 It's the Same Old Dream
2.3 They Can't Convince Me (MT)
2.4 Love of My Life
2.5 In the Still of the Night

SOC 1001

Sarah Vaughan, Mel Tormé & George Chakiris.
Artie Shaw and his orchestra with Mel Tormé are on 2 tracks, as below. The remaining tracks are by Dennis Wilson (4 items), George Chakiris (2 items) and Sarah Vaughan (2 items).
2.2 For You, for Me, for Ever More (sic)
2.3 Changing My Tune

SOUNDS GREAT (USA)

SG-5006

Mel Tormé Live: Volume One
1.1 Dear Old Fairmont
1.2 You're Driving Me Crazy
1.3 You're the Top
1.4 When the Red, Red Robin Comes Bob, Bob, Bobbin' Along
1.5 Everything Happens to Me
1.6 It's a Most Unusual Day
1.7 Pythagoras, How You Stagger Us
2.1 The French Lesson
2.2 It's Dark on Observatory Hill
2.3 I've Got the Sun in the Morning and the Moon at Night
2.4 On a Slow Boat to China
2.5 Brahm's Lullaby
2.6 Malt Shop Special
2.7 Wish I May, Wish I Might
2.8 Dear Old Fairmont (Reprise)

SG-5012

Mel Tormé Live: Volume Two
1.1 Fine and Dandy
1.2 Isn't It Romantic?
1.3 What Is This Thing Called Love?
1.4 Let's Fall in Love
1.5 The Money Song
1.6 Ah, But It Happens
1.7 Get Out and Get Under
2.1 You're the Cream in My Coffee
2.2 It's the Sentimental Thing to Do
2.3 A Fine Romance
2.4 Wrap Your Trouble in Dreams
2.5 Back in Your Own Back Yard
2.6 I Get Along Without You Very Well
2.7 How High the Moon

SOUNTRAK (USA)

STK-111

Good News June Allyson • Peter Lawford • Mel Tormé
1.1 Good News Medley
1.2 Be a Lady's Man
1.3 Lucky in Love
1.4 The French Lesson
1.5 The Best Things in Life Are Free
2.1 Pass That Peace Pipe
2.2 Just Imagine
2.3 The Best Things in Life Are Free
2.4 Varsity Drag/Finale

SPINORAMA (USA)

S-113

Mel Tormé Velvet Moods
Details wanted.
Stereo.

STASH (USA)

ST252
Mel Tormé 'Round Midnight
1.1 Lulu's Back in Town
1.2 When the Sun Comes Out
1.3 From Now On
1.4 The Lady Is a Tramp
1.5 Hello, Young Lovers
1.6 Marie
1.7 Porgy and Bess Medley
2.1 Hey, Look Me Over
2.2 A Foggy Day
2.3 The Surrey with the Fringe on Top
2.4 The Lady's in Love with You
2.5 Sugar Loaf (pâo de assucar)
2.6 Lulu's Back in Town (reprise)
2.7 'Round Midnight Track

1.3 is an instrumental by Marty Paich. 1.6 and 2.5 are instrumentals by Shorty Rogers.

STRAND (USA)

SL 1076
Mel Tormé: Sings
1.1 I'm Getting Sentimental Over You
1.2 I Can't Believe That You're in Love with Me
1.3 Prelude to a Kiss
1.4 I've Got the World on a String
1.5 Between the Devil and the Deep Blue Sea
2.1 I Surrender Dear
2.2 I Let a Song Go Out of My Heart
2.3 Don't Worry 'Bout Me
2.4 One Morning in May
2.5 I Can't Give You Anything But Love.

No dialogue between tracks.

SLS 1076
Mel Tormé: Sings
Stereo version of SL 1076. No dialogue between tracks.

SUMMIT (UK)

ATL 4123
Mel Tormé: The Fabulous Mel Tormé
1.1 I Can't Give You Anything but Love
1.2 Don't Worry 'Bout Me
2.1 I Surrender Dear
2.2 I Don't Stand a Ghost of a Chance

No dialogue between tracks. Tormé is not on the remaining tracks of this record.

SUTTON (USA)

SU-208
  Mel Tormé
    Same as Viking VK-006
SU-281
  Details required
SU-295
  Details wanted. This compilation includes one track by Artie Shaw with a Mel Tormé vocal:
  I Got the Sun in the Morning
SU-381
  Details wanted. This compilation includes one track by Artic Shaw with a Mel Tormé vocal:
  Guilty
SSU-208
  Mel Tormé
  Pseudo-stereo version of SU-208
SSU-281
  Pseudo-stereo version of SU-281
SSU-295
  Pseudo-stereo version of SU-295
SSU-381
  Pseudo-stereo version of SU-381

TELARC JAZZ

TEL-83315
  Christmas Songs
  Christmas Medley: Jingle Bells, Santa Claus Is Coming to Town, Winter Weather, Winter Wonderland
  Christmastime Is Here
  Good King Wenceslas
  What Child Is This?
  God Rest Ye Merry Gentlemen

Sleigh Ride
The Christmas Song
Glow Worm
The Christmas Feeling
It Happened in Sun Valley
Silver Bells
Christmas Was Made for Children
The Christmas Waltz
Medley: Just Look Around, Have Yourself a Merry Little Christmas
Medley: Happy Holiday, Let's Start the New Year Right, What Are You Doing New Year's Eve?
White Christmas

Stereo. Not checked.

TEL-83328
  The Great American Song Book
  Medley: Ridin' High, I'm Shooting High
  Stardust
  I'm Gonna Go Fishin'
  Medley: Don't Get Around Much Anymore, I Let a Song Go Out of My Heart
  Medley: Sophisticated Lady, I Didn't Know About You
  Rockin' in Rhythm
  A Lovely Way to Spend an Evening
  Autumn in New York
  All God's Chillun' Got Rhythm
  You Make Me Feel So Young

Stereo. Not checked.

TELE HOUSE / TELEHOUSE (USA)

TS 772 (Telehouse)
  Getting Sentimental: Mel Tormé
  1.1 Ghost of a Chance
  1.2 Getting Sentimental Over You
  1.3 I Can't Believe That You're in Love with Me
  1.4 Prelude to a Kiss
  1.5 I've Got the World on a String
  2.1 Between the Devil and the Deep Blue Sea
  2.2 I Surrender Dear
  2.3 Don't Worry 'Bout Me
  2.4 One Morning in May
  2.5 I Can't Give You Anything But Love

Stereo with no dialogue between the tracks. This record has no catalog number on the sleeve and no label name on the disc labels.

TS 7737 (Telehouse)
  Mel Tormé: Mel Swings with Lena
  1.1 I Can't Believe That You're in Love with Me
  1.4 I Don't Stand a Ghost of a Chance
  2.3 Prelude to a Kiss
  2.4 I Surrender Dear

Stereo with no dialogue between the tracks. The remaining six tracks on the record are by Lena Horne. This record has no catalog number on the sleeve and no label name on the disc labels.

TELLER HOUSE (USA)

TS 79-402
  With Love from Dick Haymes, Johnny Desmond, Mel Tormé
  1.3 Prelude to a Kiss
  2.1 Don't Worry 'Bout Me
  2.4 I Surrender Dear

Stereo, no dialogue between tracks. The other 7 tracks on the record are by Dick Haymes (4 tracks) and Johnny Desmond (3 tracks)

TIARA (USA)

TMT 7515
  Mel Tormé: Spotlight on Mel Tormé in Love Potions with the Velvet Strings
  1.1 A Cottage for Sale
  1.2 Until the Real Thing Comes Along
  1.3 Try a Little Tenderness

Tormé is not on the remaining tracks which are by an orchestra, presumably "The Velvet Strings."

TMT 7517
  Label details wanted. This compilation

includes two tracks by Artie Shaw one of which has a vocal by Mel Tormé: Get Out of Town.

TMT 7560
  Label details wanted. This compilation includes three tracks by Artie Shaw one of which has a vocal by Mel Tormé: I Got the Sun in the Morning

TST 515
  Mel Tormé: Spotlight on Mel Tormé in Love Potions with the Velvet Strings.
Pseudo-stereo version of TMT 7515

TST 517
  Label details wanted.
Pseudo-stereo version of TMT 7517

TST 560
  Label details wanted.
Pseudo-stereo version of TMT 7560

TOPS (USA)

L-975 (10-inch)
  Artie Shaw Label details wanted. Eight tracks by Artie Shaw, three of which have vocals by Mel Tormé:
  What Is This Thing Called Love?
  They Can't Convince Me
  Guilty

L1615
  Mel Tormé: Prelude to a Kiss
  1.1 Something to Live For
  1.2 I'm Getting Sentimental Over You
  1.3 I Don't Stand a Ghost of a Chance with You
  1.4 I Can't Believe That You're in Love with Me
  1.5 Prelude to a Kiss
  1.6 I've Got the World on a String
  2.1 Between the Devil and the Deep Blue Sea
  2.2 I Surrender Dear
  2.3 I Let a Song Go Out of My Heart
  2.4 Don't Worry 'Bout Me
  2.5 One Morning in May
  2.6 I Can't Give You Anything But Love

With dialogue between the tracks

VERNON (USA)

MVM 503
  That Ever Swingin' Artie Shaw
  All tracks are by Artie Shaw and his orchestra. Vocals by Mel Tormé as indicated.
  1.1 What Is This Thing Called Love? (MT)
  1.2 Get Out of Town (MT)
  1.3 I've Got the Sun in the Morning (MT)
  1.4 Night and Day
  1.5 Get Out of Town
  2.1 Love for Sale
  2.2 My Heart Belongs to Daddy
  2.3 Changing My Tune (MT)
  2.4 I've Got You Under My Skin

MVS 503
  That Ever Swingin' Artie Shaw
Pseudo-stereo version of MVM 503

VERSAILLES (?USA?)

LP 503
  Label details wanted. Identical to Vernon MVM 503

VERVE (USA)

MG V-2105
  "Tormé"
  1.1 That Old Feeling
  1.2 Gloomy Sunday
  1.3 Body and Soul
  1.4 Nobody's Heart
  1.5 I Should Care
  1.6 House Is Haunted by the Echo of Your Last Goodbye
  2.1 Blues in the Night
  2.2 I Don't Want to Cry Anymore
  2.3 Where Can I Go Without You?
  2.4 How Did She Look?
  2.5 'Round Midnight
  2.6 I'm Gonna Laugh You Out of My Life

MGV 2117
¡Olé Tormé!
1.1 At the Crossroads (Malagueña)
1.2 Frenesi
1.3 Adios
1.4 Baia
1.5 Six Lessons from Madam La Zonga
1.6 Rosita
2.1 South of the Border
2.2 Nina
2.3 Cuban Love Song
2.4 Perfidia
2.5 The Rhumba Jump
2.6 Vaya Con Dios

MG V-2120
Back in Town — Mel Tormé with the Mel-Tones
1.1 Makin' Whoopee
1.2 Baubles, Bangles and Beads
1.3 What Is This Thing Called Love?
1.4 I've Never Been in Love Before
1.5 Truckin'
1.6 A Bunch of the Blues: Keester Parade, TNT, Tiny's Blues
2.1 It Happened in Monterey
2.2 I Hadn't Anyone Till You
2.3 A Smooth One
2.4 Don't Dream of Anybody but Me
2.5 Some Like It Hot
2.6 Hit the Road to Dreamland

MG V-2132
Mel Tormé Swings Shubert Alley
1.1 Hello, Young Lovers
1.2 The Surrey with the Fringe on Top
1.3 Old Devil Moon
1.4 Whatever Lola Wants
1.5 Too Darn Hot
1.6 Lonely Town
2.1 Too Close for Comfort
2.2 Once in Love with Amy
2.3 A Sleepin' Bee
2.4 On the Street Where You Live
2.5 All I Need Is a Girl
2.6 Just in Time

MG V-2144
Swingin' on the Moon
1.1 Swingin' on the Moon
1.2 Moonlight Cocktail
1.3 I Wished on the Moon
1.4 Moon Song
1.5 How High the Moon
1.6 Don't Let That Moon Get Away
2.1 Blue Moon
2.2 Velvet Moon
2.3 No Moon at All
2.4 Moonlight in Vermont
2.5 Oh, You Crazy Moon
2.6 The Moon Was Yellow

Track 2.2, although labeled Velvet Moon, *actually plays* A Velvet Affair *on this record and on all its LP reissues.*

MG V-2146
Broadway, Right Now! Mel Tormé & Margaret Whiting
1.1 Fireworks
1.2 Make Someone Happy
1.3 Tall Hopes
1.4 I Loved You Once in Silence
1.5 Like the Wind
1.6 Hey, Look Me Over
2.1 All You Need Is a Quarter
2.2 If Ever I Would Leave You
2.3 Our Language of Love
2.4 From a Prison Cell
2.5 What's New at the Zoo
2.6 Medley from "Wildcat": Far Away from Home, Angelina.

Tracks 1.1, 1.3, 1.5, 1.6, 2.1, 2.3 2.5 and 2.6 are duets between Tormé and Whiting. Tracks 1.2 and 2.2 are solos by Whiting. Tracks 1.4 and 2.4 are solos by Tormé.

MG V6-2105
"Tormé"
Stereo version of MGV 2105

MG V6-2117 1
¡Olé Tormé!
Stereo version of MGV 2117

MG V6-2120
Back in Town — Mel Tormé with the Mel-Tones
Stereo version of MGV 2120

MG V6-2132
:   *Mel Tormé Swings Shubert Alley*
    Stereo version of MGV 2132
MG V6-2144
:   *Swingin' on the Moon*
    Stereo version of MGV 2144
MG V6-2146
:   *Broadway, Right Now! Mel Tormé & Margaret Whiting*
    Stereo version of MGV 2146
MG VS 6015
:   *"Tormé"*
    Stereo version of MGV 2105
MG VS 6058
:   *¡Olé Tormé!*
    Stereo version of MGV 2117. The sequence of titles on the sleeve of this record differs from that on the actual record.
MG VS 6083
:   *Back in Town — Mel Tormé with the Mel-Tones*
    Stereo version of MGV 2120
MG VS 6146
:   *Mel Tormé Swings Shubert Alley*
    Stereo version of MGV 2132
V-8440
:   *Mel Tormé My Kind of Music*
    1.1 You and the Night and the Music
    1.2 A Stranger in Town
    1.3 I Guess I'll Have to Change My Plan
    1.4 Born to Be Blue
    1.5 County Fair
    2.1 Dancing in the Dark
    2.2 Welcome to the Club
    2.3 By Myself
    2.4 The Christmas Song
    2.5 Alone Together
    2.6 A Shine on Your Shoes
MG V-8491
:   *Mel Tormé: I Dig the Duke, I Dig the Count*
    1.1 I'm Gonna Go Fishin'
    1.2 Don't Get Around Much Anymore
    1.3 I Like the Sunrise
    1.4 Take the "A" Train
    1.5 Reminiscing in Tempo
    1.6 Just a Sittin' and a Rockin'
    2.1 Down for Double
    2.2 I'm Gonna Move to the Outskirts of Town
    2.3 Blue & Sentimental
    2.4 Oh What a Night for Love
    2.5 Sent for You Yesterday (And Here You Come Today)
    2.6 In the Evening (When the Sun Goes Down)
V-8593
:   *Verve's Choice! The Best of Mel Tormé*
    1.1 On the Street Where You Live
    1.2 Blue Moon
    1.3 Just in Time
    1.4 South of the Border
    1.5 Take the "A" Train
    1.6 I'm Gonna Go Fishing
    2.1 Too Close for Comfort
    2.2 Moonlight in Vermont
    2.3 Perfidia
    2.4 Old Feeling
    2.5 The Christmas Song
    2.6 You and the Night and the Music
V6-8440
:   *Mel Tormé. My Kind of Music*
    Stereo version of V 8440
MG V6-8491
:   *Mel Tormé: I Dig the Duke, I Dig the Count*
    Stereo version of MG V 8491
V6-8593
:   *Verve's Choice! The Best of Mel Tormé*
    Stereo version of V 8593
SW-90443
:   *Verve's Choice! The Best of Mel Tormé*
    Stereo
    (Reissue of V6-8593. Manufactured by Capitol on behalf of M-G-M.)
823 010-1
:   *Tormé*
    Stereo.
    Reissue of Verve MG V6-2105)
823 248-1
:   *The Duke Ellington and Count Basie Songbooks*
    Stereo
    (Reissue of MGV6 8491.)

RECORD ISSUES: LPs (ALBUMS) • 119

VERVE (FRANCE)
 The next four issues are listed because they were distributed in the UK although manufactured in France.

2304 235
 Mel Tormé Swings Shubert Alley
Stereo.
(Reissue of Verve MG V6-2132.)
2304 384
 Back in Town
Stereo
(Reissue of Verve MG V6-2120.)
2304 402
 Mel Tormé: I Dig the Duke, I Dig the Count
Stereo
(Reissue of Verve MG V6-8491.)
2304 500
 "Tormé"
Stereo
(Reissue of Verve MG V6-2105.)

VERVE (UK)

VLP 9027
 I Dig the Duke, I Dig the Count
(Reissue of Verve MGV 8491.)
SVLP 9027
 I Dig the Duke, I Dig the Count
Stereo version of VLP 9027
VRV 8
 Dig the Duke, I Dig the Count
(Reissue of MGV6 8491.)
Stereo
823 010-1
 Tormé
Stereo
(Reissue of Verve MG V6-2105.)
823 248-1
 The Duke Ellington and Count Basie Songbooks
Stereo
(Reissue of Verve MGV6 8491.)
2317 076
 The Special Magic of Mel Tormé
 1.1 A Shine on Your Shoes
 1.2 Blue Moon
 1.3 Just a Sittin' and a Rockin'
 1.4 How High the Moon
 1.5 The Surrey with the Fringe on Top
 1.6 By Myself
 1.7 Lonely Town
 2.1 Just in Time
 2.2 Oh What a Night for Love
 2.3 Moonlight in Vermont
 2.4 Once in Love with Amy
 2.5 The Christmas Song
 2.6 I Guess I'll Have to Change My Plan
 2.7 All I Need Is a Girl.
Stereo

VIKING (USA)

VK-006
 Mel Tormé
 1.1 I Can't Give You Anything but Love
 1.2 I Don't Stand a Ghost of a Chance with You
 1.3 This Cottage for sale
 1.4 Until the Real Thing Comes Along
 1.5 Try a Little Tenderness
Although side 2 (like side 1) is labeled as by Mel Tormé and the Del Shaw Orchestra, it is entirely instrumental and has no connection with Tormé at all.

VOCALIAN (USA)

VL 73905
 Mel Tormé: The Velvet Fog
 1.1 All of You
 1.2 Cement Mixer (Put-ti, Put-ti)
 1.3 Tutti Frutti
 1.4 Just One More Chance
 1.5 Hold Tight (Want Some Sea Food Mama)
 2.1 The Hut-Sut Song (A Swedish Rhapsody)
 2.2 Blue Skies
 2.3 Rose O'Day
 2.4 Spellbound

2.5 It Don't Mean a Thing (If It Ain't Got That Swing)

This record is in pseudo-stereo.

VOGUE (UK)

LDE 007 (10-inch)
   Jazz Off the Air, Vol. 1. (Title sequence and division between sides required.)
   Flip and Jazz
   Buck Still Jumps
   Lover
   Honeysuckle Rose
   How High the Moon

VOGUE CORAL (UK)

LVA 9004
   Gene Norman Presents: Mel Tormé Actually Recorded Live at the Crescendo, Dec. 15, 1954.
(Reissue of Coral CRL 57012.)
LVA 9032
   Mel Tormé: "Musical Sounds Are the Best Songs"
(Reissue of Coral CRL 57044.)
LVA 9098
   We Like Guys (Details wanted. Includes Tormé's Mountain Greenery)
LVA 9137
   Merry Christmas (Details wanted. Includes Tormé's The Christmas Song)

VSP VERVE (UK)

VSP.17/VSP.18 (Double album)
   Mel Tormé Swings.
(Reissue of Verve MGV2132 and MGV8491. VSP.17 corresponds to MGV2132, VSP.18 corresponds to MGV8491.)

WESTERFIELD (USA)

1005-10021
   Mel Tormé Sings
Stereo version of Tops L-1615 but without dialogue between the tracks. This record is part of a set "D-1" but the other records in the set are untraced

WORLD RECORD CLUB (UK)

   World Record Club started with that name on the record labels but eventually used **World Sound** for mono issues and **World Stereo** for stereo issues.

R-23
   (10-inch) The label name is World Record Club; other label details wanted. Includes these tracks by Artie Shaw and his orchestra:
   You Do Something to Me
   What Is This Thing Called Love? (vocal MT)
   Get Out of Town (vocal MT)
   Love for Sale
The take used for What Is This Thing Called Love? *is not yet determined. The remainder of the LP is not by Shaw and is thought to be by Georgia Gibbs.*

World Record Club TP 350
   Tormé
(Reissue of Verve MGV 2105.)
World Sound T 388
   South of the Border
(Reissue of Verve MGV 2117.)
World Sound T 473
   Mel Tormé Swings Shubert Alley
(Reissue of His Master's Voice CLP 1405.)
World Sound T 550
   Swingin' on the Moon
(Reissue of Verve MGV 2144.)
World Stereo ST 550
   Swingin' on the Moon
Stereo
(Reissue of Verve MG V6-2144.)

Tapes

CASSETTE

The cassettes are the Philips compact cassette type.

AFFINITY (UK)

TCAFF 107
Mel Tormé Sings Fred Astaire
Cassette equivalent of AFF 107 [LP]

ARISTA (GERMANY)

406 496
2:00 am — Paradise Cafe, Barry Manilow
Cassette version of 206 496 [LP]

AUDIO FIDELITY (UK)

ZCGAS 740
Mel Tormé (Details required)

CAPITOL (UK)

TCEMS 1447
The Capitol Years (Cassette version of Capitol CDEMS 1447 [CD])

CHARLY (CLASSIC JAZZ) (UK)

CDMC 1076
The Song Stylists: Mel Tormé and Tony Bennett (Cassette version of Classic Jazz CDCD [CD])

CITY SONGS (USA)

This is a series of cassettes devoted to cities and is intended as much for promotional purposes for the cities concerned as for conventional retail sale. These compilations are also issued in CD format.

NEW YORK: With Fondest Memories
(This compilation includes one track by Mel Tormé: track 14, 42nd Street)
SAN FRANCISCO: With Fondest Memories
(This compilation includes one track by Mel Tormé: track 6, Got the Gate on the Golden Gate)
SOUTHERN CALIFORNIA: With Fondest Memories
(This compilation includes one track by Mel Tormé: track 15, They Go to San Diego)

CONCORD JAZZ (USA)

All Concord Jazz cassettes are stereo. While the cassettes all have the same content as the equivalent LP or CD, I have marked some cassettes derived from CDs as "not checked" to indicate that I do not know the division of the tracks between the sides of the cassette.

CJC-190
An Evening with George Shearing & Mel Tormé (Cassette equivalent of CJ-190 [LP])
CJC-219
Top Drawer George Shearing Mel Tormé (Cassette equivalent of CJ-219 [LP])
CJC-248
Mel Tormé / George Shearing: An Evening at Charlie's (Cassette equivalent of CJ-248 [LP])
CJC-294
An Elegant Evening: George Shearing / Mel Tormé (Cassette equivalent of CJ-294 [LP])
CJC-306
Mel Tormé, Rob McConnell and the Boss Brass (Cassette equivalent of CJ-306 [LP])
CJC-341
Mel Tormé / George Shearing: a Vintage Year (Cassette equivalent of CJ-341 [LP])
CJ-190-C
An Evening with George Shearing & Mel Tormé (Reissue of cassette CJC-190)
CJ-219-C
Top Drawer: George Shearing / Mel Tormé (Reissue of cassette CJC-219)
CJ-248-C
Mel Tormé / George Shearing: An

Evening at Charlie's (Reissue of cassette CJC-248)

CJ-294-C
An Elegant Evening: George Shearing / Mel Tormé (Reissue of cassette CJC-294)

CJ-306-C
Mel Tormé / Rob McConnell and the Boss Brass (Reissue of cassette CJC-306)

CJ-341-C
Mel Tormé / George Shearing: a Vintage Year (Reissue of cassette CJC-341)

CJ-360-C
Mel Tormé and the Marty Paich Dek-Tette Reunion
(Cassette equivalent of CCD-4360 [CD] [Not checked.])

CJ-382-C
Mel Tormé and the Marty Paich Dek-Tette in Concert, Tokyo Fujitsu-Concord Jazz Festival in Japan '88
(Cassette equivalent of CCD-4382 [CD] [Not checked.])

CJ-433-C
Mel Tormé: Night at the Concord Pavilion
(Cassette equivalent of CCD-4433 [CD] [Not checked.])

CJ-471-C
Mel Tormé / George Shearing: Mel & George "Do" World War II
(Cassette equivalent of CCD-4433 [CD] [Not checked.])

CJ-481-C
Mel Tormé Recorded Live at the Fujitsu-Concord Jazz Festival in Japan '90
(Cassette equivalent of CCD-4481 [CD] [Not checked.])

CJ-515-C
Mel Tormé / Cleo Laine: Nothing Without You
(Cassette equivalent of CCD-4515 [CD] [Not checked.])

CJ-542-C
Fujitsu Presents Mel Tormé and His All-Star Quintet
(Cassette equivalent of CCD-4542 [CD] [Not checked.])

CJ-614-C
Mel Tormé: A Tribute to Bing Crosby
(Cassette equivalent of CCD-4614 [CD] [Not checked.])

CJ-667
Mel Tormé, Rob McConnell and the Boss Brass: Velvet and Brass
(Cassette equivalent of CCD-4667 [CD] [Not checked.])

CJ-736-C
An Evening with Mel Tormé
(Cassette equivalent of CCD-4736 [CD] [Not checked.])

CJ-790-C
My Night to Dream
(Cassette equivalent of CCD-4790-2 [CD] [Not checked.])

FINESSE (USA)

ZCFID 5561
Mel Tormé and Friends
(Cassette version of FIND 5561 [LP])

GRP (USA)

GRP-C-1002
The Glenn Miller Orchestra "In the Digital Mood"
(Cassette version of GRP-A-1002 [LP])

JASMINE (UK)

JASMC 2529
Cassette equivalent of JASM 2529 (LP)

KINGFISHER (AUSTRALIA)

STAR-23
Mel Tormé / Billy Banks
(Mel Tormé appears only on the three tracks listed below. The remaining

tracks on this cassette are by Bob Gibson and the Ford Show Orchestra and by Billy Banks.)
Walking My Baby Back Home
It's a Blue World
Love Walked In

LASERLIGHT (USA)

These cassettes have also be reported as having catalog numbers in a 72 xx series, e.g. 72 222 but this has not been confirmed.

12 222
Swingin' on the Moon
(Cassette equivalent of 12 222 [CD])
12 223
'Round Midnight
(Cassette equivalent of 12 223 [CD])
12 224
Luck Be a Lady
(Cassette equivalent of 12 224 [CD])

MUSIC CLUB (UK)

MCTC 198
Cassette equivalent of MCCD 198 (CD)

POLYDOR (UK)

3113 146
The Special Magic of Mel Tormé
(Cassette equivalent of 2317 076 [LP])

PRISM (UK)

PLA C 466
In the Mood for Love
(Cassette equivalent of PLATCD 466 [CD])
PLA C 467
When I Fall in Love
(Cassette equivalent of PLATCD 467. *Polka Dots and Moonbeams* on the cassette is mislabeled *Polka Dust and Moonbeams*)
PLACBX 821
Late Night Love
(This is a box set containing 8 cassette including PLA C 466 and 467)

STAR LINE (USA)

SLC-61005
Mel Tormé the Smooth One
1.1 April Showers
1.2 Easy to Remember
1.3 Blues in the Night
1.4 Don't Take Your Love from Me
1.5 County Fair
2.1 Love Me or Leave Me
2.2 A Cottage for Sale
2.3 I Cover the Waterfront
2.4 It's Sleepy Time Down South
2.5 Gone with the Wind

SUPERSCOPE (USA)

1-A082
All About Love
Details required

TELARC (USA)

CS 33315
Christmas Songs
(Cassette version of 83315 [CD])
CS 33328
The Great American Song Book
(Cassette version of 83328 [CD])

VARI/SONICS (USA)

3510
Remembering the Memorable Years with the Shep Fields Orchestra and Mel Tormé
1.1 Ghost of a Chance
1.3 I Can't Believe That You're in Love with Me

1.6 I've Got the World on a String
2.3 I Surrender Dear
2.6 Getting Sentimental Over You
Stereo

No dialogue between tracks. The remaining seven tracks are by Shep Fields.

VERVE (USA)

823 010-4
   Tormé
   (Cassette version of Verve 823 010-1 [LP])

823 248-4
   Mel Tormé: The Duke Ellington & Count Basie Songbooks
   (Cassette version of Verve 823 248-1 [LP])

VERVE (UK)

VRVC 8
   I Dig the Duke, I Dig the Count
   (Cassette version of Verve 823 248-1 [LP])

833 282-4
   Walkman Jazz
   (Cassette version of Verve 833 282-2 [CD])

OTHER TAPES: 8-TRACK CARTRIDGE

POLYDOR (UK)

3808 114 (8 track cartridge)
   The Special Magic of Mel Tormé
   (8-track equivalent of 2317 076 [LP])

SUPERSCOPE (USA)

2-A082
   All About Love (8 track cartridge)
   (Details required. This may also have been issued on a reel-to-reel tape.)

CDs

This section lists CDs on which Mel Tormé is present. Principally there are those under his own name but also listed are CDs by other artists and CDs that are compilations where he is present on one or more tracks. In these latter cases, only the tracks that have Tormé present are given.

Some non–USA and UK issues are listed where they are the original issues or where they derive from USA LPs and have no USA or UK equivalent.

AERO SPACE (USA)

Ray Anthony: Dream Dancing Christmas. All tracks are by Ray Anthony and his orchestra. Mel Tormé appears only on track 1:
My Christmas Dream
track 3: I'll Be Home for Christmas

AFFINITY (UK)

CD CHARLY 5
   Lulu's Back in Town
   (Details wanted. CD version of Bethlehem BCP-34 [LP])

CD CHARLY 60
   Mel Tormé: Live at the Crescendo

1. It's Only a Paper Moon
2. What Is This Thing Called Love?
3. One for My Baby
4. Love Is Just a Bug
5. Nightingale Sang in Berkeley Square
6. Autumn Leaves
7. Just One of Those Things
8. The Girl Next Door
9. Lover Come Back to Me
10. Looking at You
11. The Tender Trap
12. I'm Beginning to See the Light
13. Autumn Leaves
14. Tenderly

15. I Wish I Was in Love Again
16. It's D'Lovely
17. It's Alright with Me
18. Manhattan
19. Taking a Chance on Love
20. Home by the Sea
21. I Got Plenty of Nothin'
22. Nobody's Heart

CD CHARLY 96
Mel Tormé Sings Fred Astaire
1. Nice Work If You Can Get It
2. Something's Gotta Give
3. A Foggy Day
4. A Fine Romance
5. Lets Call the Whole Thing Off
6. Top Hat, White Tie & Tails
7. The Way You Look Tonight
8. The Piccolino
9. They Can't Take That Away from Me
10. Cheek to Cheek
11. Let's Face the Music and Dance
12. They All Laughed

ARISTA (USA)

07822-18945-2
Barry Manilow: 2:00 am — Paradise Cafe
(All tracks are by Barry Manilow. Mel Tormé is present on one track in a duet with Manilow. Track 8: Big City Blues. This CD was also pressed in the EU and distributed throughout Europe using the same catalog number.)

ATLANTIC JAZZ (USA)

80078-2
Mel Tormé Songs of New York
1. Sunday in New York
2. Autumn in New York
3. Lullaby of Birdland
4. Broadway
5. The Brooklyn Bridge
6. Let Me Off Uptown
7. 42nd Street
8. Sidewalks of New York
9. Harlem Nocturne
10. New York, New York
11. There's a Broken Heart for Every Light on Broadway
12. Manhattan
13. My Time of Day

ATLANTIC JAZZ (GERMANY) (DISTRIBUTED IN THE UK)

780 078-2
Mel Tormé Songs of New York
(Reissue of Atlantic Jazz 80078-2)

ATLANTIC (JAPAN)

30P2-2322
Comin' Home Baby
Details wanted. CD version of SD 8069 (LP)

AVENUE JAZZ (USA)

R2 75732
Mel Tormé with the Marty Paich Dek-Tette: Lulu's Back in Town
1. Lulu's Back in Town
2. When the Sun Comes Out
3. I Love to Watch the Moonlight
4. Fascinating Rhythm
5. The Blues
6. The Carioca
7. The Lady Is a Tramp
8. I Like to Recognize the Tune
9. Keeping Myself for You
10. Lullaby of Birdland
11. When April Comes Again
12. Sing for Your Supper

This CD also carries a "Bethlehem Archives" logo and is manufactured and distributed by Rhino Records.

75828
Porgy & Bess (2 CD set)

(This is the complete recording from Bethlehem. The cast includes Mel Tormé, Frances Fay, Betty Roche, George Kirby, Johnny Hartman, Sallie Blair and Frank Rosolino. Music by Russ Garcia, Duke Ellington, the Australian Jazz Quartet and the Stan Levey Quartet. The musical content is the same as the equivalent LP version (EXLP-1) but shows some changes to the titles of the scenes and songs.)

75961
A Very Special Time (3 CD set)
(This CD set contains the equivalent of the three Bethlehem LPs, BCP-34 It's a Blue World; BCP-52 Mel Tormé and the Marty Paich Dek-Tette; BCP-6013 Mel Tormé Sings Fred Astaire.)

AVID (UK)

AMSC 640
George Gershwin — A Celebration — 'S Wonderful
This compilation contains one track by Mel Tormé. Track 4: How Long Has This Been Going On?

AMSC 641
George Gershwin — A Celebration — Summertime
This compilation contains one track by Artie Shaw and his orchestra with vocal by Mel Tormé. Track 5: Changing My Tune

AMSC 692 (2 CDs)
Timeless Classics
Details wanted. This compilation contains one track by Artie Shaw with Mel Tormé: What Is This Thing Called Love?

BBC (UK)

CJCD 833
Mel Tormé & Buddy Rich: Together Again — For the First Time

1. When I Found You
2. Here's That Rainy Day
3. Blues in the Night
4. Bluesette
5. You Are the Sunshine of My Life
6. I Won't Last a Day Without You
7. Lady Be Good

BEAR FAMILY (GERMANY)

BCD 16117 (4 CD set)
Ella Mae Morse
All tracks are by Ella Mae Morse. Mel Tormé is present (as a drummer) only on these three tracks: Disc 1, track 16, The Patty Cake Man, track 17, Hello Suzanne, track 18, Take Care of Me for You

BETHLEHEM (USA)

30082 (20-30082)
Mel Tormé Sings Fred Astaire
1. Nice Work If You Can Get It
2. Something's Gotta Give
3. A Foggy Day
4. A Fine Romance
5. Let's Call the Whole Thing Off
6. Top Hat, White Tie & Tails
7. The Way You Look Tonight
8. The Piccolino
9. Can't Take That Away from Me
10. Cheek to Cheek
11. Face the Music and Dance
12. They All Laughed

R2 75732 *see Avenue Jazz*

The BR series of CDs listed below were made in Japan but distributed in the U.S.A.

BR-5003/BCP-6013
Mel Tormé Sings Fred Astaire
(CD version of BCP-6013 (LP) details wanted)

BR-5004/BCP-6040
Porgy and Bess

(This CD contains a selection of tracks taken from the complete work available on BR-5014-2/EXLP-1. Mel Tormé is present only on the tracks listed.)
Track 7: I Got Plenty of Nothin'
Track 9: Bess, You Is My Woman Now
Track 15: Oh, Where's My Bess?
Track 16: I'm on My Way

BR-5007/BC-52
Mel Tormé and the Marty Paich "Dek-Tette"
1. Lulu's Back in Town
2. When the Sun Comes Out
3. I Love to Watch the Moonlight
4. Fascinating Rhythm
5. The Blues
6. The Carioca
7. The Lady Is a Tramp
8. I Like to Recognize the Tune
9. Keeping Myself for You
10. Lullaby of Birdland
11. When April Comes Again
12. Sing for Your Supper

BR-5014-2/EXLP-1
The Complete George Gershwin: Porgy and Bess (2 CD set)
The printed insert of the set shows the catalog number as BR-5014-3/EXLP-1. The discs show only the name of the work, Porgy and Bess, without individual track titles. The cast includes Mel Tormé, Frances Fay, Betty Roche, George Kirby, Johnny Hartman, Sallie Blair and Frank Rosolino. Music by Russ Garcia, Duke Ellington, the Australian Jazz Quartet and the Stan Levey Quartet. The musical content is the same as the equivalent LP version (EXLP-1).

BR-5015/BCP-34 *Mel Tormé: It's a Blue World*
1. I Got It Bad and That Ain't Good
2. Till the Clouds Roll By
3. Isn't It Romantic?
4. I Know Why
5. All This and Heaven Too
6. How Long Has This Been Going On?
7. Polka Dots and Moonbeams
8. You Leave Me Breathless
9. I Found a Million Dollar Baby (in a 5 and 10 ¢ store)
10. Wonderful One
11. It's a Blue World
12. Stay as Sweet as You Are

XLP-4016/BR-5026
Mel Tormé's California Suite
(No individual titles listed on the CD label)

BETHLEHEM (JAPAN)

COCY-06492
Songs for Any Taste
(Details wanted. Probably the same as COCY-9918)

COCY-09917
At the Crescendo
(Details wanted. Probably a CD version of BCP-6020 [LP])

COCY-9918
Songs for Any Taste
1. It's All Right with Me
2. Manhattan
3. Taking a Chance on Love
4. Home by the Sea
5. I Got Plenty o' Nuttin'
6. De Lovely
7. Tenderly
8. I Wish I Were in Love Again
9. Autumn Leaves (part ii)
10. Nobody's Heart

Track 9, Autumn Leaves, runs for 1' 38" and is the mock Chevalier portion of the song.

COCY-78656
At the Crescendo
(Details wanted. Probably the same as COCY-09917)

COCY-80069
Songs for Any Taste
(Details wanted. Probably the same as COCY-9918)

CY-2191
> *Mel Tormé / Live* (on the CD label)
> 30CY-2191 *Gene Norman Presents Mel Tormé at the Crescendo Plus "Songs for Any Taste"* (on the insert booklet)
> 1. It's Only a Paper Moon
> 2. What Is This Thing Called Love?
> 3. One for My Baby
> 4. Love Is Just a Bug
> 5. A Nightingale Sang in Berkeley Square
> 6. Autumn Leaves
> 7. Just One of Those Things
> 8. The Boy Next Door
> 9. Lover Come Back to Me
> 10. Looking at You
> 11. The Tender Trap
> 12. I'm Beginning to See the Light
> 13. It's All Right with Me
> 14. Manhattan
> 15. Taking a Chance on Love
> 16. Home by the Sea
> 17. De Lovely
> 18. Tenderly
> 19. I Wish I Were in Love Again
> 20. Autumn Leaves (part ii)
> 21. Nobody's Heart
>
> *Track 6, Autumn Leaves, runs for 1'27" and is the French language part of the song. Track 20 runs for 1'38" and is the mock Chevalier component. The English language part is omitted.*

CY-4594
> *At the Crescendo*
> (Details wanted. Probably the same as CY-2191)

BETHLEHEM ARCHIVE (USA)
SEE AVENUE JAZZ

THE BIG BAND ERA (USA)
This is a series of CDs each of which is a compilation of tracks by a variety of artists. Only those that contain a Mel Tormé track are listed

Volume 1
> Track 8: I'm Getting Sentimental Over You

Volume 2
> Track 10: I Surrender Dear

Volume 3
> Track 11: Between the Devil and the Great Blue Sea

Volume 4
> Track 2: Ghost of a Chance

Volume 5
> Track 4: I've Got the World on a String

Volume 7
> Track 14: Don't Worry 'Bout Me

Volume 9
> Track 13: I Can't Believe That You're in Love with Me

Volume 10
> Track 5: I Can't Give You Anything But Love

CAPITOL (USA)

7243 8 29384 2 2
> *Capitol Sings Broadway* (Vol. 19).
> This compilation contains one track by Mel Tormé.
> Track 14: I Like to Recognize the Tune

7243 8 32592 2 9
> *Capitol Sings Volume 15 Hoagy Carmichael.*
> This compilation contains one track by Mel Tormé.
> Track 5: Heart and Soul

72434-94749-0-1
> *Mel Tormé: A [Musical] Anthology*
> 1. Careless Hands
> 2. It Happened in Monterey
> 3. Strangers in the Night
> 4. I Like to Recognize the Tune
> 5. Blue Moon
> 6. It Don't Mean a Thing (If It Ain't Got That Swing)
> 7. Again
> 8. Love Is Such a Cheat (The Gypsy Song)

9. Bewitched
10. A Lonesome Cup o' Coffee
11. Got the Gate on the Golden Gate
12. Anywhere I Wander
13. The Four Winds and the Seven Seas
14. The Old Master Painter (*with Peggy Lee*)
15. The Christmas Song (Chestnuts Roasting on An Open Fire)
16. Goodbye

This disc also has an audio-visual track that is a biography of Mel Tormé spoken by Jack Perkins over pictures from phases in Mel Tormé's life. It is introduced by a few seconds of Tormé singing "Bewitched."

CDP 7 89941 2
Great Gentlemen of Song: Spotlight on Mel Tormé
1. Oh, You Beautiful Doll
2. My Buddy
3. Stompin' at the Savoy
4. Blue Moon
5. I Love Each Move You Make
6. You're Getting to Be a Habit with Me
7. It's Too Late Now
8. Heart and Soul
9. Lullaby of the Leaves
10. Do Do Do
11. Sonny Boy
12. Bewitched
13. You're a Heavenly Thing
14. Skylark
15. Careless Hands
16. I Hadn't Anyone Till You
17. I've Got a Feeling I'm Falling
18. Recipe for Romance

CDP 7 93195 2
peggy Lee Collectors Series.
All tracks are by Peggy Lee. Mel Tormé is present only on one track (in duet).
Track 24: The Old Master Painter

CDP 7 95288 2
ella eae Morse Collectors Series.
All tracks are by Ella Mae Morse. Mel Tormé is present only on one track (as the drummer).
Track 9: The Patty Cake Man

CDP 7243 8 31774 2 4
Great Gentlemen of Song Vol. 1. Hooray for Love.
This compilation contains one track by Mel Tormé.
Track 3: My Buddy

CDP 7243 8 31775 2 3
Great Gentlemen of Song Vol. 2. Pennies from Heaven.
This compilation contains one track by Mel Tormé.
Track 20: Good-Bye

CDP 7243 8 55161 2 2
Rock 'n' Roll Hits — On the Rocks Part One.
This compilation contains one track by Mel Tormé.
Track 2: Sunshine Superman

CAPITOL (UK)

CDEMS 1447
The Best of the Capitol Years: Mel Tormé
1. A Stranger in Town
2. Blue Moon
3. Again
4. Do Do Do
5. The Carioca
6. I've Got a Feeling I'm Falling
7. The Old Master Painter (*with Peggy Lee*)
8. Bewitched, Bothered and Bewildered
9. You're a Heavenly Thing
10. I Hadn't Anyone But You
11. It's Too Late Now
12. Oh You Beautiful Doll
13. Skylark
14. Heart and Soul
15. You're Getting to Be a Habit with Me
16. On a Little Street in Singapore
17. I Like to Recognize the Tune

18. My Buddy
19. Don't Fan the Flame (*with Peggy Lee*)
20. The Four Winds and the Seven Seas
21. Lullaby of the Leaves

CDEMS 1565
Capitol Sings Volume 15 Hoagy Carmichael
(Reissue of 7243 8 32592 2 9.)

CDP789941 2
Great Gentlemen of Song: Spotlight on Mel Tormé
(Reissue of CDP 7 89941 2 [USA].)

CDP 7 95288 2
ella mae Morse Collectors Series
(Reissue of CDP 7 95288 2 [USA].)

0777 7 89941 2 1
Great Gentlemen of Song: Spotlight on Mel Tormé
(This is the export number of CDP 7 89941-2.)

0777 7 99426 2 6
The Best of the Capitol Years: Mel Tormé
(This is the export number for CDEMS 1447.)

CBS (HOLLAND)

(Distributed in the U.K.)

474396-2
16 Most Requested Songs: Mel Tormé
(Reissue of Columbia CK 53779.)

CDCARD (UK)

This company issues a series of CDs called "A Time to Remember" commemorating the years from 1948. Each CD contains a selection of tracks from the relevant year and is available in two formats: the CD is either in a conventional plastic case or is in a folder designed as a greeting card. The CDs are identical irrespective of the format.

CD536
A Time to Remember 1948.
This compilation contains one track by Mel Tormé.
Track 11: You're Getting to Be a Habit with Me

CD537
A Time to Remember 1949.
This compilation contains one track by Mel Tormé.
Track 13: Blue Moon

CD538
A Time to Remember 1950.
This compilation contains one track by Mel Tormé.
Track 9: Bewitched

CD539
A Time to Remember 1951
This compilation contains one track by Mel Tormé.
Track 8: Heart and Soul

CHARLY (UK)

CDGR 135
It's a Blue World
(Details wanted. CD version of Bethlehem BCP-34 [LP])

CDGR 200-2 (2 CDs)
Songs for Sophisticats.
Details wanted. This compilation contains one track by Mel Tormé: Lulu's Back in Town

CLASSIC JAZZ (UK)

CDCD 1076
Mel Tormé & Tony Bennett: The Song Stylists
1. I'm Getting Sentimental Over You
2. I Can't Believe That You're in Love with Me
3. Prelude to a Kiss
4. I've Got the World on a String
5. (You've Got Me Between) the Devil and the Deep Blue Sea
6. I Surrender Dear
7. I Let a Song Go Out of My Heart

8. Don't Worry About Me
9. One Morning in May
10. I Can't Give You Anything but Love

There is no dialogue between the tracks. Tracks 11 to 20 are by Tony Bennett and the Count Basie Band

CDCD 1158
The Stars Salute Cole Porter.
This compilation contains one track by Artie Shaw with Mel Tormé.
Track 18: What Is This Thing Called Love?

COLLECTORS' CHOICE MUSIC (USA)

CCM0074-2
Two Classic Albums from Mel Tormé
(This CD also carries the Rhino logo and the catalog number R2 7295)
At the Red Hill:
1. Shakin' the Blues Away
2. I'm Beginning to See the Light
3. In Other Words
4. Medley: A Foggy Day, A Nightingale Sang in Berkeley Square
5. Love for Sale
6. It's Delovely
7 Mountain Greenery
8. Nevertheless
9. Early Autumn
10. Anything Goes
11. (Ah, the Apple Trees) When the World Was Young
12. Love Is Just Around the Corner

Live at the Maisonette
13. Introduction
14. Jet Set
15. What Are You Doing the Rest of Your Life?
16. Mountain Greenery
17. It Takes Too Long to Learn to Live Alone
18. (Get Your Kicks On) Route 66
19. Gershwin Medley

20. Superstition
21. The Party's Over

COLUMBIA (EUROPE)

COL 487890 2
Jazz Singers.
This compilation contains one track by Mel Tormé.
Track 2: All That Jazz (2'11")

COLUMBIA LEGACY (USA)

CK 53779 16
Most Requested Songs: Mel Tormé
1. P.S. I Love You
2. The Second Time Around
3. Haven't We Met?
4. The Nearness of You
5. My Romance
6. Do I Love You Because You're Beautiful?
7. Isn't It a Pity?
8. I Know Your Heart
9. I've Got You Under My Skin
10. That's All
11. What Is There to Say?
12. The Folks Who Live on the Hill
13. Everyday's a Holiday
14. You'd Better Love Me
15. Strangers in the Night
16. The Christmas Song (Chestnuts Roasting On An Open Fire)

CK 65164
Right Now!
1. Comin' Home Baby
2. Homeward Bound
3. My Little Red Book
4. Walk on By
5. If I Had a Hammer
6. Strangers in the Night
7. Better Use Your Head
8. Time
9. Secret Agent Man
10. Pretty Flamingo
11. Red Rubber Ball

12. All That Jazz
13. You Don't Have to Say You Love Me
14. Dominique's Discotheque
15. The Power of Love
16. Lover's Roulette
17. Ciao Baby
18. Molly Marlene
19. The King
20. Lima Lady
21. Wait Until Dark
22. Only When I'm Lonely

CK 65165
That's All
1. I've Got You Under My Skin
2. That's All
3. What Is There to Say?
4. Do I Love You Because You're Beautiful?
5. Folks Who Live on the Hill
6. Isn't It a Pity?
7. Ho-Ba-La-La
8. P.S. I Love You
9. The Nearness of You
10. My Romance
11. The Second Time Around
12. Haven't We Met?
13. I Know Your Heart
14. You'd Better Love Me
15. I See It Now
16. Once in a Lifetime
17. Hang on to Me
18. Seventeen
19. I Remember Suzanne
20. Only the Very Young
21. Paris Smiles
22. Ev'ry Day's a Holiday
23. One Little Snowflake
24. The Christmas Song (Chestnuts Roasting on an Open Fire)

SK 46595
Home Alone.
Details wanted. This compilation contains one track by Mel Tormé: Have Yourself a Merry Little Christmas

CONCORD JAZZ (USA)

CCD-4190
An Evening with George Shearing & Mel Tormé
1. All God's Chillun Got Rhythm
2. Born to Be Blue
3. Give Me the Simple Life
4. Good Morning Heartache
5. Manhattan Hoedown
6. You'd Be So Nice to Come Home To
7. A Nightingale Sang in Berkeley Square
8. Love
9. It Might As Well Be Spring
10. Lullaby of Birdland

CCD-4219
Top Drawer: George Shearing / Mel Tormé
1. Shine on Your Shoes
2. How Do You Say Auf Wiedersehen?
3. Oleo
4. Stardust
5. Hi Fly
6. Smoke Gets in Your Eyes
7. What's This?
8. Away in a Manger
9. Here's to My Lady

CCD-4248
Mel Tormé / George Shearing: An Evening at Charlie's
1. Medley: Just One of Those Things, On Green Dolphin Street
2. Dream Dancing
3. I'm Hip
4. Then I'll Be Tired of You
5. Medley: Caught in the Middle of My Years, Welcome to the Club
6. Nica's Dream
7. Chase Me Charlie
8. Love Is Just Around the Corner

CCD-4294
An Elegant Evening: George Shearing and Mel Tormé
1. I'll Be Seeing You

2. Moon Medley: Love and the Moon, Oh, You Crazy Moon, No Moon At All
3. After the Waltz Is Over
4. This Time the Dream's on Me
5. Last Night, When We Were Young
6. You Changed My Life
7. Dream Medley: I Had the Craziest Dream, Darn That Dream
8. Brigg Fair
9. My Foolish Heart
10. You're Driving Me Crazy

CCD-4306

Mel Tormé, Rob McConnell and the Boss Brass
1. Just Friends
2. September Song
3. Don'cha Go 'Way Mad
4. A House Is Not a Home
5. The Song Is You
6. Cow Cow Boogie
7. A Handful of Stars/Stars Fell on Alabama
8. Duke Ellington Medley: It Don't Mean a Thing (If It Ain't Got That Swing), Do Nothing Till You Hear From Me, Mood Indigo, Take the "A" Train, Sophisticated Lady, Satin Doll

CCD-4341

Mel Tormé, George Shearing: A Vintage Year
1. Whisper Not/ Love Me or Leave Me
2. Out of This World
3. Someday I'll Find You
4. The Midnight Sun
5. New York, New York Medley: Me and My Girl, Mack the Knife, Birth of the Blues, Send a Little Love My Way, How High the Moon, New York, New York
6. Folks Who Live on the Hill
7. Bitter Sweet
8. Since I Fell for You
9. The Way You Look Tonight
10. Anyone Can Whistle/A Tune for Humming
11. When Sunny Gets Blue
12. Little Man You've Had a Busy Day

CCD-4360

Mel Tormé and the Marty Paich Dek-Tette Reunion
1. Sweet Georgia Brown
2. Walk Between Raindrops
3. When You Wish Upon a Star/I'm Wishing
4. Bossa Nova Potpourri: The Gift, One Note Samba, How Insensitive
5. The Trolley Song/Get Me to the Church on Time
6. More Than You Know
7. The Goodbye Look
8. The Blues
9. For Whom the Bell Tolls/Spain (I Can Recall)

CCD-4382

Mel Tormé and the Marty Paich Dek-Tette in Concert, Tokyo, Fujitsu-Concord Jazz Festival in Japan '88
1. It Don't Mean a Thing (If It Ain't Got That Swing)
2. Sweet Georgia Brown
3. Just in Time
4. When the Sun Comes Out
5. The Carioca
6. More Than You Know
7. Too Close for Comfort
8. The City
9. Bossa Nova Potpourri: The Gift, One Note Samba, How Insensitive
10. On the Street Where You Live
11. Cotton Tail
12. The Christmas Song
13. It Don't Mean a Thing (If It Ain't Got That Swing)

CCD-4433

Mel Tormé: Night at the Concord Pavilion
1. Sing for Your Supper/ Sing, Sing, Sing/Sing (Sing a Song)
2. You Make Me feel So Young
3. Early Autumn
4. Guys and Dolls Medley: Guys and Dolls, Fugue for Tinhorns, The Oldest

Established, If I Were a Bell, My Time of Day, I've Never Been in Love Before, Sit Down, You're Rockin' the Boat, Luck Be a Lady
5. I Could Have Told You/Losing My Mind/Deep in a Dream/Goin' Out of My Head
6. Too Darn Hot
7. Day In — Day Out
8. Down for Double
9. You're Driving Me Crazy (What Do I Do)
10. Sent for You Yesterday and Here You Come Today

CCD-4471

Mel Tormé / George Shearing: Mel & George "Do" World War II
1. Lili Marlene
2. (It Seems to Me) I've Heard That Song Before
3. I Know Why and So Do You
4. Love
5. Aren't You Glad You're You?
6. Ellington Medley: Cotton Tail, I Didn't Know About You, Don't Get Around Much Anymore, I'm Beginning to See the Light
7. Walk Medley: I Don't Want to Walk Without You Baby, I'll Walk Alone
8. I Could Write a Book
9. (This Is) a Lovely Way to Spend An Evening
10. On the Swing Shift/ The Five O'clock Whistle
11. Ac-cent-tchu-ate the Positive
12. This Is the Army Mister Jones
13. We Mustn't Say Goodbye

CCD-4481

Mel Tormé Recorded Live at the Fujitsu-Concord Jazz Festival in Japan '90
1. Shine on Your Shoes
2. Looking At You/Look at That Face
3. A Nightingale Sang in Berkeley Square
4. Wave
5. Star Dust
6. Don't'cha Go 'Way Mad/Come to Baby Do
7 The Christmas Song/Autumn Leaves
8. You're Driving Me Crazy/Moten Swing
9. Sent for You Yesterday and Here You Come Today
10. Swingin' the Blues
11. New York State of Mind

CCD-4515

Mel Tormé / Cleo Laine: Nothing Without You
1. I'm Nothing Without You (You're Nothing Without Me)
2. I Thought About You
3. Where or When
4. I Wish I Were in Love Again
5. Girl Talk
6. After You've Gone
7. Brazil/ Baia
8. Birdsong
9. Isn't It a Pity?
10. Love You Madly
11. Angel Eyes
12. Two Tune Medley: Two Tune Verse, Sweet Sue, Honeysuckle Rose, I May Be Wrong (But I Think You're Wonderful), The Nearness of You, There's No You, Blue Moon, Heart and Soul, Watch What Happens, Exactly Like You, Take the "A" Train, I Found a Million Dollar Baby, On the Alamo, Fly Me to the Moon, Autumn Leaves, Yesterday When I Was Young, You and the Night and the Music, Sing (Sing a Song), Guilty, Feelin' Groovy (The 59th Street Bridge Song)
13. I Don't Think I'll Fall in Love Today
14. Ev'ry Time We Say Goodbye

CCD-4542

Fujitsu Presents Mel Tormé and His All-Star Quintet
1. Lulu's Back in Town
2. Memories of You

3. It's All Right with Me/Love
4. These Foolish Things
5. "All" Medley: All the Things You Are, All of You, All of Me
6. Tribute to Benny Goodman: Stompin' at the Savoy, Don't Be That Way, And the Angels Sing, Gotta Be This Or That, Jersey Bounce, Why Don't You Do Right?, Air Mail Special, Avalon, Sing, Sing, Sing
7. Get Happy
8. Three Little Words
9. Guess I'll Hang My Tears Out to Dry
10. Love, Come Back to Me
11. Ev'ry Time We Say Goodbye

CCD-4614
Mel Tormé: A Tribute to Bing Crosby
1. This Must Be My Night to Dream/It Must Be True
2. Moonlight Becomes You
3. I Can't Escape from You
4. With Every Breath I Take
5. A Man and His Dreams
6. Without a Word of Warning
7. May I?
8. Please
9. Thanks
10. Don't Let That Moon Get Away
11. Soon
12. It's Easy to Remember
13. Love in Bloom
14. The Day You Came Along
15. Pennies from Heaven
16. Learn to Croon

CCD-4667
Mel Tormé, Rob McConnell and the Boss Brass: Velvet and Brass
1. Nobody Else but Me
2. Liza (All the Clouds'll Roll Away)
3. If You Could See Me Now
4. I Get a Kick Out of You
5. Have You Met Miss Jones?
6. Love Walked In
7. Autumn Serenade
8. My Sweetie Went Away
9. I'll Be Around

10. On the Swing Shift
11. High and Low
12. In the Still of the Night
13. I'm Glad There's You

CCD-4720 A
Concord Jazz Christmas 2.
This compilation contains one track by Mel Tormé.
Track 17: The Christmas Song

CCD-4736
An Evening with Mel Tormé
1. Just One of Those Things/On Green Dolphin Street
2. You Make Me Feel So Young
3. A Nightingale Sang in Berkeley Square
4. Pick Yourself Up
5. Stardust
6. Love for Sale
7. Since I Fell for You
8. Three Little Words/Slipped Disc/Smooth One/Rachel's Dream
9. I Remember You/It's Easy to Remember
10. Love Come Back to Me
11. Stairway to the Stars
12. Oh, Lady Be Good
13. Ev'ry Time We Say Goodbye

CCD-4790-2
Mel Tormé: My Night to Dream
1. Medley: This Is My Night to Dream, …It Must Be True
2. My Foolish Heart
3. More Than You Know
4. Here's to My Lady
5. Moonlight Becomes You
6. After the Waltz Is Over
7. Angel Eyes
8. How Do You Say Auf Wiedersehen?
9. If You Could See Me Now?
10. House Is Not a Home
11. I'll Be Seeing You
12. I'll Be Around

CCD-4811-2
Mel Tormé: The Concord Jazz Heritage Series

1. Just Friends
2. Hi Fly
3. I'll Be Seeing You
4. I Get a Kick Out of You
5. I Thought About You
6. It's Easy to Remember/Adios
7. Sweet Georgia Brown
8. Born to Be Blue
9. New York, New York Medley: For Me and My Gal, Mack the Knife, Birth of the Blues, Send a Little Love My Way, How High the Moon, New York, New York
10. Stardust
11. Too Close for Comfort
12. You're Driving Me Crazy (What Did I Do?)
13. Love, Come Back to Me
14. Ev'ry Time We Say Goodbye

CCD-7005
    A Tribute to Carl Jefferson.
      Details wanted. This compilation contains one track by Mel Tormé: Ev'ry Time We Say Goodbye

CONCORD JAZZ (GERMANY)

(Distributed in the UK) The first few Concord Jazz issues were imported into Europe from the U.S.A. or Japan but then issues were pressed in Germany for release throughout Europe. The second Christmas album (CCD-4720) and the Tribute to Carl Jefferson (CCD-7005) do not seem to have been released in Europe.

CORAL (JAPAN)

30P2-2323
    At the Crescendo 1954.
      Details wanted. Reissue of MCA GRP 16172 (USA) "Mel Tormé in Hollywood" but with the missing track, "You're Driving Me Crazy" included

MVCM-274
    At the Crescendo
      (Details wanted. CD version of Coral CRL 57012 [LP])

MVCM-275
    Musical Sounds Are the Best Songs
      (Details wanted. CD version of Coral CRL 57044 [LP])

CRIMSON (UK)

CRIMICD 011
    Things Are Swinging.
      This compilation contains two tracks by Mel Tormé.
    Track 5: Nice Work If You Can Get It
    Track 17: All of You

CURB (USA)

D2-77618
    Best of Mel Tormé
1. Windmills of Your Mind
2. Spinning Wheel
3. Raindrops Keep Falling on My Head
4. A Time for Us
5. You've Made Me So Very Happy
6. Yesterday When I Was Young
7. Traces
8. Happy Together
9. Stranger in Town
10. Four Winds and the Seven Seas.

These is a report of a Curb CD issued in 1993 that includes material from Atlantic. I have not been able to confirm its existence.

CD???
    The Best of Mel Tormé. Issued 1993 and including tracks from Atlantic

DCC JAZZ (USA)

DJZ-621
    Tormé Encore at Marty's, New York
1. Lulu's Back in Town
2. Looking at You
3. That Face
4. I'm Gonna Miss You

5. Medley: A Tribute to Fred Astaire
6. What Are You Doing the Rest of Your Life?
7. Sophisticated Lady
8. Stormy Weather
9. When the Sun Comes Out
10. Autumn Leaves
11. Pieces of Dreams
12. I Like to Recognize the Tune
13. Day In, Day Out
14. Watch What Happens

631
Mel Tormé and Friends
(CD version of Finesse W2X 37848)

DISKY (HOLLAND)
(Distributed in the U.K.)

TC 885732
Mel Tormé: A Touch of Class
1. Careless Hands
2. Again
3. The Four Winds and the Seven Seas
4. The Old Master Painter (*w Peggy Lee & The Mellow Men*)
5. A Stranger in Town (*w The Jud Conlon Singers*)
6. Blue Moon
7. I've Got a Feeling I'm Falling (*w The Red Norvo Trio*)
8. Bewitched, Bothered and Bewildered
9. Don't Fan the Flame (*w Peggy Lee & Orchestra*)
10. My Buddy (*w Orchestra & Chorus*)
11. On a Little Street in Singapore (*w The Red Norvo Trio*)
12. Oh You Beautiful Doll
13. You're Getting to Be a Habit with Me
14. Heart and Soul
15. Lullaby of the Leaves

ECLIPSE (UK)
820 642-2
Matt 'n' Mel: Matt Monro & Mel Tormé
4. Waltz for Young Lovers
8. I Don't Want to Walk Without You
12. Walkin' Shoes
16. Cuckoo in the Clock
20. Shenandoah Valley
24. Hooray for Love.

The other 18 tracks on this CD are by Matt Monro

FAT BOY (HOLLAND)
(Distributed in the U.K.)

FATCD 164
Life Is a Song
(Content identical to Classic Jazz CDCD 1076)

FINESSE (JAPAN)

30JD-20/21
Tormé
(Recorded at Marty's New York CD version of W2X 37484)

FLASHBACK
SEE RHINO FLASHBACK

FRESH SOUNDS (SPAIN)
(Distributed in the U.K.)

FSR-CD 109
Mel Tormé: Prelude to a Kiss
1. I've Got the World on a String
2. Don't Worry 'Bout Me
3. One Morning in May
4. I Can't Give You Anything But Love
5. Between the Devil and the Deep Blue Sea
6. I Don't Stand a Ghost of a Chance with You
7. I'm Getting Sentimental Over You
8. I Can't Believe That You're in Love with Me

9. Prelude to a Kiss
10. Something to Live For
11. I Surrender Dear
12. I Let a Song Go Out of My Heart.
Has dialogue between the tracks.

GEFFEN (USA)

GHS-4016
Born to Laugh at Tornadoes.
This is an album by the group Was (Not Was) with one track on which Tormé is present.
Track 10: Zaz Turned Blue

GIANTS OF JAZZ (ITALY)
(Distributed in the U.K.)

CD 0230
Lulu's Back in Town
1. Lulu's Back in Town
2. They Can't Take That Away from Me
3. Nice Work If You Can Get It
4. The Way You Look Tonight
5. A Foggy Day
6. Lullaby of Birdland
7. The Lady Is a Tramp
8. Let's Call the Whole Thing Off
9. When April Comes Again
10. A Fine Romance
11. Cheek to Cheek
12. Let's Face the Music and Dance
13. The Piccolino
14. The Blues
15. Top Hat, White Tie & Tails
16. Something's Gotta Give
17. The Carioca
18. Sing for Your Supper
19. When the Sun Comes Out
20. I Love to Watch the Moonlight
21. I Like to Recognize the Tune
22. Keeping Myself for You
23. Fascinatin' Rhythm

CD 53343
George Gershwin: By the Giants of Jazz.
Full details wanted. This compilation contains at least one track by Mel Tormé.

CD 53343
Mel Tormé with Marty Paich and Dave Barbour "I Let a Song Go Out of My Heart"
1. I Let a Song Go Out of My Heart
2. I'm Getting Sentimental Over You
3. I Can't Believe That You're in Love with Me
4. I Surrender Dear
5. I've Got the World on a String
6. (I Don't Stand) a Ghost of a Chance with You
7. I Can't Give You Anything but Love
8. Between the Devil and the Deep Blue Sea
9. Prelude to a Kiss
10. Something to Live For
11. Don't Worry 'Bout Me
12. One Morning in May
13. I Cover the Waterfront
14. Love Me or Leave Me
15. When It's Sleepy Time Down South
16. Three Little Words
17. Gone with the Wind
18. Don't Take Your Love from Me
19. Blues in the Night
20. A Cottage for Sale
21. The Blues

GREAT MOVIE THEMES (?ITALY?)
(Distributed in the U.K.)

CD 60004
Original Soundtracks — Higher and Higher & Step Lively.
Mel Tormé is only audible on these tracks from "Higher and Higher" and does not appear in "Step Lively."
Track 1: It's a Most Important Affair
Track 2: Today I'm a Debutante
Track 7: You're on Your Own
Track 8: Minuet in Boogie/I Saw You First/Finale

GREAT VOICES OF THE CENTURY (UK)

GVC 2005
Mel Tormé and the Mel-Tones: That's Where I Came From (2 CD set)
DISC ONE
Tracks 1 to 11 and 13 Mel Tormé. Tracks 12 and 14 to 22 Artie Shaw with Mel Tormé.
1. Willow Road
2. There's No One but You
3. Try a Little Tenderness
4. South America Take It Away
5. Born to Be Blue
6. It Happened in Monterey
7. Dream Awhile
8. There's No Business Like Show Business
9. A Little Kiss Each Morning
10. When Is Sometime
11. It's Easy to Remember
12. They Can't Convince Me
13. I Got the Sun in the Morning
14. Along with Me
15. What Is This Thing Called Love?
16. For You, for Me, for Evermore
17. Changing My Tune
18. Guilty
19. And So to Bed
20. Don't You Believe It Dear
21. It's the Same Old Dream
22. I Believe

DISC TWO
Tracks 1 to 12 Mel Tormé, tracks 13 to 22 from the Mel Tormé radio show of 1948.
1. Love Is the Sweetest Thing
2. How Long Has This Been Going On?
3. Three Little Words
4. I Can't Give You Anything but Love
5. Fine and Dandy
6. The Day You Came Along
7. County Fair
8. That's Where I Came In
9. I Cover the Waterfront
10. The Best Things in Life Are Free
11. Little White Lies
12. Night and Day
13. You're Driving Me Crazy
14. When the Red, Red Robin Comes, Bob, Bob, Bobbin' Along
15. Everything Happens to Me
16. It's a Most Unusual Day
17. Pythagoras, How You Stagger Us
18. I Got the Sun in the Morning
19. On a Slow Boat to China
20. Brahm's Lullaby
21. Malt Shop Special
22. Wish I May, Wish I Might

GRP (USA)

GRP 16172
Mel Tormé in Hollywood
(See MCA GRP 16172)

GRD-2004
The Glenn Miller Orchestra "In the Digital Mood"
This is a Limited Gold Edition with an extra track over the original CD (see GRP-D-9502 below) but this extra track does not involve Tormé. All tracks are by the Glenn Miller Orchestra and Mel Tormé is present as a member of the vocal group only on two tracks:
Track 2: Chattanooga Choo-Choo
Track 6: (I've Got a Gal in) Kalamazoo

GRD-9679
Gerry Mulligan. Re-Birth of the Cool
All tracks are by Gerry Mulligan. Mel Tormé is present only on one track:
Track 11: Darn That Dream

GRP-D-9502
The Glenn Miller Orchestra "In the Digital Mood."
All tracks are by the Glenn Miller Orchestra and Mel Tormé is present as a member of the vocal group on only two tracks:

Track 2: Chattanooga Choo-Choo
Track 6: Kalamazoo

HEP (UK)

HEP CD-1
> *Boyd Raeburn and His Orchestra. Jubilee Performances — 1946.*
> All tracks are by Boyd Raeburn and his orchestra. Mel Tormé and the Mel-Tones are present only on one track:
> Track 16: That's Where I Came In

HINDSIGHT (USA)

HCD-253
> *Mel Tormé "Easy to Remember"*
> 1. Don't Let That Moon Get Away
> 2. Day in Day Out
> 3. I'll Be Seeing You
> 4. It's Easy to Remember
> 5. 'Round Midnight
> 6. I Could Have Told You
> 7. I Concentrate on You
> 8. The Moon Was Yellow
> 9. The Night We Called It a Day
> 10. I'm Gonna Miss You
> 11. In Love in Vain
> 12. Swingin' on the Moon
> 13. Where Are You?
> 14. Portia Brown
> 15. Long Ago and Far Away
> 16. All I Need Is the Girl

HCD-272 *Mel Tormé with the Buddy Rich Orchestra: When I Found You*
> 1. When I Found You
> 2. Here's That Rainy Day
> 3. Cape Verdean Blues
> 4. Blues in the Night
> 5. Bluesette
> 6. You Are the Sunshine of My Life
> 7. Funk City Ola
> 8. I Won't Last a Day Without You
> 9. Lady Be Good

Tracks 3 and 7 are instrumentals without Tormé

HOLLYWOOD NITES (USA)

HNC 0049
> *The Jazz Singers*
> This compilation contains one track by Artie Shaw with Mel Tormé:
> Track 10: Guilty

INTERSOUND (USA)

CDS 3505
> *Peter Nero & Friends: It Had to Be You*
> All tracks are by Peter Nero's Trio with a number of guests. Mel Tormé is present on only one track:
> Track 9: Long Ago and Far Away

JUDY DUETS
SEE WILEY ENTERTAINMENT

LASERLIGHT (USA)

12 222
> *Mel Tormé: Swingin' on the Moon*
> 1. Because of You
> 2. Swinging on the Moon
> 3. Blues in the Night
> 4. You Oughta Be in Pictures
> 5. I'm Gonna Miss You
> 6. Love Me or Leave Me
> 7. I Hadn't Anyone Till You
> 8. Something's Gotta Give
> 9. County Fair
> 10. Back in Your Backyard
> 11. Don't Let That Moon Get Away
> 12. Don't Take Your Love From Me

12 223
> *Mel Tormé: 'Round Midnight*
> 1. Gone with the Wind
> 2. Johnny One Note
> 3. Portia Brown
> 4. The Money Song
> 5. When It's Sleepy Time Down South
> 6. A Fine Romance
> 7. 'Round Midnight

8. April Showers
9. Don't Get Around Much Anymore
10. The Blues
11. Baby, Don't You Go Away Mad
12. Isn't It a Lovely Day (To Be Caught in the Rain)

12 224
Mel Tormé: Luck Be a Lady
1. All I Need Is the Girl
2. Easy to Remember
3. Isn't It a Lovely Day (To Be Caught in the Rain)
4. Luck Be a Lady
5. A Cottage for Sale
6. You're the Cream in My Coffee
7. The Moon Was Yellow
8. April in Paris
9. Lover's Delight
10. I Cover the Waterfront
11. I'll Be Seeing You
12. Wrap Your Troubles in Dreams (and Dream Your Troubles Away)

The above three CDs (12 222 to 224) were also available in an outer sleeve as a set that did not have an additional catalog number

15 467
The Judy Garland Christmas Album.
This CD includes most of the soundtrack from Ms. Garland's Christmas Show on CBS in December 1963. Tormé is only on one track and in part of the Christmas Carol medley:
Track 9: The Christmas Song (Garland and Tormé)
Track 10: The Christmas Carol Medley includes Hark! The Herald Angels Sing (Tormé and Jack Jones), Deck the Halls (Garland and all the guests including Tormé)

15 381
Mel Tormé: Smooth as Velvet
(Reissue of Pickwick PMDT 16009.)

15 463
Christmas Favorites.
Details wanted. This compilation contains one track by Mel Tormé: The Christmas Song

15 767
Big Bands of Hollywood: Desi Arnaz and Chico Marx
Tracks 1 to 7 are by Desi Arnaz. The remaining tracks are by The Chico Marx Orchestra and Mel Tormé is present only on the indicated tracks.
8. Abraham (MT)
9. Velvet Moon
10. Pagliacci (MT)
11. Swing Stuff
12. Beer Barrel Polka
13. Mr. Five by Five
14. Chicago Strut

16 504
Home for the Holiday.
Details wanted. This compilation contains at least one track by Mel Tormé.

LIFE, TIMES AND MUSIC (USA)

Jazz Duets (ISBN 1 56799 360-5)
Details wanted. This is a package of CD and book. It contains one track by Mel Tormé and Cleo Laine, "I'm Nothing Without You" from Concord

MAGIC (UK)

DAWE85
Jerry Gray and His Band of the Day: Stand By for Music
All tracks are by Jerry Gray and his band. The CD contains six programs taken from US Navy transcriptions. Mel Tormé is present on one program and only on the indicated tracks:
29. Theme — Desert Serenade
30. You Ought to Be in Pictures (MT)
31. Interview (MT)
32. All of You (MT)
33. Coronado Cruise

34. I Cover the Waterfront (MT)
35. Theme — Desert Serenade

MCA (USA)

GRP-16172
Mel Tormé in Hollywood
1. From This Moment On
2. September Song
3. That Old Black Magic
4. Get Out of Town
5. My Shining Hour
6. Goody, Goody
7. County Fair
8. The Christmas Song (Merry Christmas to You)
9. A Stranger in Town
10. I Wish I Were in Love Again
11. Moonlight in Vermont
12. Bernie's Tune
13. Our Love Is Here to Stay
14. Old Devil Moon
15. Blue Moon
16. Have You Met Miss Jones?
17. Jeepers Creepers
18. Mountain Greenery
19. Imagination
20. Get Happy

MCA (UK)

GRP 97482
Balladeers
This compilation contains one track by Mel Tormé.
Track 13: September Song
MCBD 19533
The Legendary Songs of Cole Porter.
This compilation contains two tracks by Mel Tormé.
Track 6: Get Out of Town
Track 19: From This Moment On
MCLD 19232
The Songs of Harry Warren: It's a Great Big World
This compilation contains one track by Mel Tormé.
Track 7: Jeepers Creepers
MCLD 19235
The Songs of Johnny Mercer: When the World Was Young
This compilation contains one track by Mel Tormé.
Track 14: Goody Goody

MCA UNIVERSAL (UK)

MCBD
The Legendary Songs of Cole Porter
This compilation includes two tracks by Mel Tormé.
Track 5: Get Out of Town
Track 19: From This Moment On
MCLD 19377
Bing Crosby: Some Fine Old Chestnuts & New Tricks
All tracks are by Bing Crosby. Mel Tormé and The Mel-Tones are present on two tracks.
Track 28: Day by Day
Track 29: Prove It by the Things You Do

MCA (GERMANY)

Distributed in the U.K.

GRP-16172
Mel Tormé in Hollywood
(Reissue of USA issue GRP-16172.)

MEMBERS EDITION (HOLLAND)

Distributed in USA & UK. Produced by United Audio Entertainment Ltd.

UAE 30652
Mel Tormé / Billy Eckstine
Tracks 1 to 12 are by Billy Eckstine.
13. I'm Getting Sentimental Over You
14. I Can't Believe That You're in Love with Me
15. Prelude to a Kiss
16. I've Got the World on a String
17. The Devil and the Deep Blue Sea
18. I Surrender Dear

19. I Let a Song Go Out of My Heart
20. Don't Worry About Me
21. One Morning in May
22. I Can't Give You Anything But Love

No dialogue between tracks.

MICHELLE (UK)

These CDs are the UK release of the "The Big Band Era" (USA) series. Only those that contain a Mel Tormé track are listed

MICH 5601: Volume 1
  track 8: I'm Getting Sentimental Over You
MICH 5602: Volume 2
  track 10: I Surrender Dear
MICH 5603: Volume 3
  track 11: Between the Devil and the Great Blue Sea
MICH 5604: Volume 4
  track 2: Ghost of a Chance
MICH 5605: Volume 5
  track 4: I've Got the World on a String
MICH 5607: Volume 7
  track 14: Don't Worry 'Bout Me
MICH 5609: Volume 9
  track 13: I Can't Believe That You're in Love with Me
MICH 5610: Volume 10
  track 5: I Can't Give You Anything but Love

MOBILE FIDELITY (USA)

UDCD-592
  Together Again — For the First Time
  (Details wanted)

MR. MUSIC (USA)

MMCD 7005
  Mel Tormé Live with the Mel-Tones Volume One
  1. Fairmont College
  2. You're Driving Me Crazy
  3. You're the Top
  4. That Old Black Magic
  5. When the Red, Red Robin Comes Bob Bob Bobbin' Along
  6. Everything Happens to Me
  7. It's a Most Unusual Day
  8. Maybe You'll Be There
  9. Geometric Blues
  10. The French Lesson
  11. It's Dark on Observatory Hill
  12. I've Got the Sun in the Morning and the Moon at Night
  13. On a Slow Boat to China
  14. Brahms' Lullaby
  15. You're the Cream in My Coffee
  16. I Gotta Eight to Sing the Blues
  17. Mountain Greenery
  18. Here I'll Stay
  19. Wish I May, Wish I Might
MMCD 7006
  Mel Tormé Live with the Mel-Tones Volume Two
  1. Fine and Dandy
  2. Isn't It Romantic?
  3. Blues in the Night
  4. What Is This Thing Called Love?
  5. Let's Fall in Love
  6. The Money Song
  7. Ah, but It Happens
  8. Hooray for Love
  9. Get Out and Get Under
  10. Lover's Delight
  11. It's the Sentimental Thing to Do
  12. A Fine Romance
  13. Wrap Your Troubles in Dreams
  14. Back in Your Own Backyard
  15. I Get Along Without You Very Well
  16. Friendship
  17. This Is the Moment
  18. How High the Moon
  19. It's Magic
  20. Fairmont College (reprise)

MUSIC CLUB (UK)

MCCD 198
  The Magic of Mel Tormé

1. A Stranger in Town
2. Day by Day (*Bing Crosby w MT*)
3. You've Laughed at Me for the Last Time
4. Am I Blue? (*Eugenie Baird w MT*)
5. My Rosemarie
6. The Anything Can Happen Mambo
7. The Hut-Sut Song
8. All of You
9. Hold Tight
10. Blue Skies
11. Rose O'Day
12. Spellbound
13. That Old Black Magic
14. Blue Moon
15. County Fair
16. The Christmas Song (Merry Christmas to You)
17. Mountain Greenery
18. You're Driving Me Crazy

MUSIC FOR PLEASURE (UK)

CDDL 1230
A Tribute to Hoagy Carmichael
This 2-CD compilation contains one track by Mel Tormé.
Disc 2, track 12: Skylark

CDDL 1236
Flashback to the 50's
This 2-CD compilation contains one track by Mel Tormé.
Disc 1, track 11: Bewitched

CDDLD 1299
Sophisticated Gentlemen
This 2-CD compilation contains these four tracks by Mel Tormé:
Disc 1, track 4: You're Getting to Be a Habit with Me
Track 14: Blue Moon
Disc 2, track 5: Again
Track 10: Bewitched

CDMFP 6162
Great Jazz Singers
Mel Tormé appears only on track 13: Got the Gate on the Golden Gate

CDMFP 6217
Mel Tormé Around the World
1. Frenesi
2. Blue Moon
3. You're Getting to Be a Habit with Me
4. Skylark
5. Perfidia
6. Autumn Leaves
7. It's D'lovely
8. Recipe for Romance
9. South of the Border
10. Vaya Con Dios
11. I Wish I Were in Love Again
12. Tenderly
13. I've Got a Feeling I'm Falling
14. Oh You Beautiful Doll
15. Sonny Boy
16. Bewitched, Bothered and Bewildered
17. Lullaby of the Leaves
18. I Hadn't Anyone Till You
19. The Piccolino
20. Black Moonlight

CDMFP 6282
The Very Thought of You
This compilation contains one track by Mel Tormé:
You're Getting to Be a Habit with Me

0777 7 80615 2 6
A Tribute to Hoagy Carmichael
(Export number for CDDL 1230)

0777 7 80618 2 3
Flashback to the 50's
(Export number for CDDL 1236)

494 3502
Favourite Capitol Classics
This compilation contains one track by Mel Tormé.
Track 11: Blue Moon

7243 4 94350 2 5
Favourite Capitol Classics
(Export number for 494 3502)

7243 8 32763 2 5
Great Jazz Singers
(Export number for CDMFP 6162)

7243 8 36547 2 7
Sophisticated Gentlemen
(Export number for CDDLD 1299)
7243 8 53503 2 0
Mel Tormé Around the World
(Export number for CDMFP 6217)
MFP 94349-2
Favourite Easy Listening
This compilation contains one track by Mel Tormé:
You're Getting to Be a Habit with Me

MUSICRAFT (USA)

Mvscd-50
Artie Shaw & His Orchestra Volume 1 "For You, for Me, Forevermore."
All tracks by Artie Shaw & his orchestra. Mel Tormé is present only on tracks where indicated.
1. Changing My Tune (MT)
2. I've Got You Under My Skin
3. For You, for Me, Forevermore (MT)
4. Along with Me (MT)
5. What Is This Thing Called Love? (MT)
6. Get Out of Town (MT)
7. Let's Walk
8. I Got the Sun in the Morning (MT)
9. And So to Bed (MT)
10. Love for Sale
11. Connecticut
12. They Can't Convince Me (MT)
13. The Glider
14. Don't You Believe It Dear (MT)

MVSCD-51
Artie Shaw and His Orchestra Volume 2 "You Do Something to Me"
All tracks by Artie Shaw & his orchestra. Mel Tormé is present only on tracks where indicated.
1. Love of My Life
2. It's the Same Old Dream (MT)
3. How Deep Is the Ocean?
4. The Hornet
5. You Do Something to Me
6. In the Still of the Night
7. Begin the Beguine
8. My Heart Belongs to Daddy
9. Night and Day
10. Guilty (MT)
11. Anniversary Song
12. Ghost of a Chance
13. When You're Around
14. I Believe (MT)

MVSCD-54
Mel Tormé and the Mel-Tones "A Foggy Day"
1. A Foggy Day
2. Do It Again
3. There's No Business Like Show Business
4. But Beautiful
5. Night and Day
6. Makin' Whoopee
7. It Happened in Monterey
8. It's Dreamtime
9. That's Where I Came In
10. Who Cares What People Say?
11. With You
12. Kokomo, Indiana
13. You're Driving Me Crazy
14. My Baby Just Cares for Me
15. I'm Yours

MVSCD-60
Mel Tormé and the Mel-Tones "There's No One But You"
1. South America Take It Away
2. Love Is the Sweetest Thing
3. The Best Things in Life Are Free
4. It's Easy to Remember
5. How Long Has This Been Going On?
6. When Is Sometime?
7. Willow Road
8. There's No One But You
9. County Fair
10. Try a Little Tenderness
11. I Cover the Waterfront
12. Three Little Words
13. A Little Kiss Each Morning
14. Little White Lies

15. I Can't Give You Anything but Love
16. The Day You Came Along

70060-2
There's No One But You
(Details wanted. Probably the same as MVSCD-60)

PADDLE WHEEL (JAPAN)

KICJ 128
Tormé: A New Album, London Sessions Complete Edition
1. All in Love Is Fair
2. The First Time Ever I Saw Your Face
3. New York State of Mind
4. Stars
5. Send in the Clowns
6. Ordinary Fool
7. Medley: When the World Was Young/Yesterday When I Was Young
8. Bye Bye Blackbird
9. It's Too Late
10. Never Look Back
11. Charade
12. Like a Lover
13. What's This?

KICJ 129
Tormé Encore at Marty's New York
1. Lulu's Back in Town
2. Looking at You
3. That Face
4. I'm Gonna Miss You
5. Medley: A Tribute to Fred Astaire
6. What Are You Doing the Rest of Your Life?
7. Too Close for Comfort
8. Sophisticated Lady
9. Stormy Weather
10. When the Sun Comes Out
11. Autumn Leaves
12. The Folks Who Live on the Hill
13. I Like to Recognize the Tune
14. Day In, Day Out
15. Watch What Happens

PADDLE WHEEL (GERMANY)
Distributed in the U.K.

KICJ 128
Tormé. A New Album London Sessions Complete Edition
(Reissue of KICJ 128 [Japan].)

KICJ 129
Tormé Encore at Marty's New York
(Reissue of KICJ 129 [Japan].)

PARADE (UK)

PAR 2006
London Mood
Details wanted.

PICKWICK (USA)

PMTD 16009
Mel Tormé Smooth as Velvet
1. One Morning in May
2. I Surrender Dear
3. Don't Worry 'Bout Me
4. (I Don't Stand) a Ghost of a Chance with You
5. Something to Live For
6. I'm Getting Sentimental Over You
7. I Can't Believe That You're in Love with Me
8. I Cover the Waterfront
9. Prelude to a Kiss
10. I've Got the World on a String
11. Between the Devil and the Deep Blues Sea
12. I Can't Give You Anything but Love
13. A Cottage for Sale
14. Don't Take Your Love from Me
15. Gone with the Wind
16. Love Me or Leave Me

PRESIDENT (UK)

PLCD 557
What Is This Thing Called Love? Artie Shaw
All tracks by Artie Shaw & his orchestra. Mel Tormé is present only on tracks where indicated.

1. Let's Walk
2. Love of My Life
3. How Deep Is the Ocean?
4. The Glider
5. The Hornet
6. They Can't Convince Me (MT)
7. I Got the Sun in the Morning (MT)
8. Along with Me (MT)
9. You Do Something to Me
10. In the Still of the Night
11. Begin the Beguine
12. My Heart Belongs to Daddy
13. Night and Day
14. What Is This Thing Called Love? (MT)
15. I've Got You Under My Skin
16. Get Out of Town (MT)
17. For You, for Me, for Evermore (MT)
18. Changing My Tune (MT)
19. Love for Sale
20. They Can't Convince Me (MT)
21. Guilty (MT)
22. And So to Bed (MT)
23. Don't You Believe It, Dear (MT)
24. It's the Same Old Dream (MT)
25. I Believe (MT)

PRISM (UK)

PLATCD 466
In the Mood for Love
This compilation contains one Tormé track.
Track 4: It's a Blue World

PLATCD 467
When I Fall in Love
This compilation contains one Tormé track.
Track 2: Polka Dust and Moonbeams (a mislabeling of "Polka Dots and Moonbeams")

PLATBX 821
Late Night Love
This is a box set containing 8 CDs including PLATCD 466 and 467

PULSE (UK)

PLS CD 342
Some tracks are with Artie Shaw and one with Bing Crosby
1. What Is This Thing Called Love?
2. Born to Be Blue
3. Night and Day
4. You're Driving Me Crazy
5. Try a Little Tenderness
6. It Happened in Monterey
7. Guilty
8. For You, for me, for Evermore
9. And So to Bed
10. A Stranger in Town
11. Get Out of Town
12. Willow Road
13. Day by Day
14. It's Dreamtime
15. I Got the Sun in the Morning
16. Changing My Tune
17. Don't You Believe It, Dear
18. Makin' Whoopee
19. Gone with the Wind
20. County Fair

RANWOOD (USA)

8270-2
Standards by Mel Tormé
1. Oh, You Beautiful Doll
2. My Buddy
3. Stompin' at the Savoy
4. Blue Moon
5. You're Getting to Be a Habit with Me
6. Heart and Soul
7. Bewitched
8. Around the World
9. Sonny Boy
10. Skylark
11. Anywhere I Wander
12. Shenandoah Valley
13. The Windmills of Your Mind
14. Raindrops Keep Fallin' on My Head

READER'S DIGEST MUSIC (USA)

RC7-012-1 (C) (3 CDs)

The Legendary Mel Tormé
(This set also has a computer stock number of 72438-19655-2-8.)

Disc 1 (RC7-012-1/1) *Careless Hands: Mel's Greatest Hits*
1. Careless Hands
2. Again
3. Blue Moon
4. The Four Winds and the Seven Seas
5. Bewitched
6. Anywhere I Wander
7. Heart and Soul
8. It's Dreamtime (*w The Mel-Tones*)
9. It's Too Late Now
10. It Happened in Monterey (*w The Mel-Tones*)

Night and Day: Classic Mel
11. Night and Day
12. My Buddy
13. Makin' Whoopee
14. County Fair
15. You're a Heavenly Thing
16. Got the Gate on the Golden Gate (*w The Mel-Tones and Chorus*)
17. The Old Master Painter (*w Peggy Lee*)
18. Cross Your Heart
19. A Foggy Day
20. P.S. I Love You

Disc 2 (RC7-012-1/2) *The Nearness of You: By Request*
1. The Nearness of You
2. Body and Soul
3. Where Can I Go Without You?
4. Forty-Second Street
5. How Did She Look?
6. Comin' Home Baby
7. Right Now
8. Lover's Roulette
9. You'd Better Love Me
10. The Folks Who Live on the Hill

A Time for Us: The Best of the '60s & '70s
11. Time for Us (Love Theme from Romeo and Juliet)
12. The Windmills of Your Mind
13. Raindrops Keep Fallin' on My Head
14. You've Made Me So Very Happy
15. Traces
16. A Stranger in Town
17. Spinning Wheel
18. Strangers in the Night
19. The Second Time Around
20. Yesterday, When I Was Young

Disc 3 (RC7-012-1/3) *That Old Feeling: Swingin' Favorites*
1. That Old Feeling
2. Too Close for Comfort
3. Swingin' on the Moon
4. Stompin' at the Savoy
5. On the Street Where You Live
6. Skylark
7. I've Got the Feeling I'm Falling
8. I Hadn't Anyone But You (*w The Mel-Tones and Chorus*)
9. Lullaby of the Leaves
10. I've Got You Under My Skin

Oh, You Beautiful Doll: The Vintage Years
11. Oh, You Beautiful Doll
12. I Love Each Move You Make
13. You're Getting to Be a Habit with Me
14. It's De-Lovely
15. I Remember Suzanne
16. I Should Care
17. 'Round Midnight
18. Paris Smiles
19. Only the Very Young
20. The Christmas Song (Chestnuts Roasting on an Open Fire)

RHAPSODY (UK)

RH CD 3
Mel Tormé: Tormé
1. All in Love Is Fair
2. The First Time Ever I Saw Your Face
3. New York State of Mind
4. Stars
5. Send in the Clowns
6. Ordinary Fool
7. Medley: When the World Was Young, Yesterday When I Was Young
8. Bye Bye Blackbird

RHINO (USA)

R2 7295
  see Collectors' Choice Music
  CCM0074-2

R2 71505
  Great American Songwriters
  This compilation contains one track by Mel Tormé:
  Mountain Greenery

R2 71507
  Great American Songwriters
  This compilation contains one track by Mel Tormé:
  Take the "A" Train

R2 71589 (4 CD box set)
  The Mel Tormé Collection

Disc One:
1. Where or When?
2. A Stranger in Town
3. Day by Day
4. Willow Road
5. Born to Be Blue
6. What Is This Thing Called Love?
7. Get Out of Town
8. For You, for Me, Forevermore
9. It's Dreamtime
10. Gone with the Wind
11. A Cottage for Sale
12. Makin' Whoopee
13. Night and Day
14. County Fair
15. Three Little Words
16. Love Me or Leave Me
17. How High the Moon
18. Careless Hands
19. Blue Moon
20. Again
21. The Four Winds and the Seven Seas
22. Got the Gate on the Golden Gate
23. Cross Your Heart
24. Bewitched
25. It Don't Mean a Thing (If It Ain't Got That Swing)
26. All of You

Disc Two:
1. That Old Black Magic
2. Mountain Greenery
3. Bernie's Tune
4. Goody, Goody
5. I Got It Bad and That Ain't Good
6. All This and Heaven Too
7. Isn't It Romantic?
8. Lulu's Back in Town
9. The Blues
10. Lullaby of Birdland
11. The Carioca
12. Fascinating Rhythm
13. The Lady Is a Tramp
14. I've Got Plenty of Nuthin'
15. Nice Work If You Can Get It
16. The Way You Look Tonight
17. A Foggy Day
18. Something's Gotta Give
19. Cheek to Cheek
20. Just One of Those Things
21. I'm Beginning to See the Light
22. It's All Right with Me
23. Autumn Leaves
24. Poor Little Extra Girl

Disc Three:
1. A Nightingale Sang in Berkeley Square
2. These Foolish Things
3. Try a Little Tenderness
4. Prelude to a Kiss
5. I Let a Song Go Out of My Heart
6. Blues in the Night
7. Vaya Con Dios
8. Frenesi
9. At the Crossroads (Malaguena)
10. It Happened in Monterey
11. Too Close for Comfort
12. Swingin' on the Moon
13. Medley from "Wildcat" (Margaret Whiting)
14. I'm Gonna Move to the Outskirts of Town
15. Sent for You Yesterday (and Here You Come Today)
16. By Myself
17. (Ah, the Apple Trees) When the World Was Young
18. It's Delovely

19. Dat Dere
20. On Green Dolphin Street
21. Walkin' Shoes

Disc Four:
1. Comin' Home Baby
2. Right Now
3. Cast Your Fate to the Winds
4. Hey, Look Me Over!
5. Forty Second Street
6. Sunday in New York
7. You'd Better Love Me
8. I've Got You Under My Skin
9. The Folks That Live on the Hill
10. Haven't We Met?
11. Strangers in the Night
12. A Day in the Life of Bonnie and Clyde
13. Yesterday When I Was Young
14. What Are You Doing the Rest of Your Life?
15. Gershwin Medley: a. I Got Rhythm, b. Mine, c. Do-Do-Do, d. 'S Wonderful, e. Embraceable You, f. Love Walked In, g. Love Is Here to Stay, h. Oh, Lady Be Good, i. A Foggy Day, j. How Long Has This Been Going On?, k. Oh Bess, O Where's My Bess?, l. Who Cares?, m. Love Is Sweeping the Country, n. Of Thee I Sing, o. Swanee, p. Strike Up the Band, q. I'll Build a Stairway to Paradise
16. Pick Yourself Up
17. The Best Is Yet to Come
18. Zaz Turned Blue
19. Big City Blues
20. Theme from Arthur (Best That You Can Do)
21. The Christmas Song

R2 72473
Masters of Jazz Vol. 6: Male Vocal Classics
This compilation includes one track by Mel Tormé:
Track 16: Whisper Not

R2 72886
see Rhino Flashback

R2 75481
Mel Tormé: At the Movies
This might also be considered a Turner issue since it has the legend "Turner Classic Movies" as well as the "Rhino" logo
1. Mrs. Whiffen (Outtake)
2. Minuet in Boogie
3. The Best Things in Life Are Free
4. Lucky in Love
5. Be a Ladies Man
6. Just Imagine (Outtake)
7. Lucky in Love (Reprise) (Outtake)
8. Blue Moon
9. Warm Hands, Cold Heart (Outtake)
10. Walk Like a Dragon
11. Sunday in New York
12. Love Is Just Around the Corner (Live)
13. These Desperate Hours
14. On Green Dolphin Street
15. The Lady's in Love with You
16. Puttin' on the Ritz
17. I Wished on the Moon
18. All That Jazz
19. Monsters Lead Such Interesting Lives
20. Live Alone and Like It

R2 75732
see Avenue Jazz

RHINO FLASHBACK (USA)

R2 72886
Mel Tormé: Comin' Home Baby and Other Hits
1. Comin' Home Baby
2. (Get Your Kicks) on Route 66
3. Mountain Greenery
4. Cast Your Fate to the Winds
5. Sunday in New York
6. Lullaby of Birdland
7. Broadway
8. New York, New York
9. It's Delovely
10. Puttin' on the Ritz

ST MICHAEL (UK)

9599 222
Voices of Jazz
This compilation contains one track by Mel Tormé
track 8: Blue Moon (Verve version)

SANDSTONE (USA)

SAN 5005
Mel Tormé: The London Sessions
1. All in Love Is Fair
2. The First Time Ever I Saw Your Face
3. New York State of Mind
4. Stars
5. Send in the Clowns
6. Ordinary Fool
7. Medley: When the World Was Young, Yesterday When I Was Young
8. Bye Bye Blackbird

SIMITAR (USA)

55002
Mel Tormé: Prelude to a Kiss
1. Dialogue
2. I've Got the World on a String
3. Dialogue
4. Don't Worry 'Bout Me
5. Dialogue
6. One Morning in May
7. Dialogue
8. I Can't Give You Anything but Love
9. Dialogue
10. Between the Devil and the Deep Blue Sea
11. Dialogue
12. I Don't Stand a Ghost of a Chance with You
13. Dialogue
14. I'm Getting Sentimental Over You
15. Dialogue
16. I Can't Believe That You're in Love with Me
17. Dialogue
18. Prelude to a Kiss
19. Dialogue
20. Something to Live For
21. Dialogue
22. I Surrender Dear
23. Dialogue
24. I Let a Song Go Out of My Heart
25. Dialogue

Has dialogue between the tracks.

SMITHSONIAN (USA)

RD-113
The Jazz Singers
Details wanted. Includes "Down for Double" by Mel Tormé

SONY (USA)

AK-47025
Good News. Motion Picture Soundtrack
The artists include The MGM Studio Orchestra, June Allyson, Peter Lawford, Joan McCracken, Patricia Marshall and Mel Tormé. Tormé can be heard on the indicated tracks.
Title Music (MGM)
Title Music
Good News (JM)
Visit to the Dean (MGM)
Varsity Drag (JA, PL)
Pass That Peace Pipe (JM)
Lucky in Love (MT, JA)
Just Imagine (MT, JA)
He's a Ladies Man (MT, PL)
Good News (Tait College) (JM)
The French Lesson (JA, PL)
Easier Way (JA, PM)
Big Game (MGM)
The Best Things in Live Are Free (JA)
The Best Things in Life Are Free (MT, PL)

SOUNDIES (USA)

SCD4110

The Complete World Transcriptions
1. I Concentrate on You
2. In Love in Vain
3. Long Ago and Far Away
4. Star Eyes
5. The Night We Called It a Day
6. Day In, Day Out
7. The Christmas Song
8. I Could Have Told You So
9. All in Fun
10. Where Are You?
11. It's Easy to Remember
12. Too Late Now
13. Isn't It Romantic?
14. You Make Me Feel So Young
15. You Took Advantage of Me
16. I Understand
17. Too Darn Hot
18. Nina
19. Sure Thing
20. It Never Entered My Mind
21. I Never Had a Chance
22. I Wish I Were in Love Again
23. The Glory of Love
24. Day Dreaming
25. Time Was

SPECTRUM (UK)

552 637-2
With a Song in My Heart — The Classic Songs of Rodgers & Hart
This compilation includes one track by Mel Tormé.
track 17: Nobody's Heart

552645-2
You're the Tops — The Classic Songs of Cole Porter
This compilation includes one track by Mel Tormé.
track 1: Too Darn Hot

ST MICHAEL (UK)

CMD007
Voices of Jazz
This compilation contains one track by Mel Tormé.
track 8: Blues Moon (Verve version)

STASH (USA)

ST-CD- 4
Mel Tormé: A Retrospective 1956–1968
1. I've Got a World That Swings
2. Quiet Nights of Quiet Stars
3. Comin' Home Baby
4. Sidney's Soliloquy
5. Dat Dere
6. When Sunny Gets Blue
7. Li'l Darlin'
8. Fascinatin' Rhythm
9. Four Brothers
10. Lonely Girl
11. Bluesette
12. That Face *interpolating* Look at That Face
13. Gone with the Wind
14. That Old Feeling
15. Don't Let That Moon Get Away
16. All I Need Is the Girl
17. I'll Be Seeing You
18. Lulu's Back in Town
19. When the Sun Comes Out
20. The Lady Is a Tramp
21. Hello, Young Lovers
22. A Foggy Day
23. Porgy and Bess Medley
24. Hey, Look Me Over
25. The Surrey with the Fringe on Top
26. The Lady's in Love with You
27. 'Round Midnight

TELARC JAZZ

CD-83315
Mel Tormé: Christmas Songs
1. Christmas Medley: Jingle Bells, Santa Claus Is Coming to Town, Winter Weather, Winter Wonderland

2. Sleigh Ride
  3. The Christmas Song
  4. Glow Worm
  5. The Christmas Feeling
  6. It Happened in Sun Valley
  7. Christmastime Is Here
  8. Good King Wenceslas
  9. What Child Is This? (instrumental)
  10. Silver Bells
  11. Christmas Was Made for Children
  12. The Christmas Waltz
  13. Just Look Around / Have Yourself a Merry Little Christmas
  14. God Rest Ye Merry Gentlemen (instrumental)
  15. Happy Holiday / Let's Start the New Year Right/ What Are You Doing New Year's Eve?
  16. White Christmas

CD-83328
Mel Tormé: The Great American Songbook — Live at Michael's Pub
  1. You Gotta Try
  2. Ridin' High/ I'm Shootin' High
  3. You Make Me Feel So Young
  4. Stardust
  5. I'm Gonna Go Fishin'
  6. Don't Get Around Much Anymore/I Let a Song Go Out of My Heart
  7. Sophisticated Lady/ I Didn't Know About You
  8. Rockin' in Rhythm
  9. It Don't Mean a Thing If It Ain't Got That Swing
  10. A Lovely Way to Spend an Evening
  11. I'll Remember April/ I Concentrate on You
  12. Autumn in New York
  13. Just One of Those Things/ Green Dolphin Street
  14. All God's Chillun' Got Rhythm
  15. The Party's Over

TURNER (USA)
SEE ALSO RHINO
7243 8 21963 2 7
  Bachelor in Paradise: Cocktail Classics from M-G-M Films
  This compilation contains one track by Mel Tormé.
  track 4: Sunday in New York

TURNER (UK)
821 963
  Bachelor in Paradise: Cocktail Classics from M-G-M Films
  (Reissue of US 7243 8 21963 2 7.)

UNITED AUDIO ENTERTAINMENT
SEE MEMBERS EDITION

VERVE (USA)
  Many of these CDs have also been pressed and issued in Europe using the same catalog numbers

311 511 070-2
  I Get a Kick Out of You — Cole Porter
  This compilation contains one track by Mel Tormé:
  Too Darn Hot
314 511 522-2
  Mel Tormé with the Meltones: Back in Town
  1. Makin' Whoopee
  2. Baubles, Bangles and Beads
  3. What Is This Thing Called Love?
  4. I've Never Been in Love Before
  5. Truckin'
  6. A Bunch of the Blues: Keester Parade, TNT, Tiny's Blues
  7. It Happened in Monterey
  8. I Hadn't Anyone 'Til You
  9. A Smooth One
  10. Don't Dream of Anybody but Me (Li'l Darlin')
  11. Some Like It Hot

12. Hit the Road to Dreamland
13. I Hadn't Anyone 'Til You (alternate version)

314 521 656-2
Jazz 'Round Midnight: Mel Tormé
1. Hello Young Lovers
2. How High the Moon
3. How Did She Look?
4. Li'l Darlin (a.k.a. "Don't Dream of Anybody But Me")
5. Alone Together
6. A Sleepin' Bee
7. Blue and Sentimental
8. I Wished on the Moon
9. Just in Time
10. Body and Soul
11. I Hadn't Anyone 'Til You
12. Moonlight in Vermont
13. Lonely Town
14. 'Round Midnight
15. Blue Moon
16. Born to Be Blue

314 557 539-2
The Complete Johnny Mercer Songbooks
This is a 3 CD set that includes the CD 553 268-2 (qv) which contains one Mel Tormé track.

511 385-2
Swingin' on the Moon: Mel Tormé
1. Swingin' on the Moon
2. Moonlight Cocktail
3. I Wished on the Moon
4. Moon Song
5. How High the Moon
6. Don't Let That Moon Get Away
7. Blue Moon
8. A Velvet Affair
9. No Moon at All
10. Moonlight in Vermont
11. Oh, You Crazy Moon
12. The Moon Was Yellow

553 268-2
Blues in the Night: The Johnny Mercer Song Book
This compilation contains one track by Mel Tormé.
track 4: Hit the Road to Dreamland

This CD was also issued as part of a 3 CD set (314 557 539-2)

821 581-2
Mel Tormé Swings Shubert Alley
1. Too Close for Comfort
2. Once in Love with Amy
3. A Sleepin' Bee
4. On the Street Where You Live
5. All I Need Is the Girl
6. Just in Time
7. Hello Young Lovers
8. The Surrey with the Fringe on Top
9. Old Devil Moon
10. Whatever Lola Wants
11. Too Darn Hot
12. Lonely Town

823 010-2
Tormé
1. That Old Feeling
2. Gloomy Sunday
3. Body and Soul
4. Nobody's Heart
5. I Should Care
6. The House Is Haunted by the Echo of Your Last Goodbye
7. Blues in the Night
8. I Don't Want to Cry Anymore
9. Where Can I Go Without You?
10. How Did She Look?
11. 'Round Midnight
12. I'm Gonna Laugh You Out of My Life
13. I'm Shooting High
14. These Desperate Hours
15. Her Face
16. Yes, Indeed

823 248-2
Mel Tormé: The Duke Ellington & Count Basie Songbooks
1. I'm Gonna Go Fishin'
2. Don't Get Around Much Anymore
3. I Like the Sunrise
4. Take the "A" Train
5. Reminiscin' in Tempo
6. Just a Sittin' and a Rockin'
7. Down for Double
8. I'm Gonna Move to the Outskirts of Town

9. Blue and Sentimental
   10. Oh, What a Night for Love
   11. Sent for You Yesterday (And Here You Come Today)
   12. In the Evening (When the Sun Goes Down)
833 282-2
   Compact Jazz: Mel Tormé
   1. Too Close for Comfort
   2. A Stranger in Town
   3. Don't Get Around Much Anymore
   4. Body & Soul
   5. The Surrey with the Fringe on Top
   6. Welcome to the Club
   7. Sent for You Yesterday
   8. Truckin'
   9. Born to Be Blue
   10. Whatever Lola Wants
   11. 'Round Midnight
   12. Take the "A" Train
   13. Blue Moon
   14. Just in Time
   15. Blue and Sentimental
   16. The Christmas Song

VERVE (UK)

No Verve CDs are manufactured in the UK but some of the Verve (USA) issues were imported into and distributed in the UK. All the issues listed under Verve (Germany) were imported into and distributed in the UK.

VERVE (GERMANY)

821 581-2
   Mel Tormé Swings Shubert Alley
   Reissue of US issue 821 581-2

823 010-2
   Tormé
   (Reissue of US issue 823 010-2.)
823 248-2
   The Duke Ellington and Count Basie Songbooks
   (Reissue of US issue 823 248-2.)
833 282-2
   Compact Jazz: Mel Tormé
   (Reissue of US issue 833 282-2.)

VERVE (JAPAN)

J25J-25136
   Olé Tormé
   CD version of Verve MG-V6 2117
POCJ-2139
   Ole Tormé
   CD version of Verve MG-V6 2117
POCJ-2665
   Ole Tormé
   CD version of Verve MG-V6 8440

WILEY ENTERTAINMENTS (USA ?)

Judy Duets / Judy at the Palace
   This set has no catalog number and no label name. "Wiley Entertainments" appears on the cardboard outer sleeve which contains two CDs. One CD is from a performance by Judy Garland at the New York Palace in February 1952. The other CD contains extracts from the soundtracks of Garland's CBS television shows in the winter season 1963–64. Mel Tormé is on only one track, a duet with Garland.
   track 5: The Trolley Song

PART 4

FILMS AND VIDEOS

Drama and Documentary

1938/9 **Unknown title** (the "star" was Paul Ash). Mel Tormé sings "Whose Sweet Patootie Are You?"

1943/4 **Higher and Higher** Mel Tormé plays the part of Marty.

1944 **Pardon My Rhythm** Mel Tormé plays the part of Ricky O'Bannon.

1944 **Ghost Catchers** Mel Tormé plays the part of a drummer.

1945 **Junior Miss** Mel Tormé plays the part of Sterling Brown.

1945 **Let's Go Steady** Mel Tormé plays the part of "Streak" Edwards.

1945 **Night and Day** Mel Tormé plays the part of a drummer in a band hired for a garden party.

1945 **Movieland Magic** Mel Tormé plays the part of a guide taking visitors on a tour of a movie lot.

1945 **Mel Tormé and His Mel-Tones** (Soundies) Mel Tormé and the Mel-Tones with Buddy Cole and his group (see The Mel-Tones Soundies p. 163).

1946 **Choo Choo Amigo** (Frank Tashlin animated short movie) Mel Tormé and his Mel-Tones perform on the soundtrack.

1946 **Janie Gets Married** Mel Tormé plays one of the G.I.s singing about being overseas.

1947 **Good News** Mel Tormé plays the part of Danny.

1948 **Words and Music** Mel Tormé plays the part of a bandleader at a party.

1950 **The Duchess of Idaho** Mel Tormé plays the part of Cyril.

1950s **Meet the Singers, Volume 2** Mel Tormé performs.

1958 **The Fearmakers** Mel Tormé plays the part of Barney Bond.

1958/9 ***The Big Operator*** Mel Tormé plays the part of Fred McAfee. Also issued as "Anatomy of the Syndicate."

1958 ***Girls' Town*** Mel Tormé plays the part of Fred Alger. Also issued as "The Innocent and the Damned."

1958/60 ***The Private Lives of Adam and Eve*** Mel Tormé plays the part of Hal Sanders.

1958 ***Night Light*** no details of Tormé's involvement.

1958 ***Stars of Jazz, Volume 1*** Mel Tormé is one of the performers.

1960 ***Walk Like a Dragon*** Mel Tormé plays the part of the Deacon.

1963 ***Sunday in New York*** Mel Tormé sings the Credit Title song.

1964 ***Patsy*** Mel Tormé appears as himself.

1966 ***A Man Called Adam*** Mel Tormé appears as himself and sings the film's theme — twice.

1970 ***Lionel Hampton's One Night Stand*** Mel Tormé performs.

1974 ***The Snowman*** (made for TV) Mel Tormé plays the part of Zak O'Brien. Also issued as "Challenge to Survive" and "Land of No Return."

1981 ***Land of No Return*** Mel Tormé is a member of the cast.

1982 ***Hotel*** (made for TV) Mel Tormé appears as himself.

1982 ***Pray TV*** (made for TV) Mel Tormé appears as himself. Also issued as "Mixed Blessings."

1983 ***Mel Torme*** (documentary) Mel Tormé performs.

1983 ***Mel Torme Special*** (documentary) Mel Tormé performs.

1984 ***Barry Manilow 2:00 AM Paradise Café*** This is a video of the rehearsal for Manilow's Arista album of the same name. Mel Tormé performs "Big City Blues" as a duet with Barry Manilow. Issued in the UK as Video Collection VC 4008.

1985 ***Artie Shaw: Time Is All You've Got*** (documentary) Mel Tormé is a contributor.

1988/9 ***Daffy Duck: Quackbusters*** (animated cartoon series) Mel Tormé provides the voice of Daffy Duck both speech and singing.

1989 ***Dick Tracy*** (animated cartoon) Mel Tormé provides an "off-screen" song.

1990 ***Colt Firearms Legends*** (documentary video) Narrated by Mel Tormé.

1991 ***Naked Gun 2½: The Smell of Fear*** (sequel to *The Naked Gun*) Mel Tormé appears as himself.

1992 ***The Return of Spinal Tap*** (a sequel to "Spinal Tap") Mel Tormé is a member of the cast. Also issued as "The Spinal Tap Reunion."

1996 ***A & E Biography Series: Mel Tormé — Smooth As Velvet*** (ISBN 1 5650 1763 3) Mel Tormé is the subject of the biography and performs.

--- ***Mel Torme*** No details. Issued in the U.K. as Video VIDSP 9.

Musical Stage Performances

Performances are listed only if a commercial video has been released.

1964 **Jazz Casual: Mel Tormé** Live show from 1964.

1981 **Mel Torme and Della Reese in Concert** Live performance filmed in Edmonton, Canada. Also available in laserdisc format.

1986 **Monterey Jazz Festival** Performers include Mel Tormé, Woody Herman and Joe Williams.

1991 **Mel Tormé: A Night At the Ambassador** On stage performance by Mel Tormé at the Ambassador Auditorium, Pasadena, California.

--- **Nat King Cole — Unforgettable** Mel Tormé is a contributor to this tribute to Nat King Cole.

--- **Buddy Rich, Jazz Legend, Part 1: 1917 to 1970; Part 2: 1970 to 1987** Mel Tormé is a contributor to this biography of Buddy Rich.

Television Shows

Performances are listed only if a commercial video has been released.

1949 **The Ed Wynn Show, Volume 1** Three shows from the TV series. Includes an appearance by Mel Tormé.

1950 **Snader film transcriptions** Mel Tormé made at least 5 Snader transcriptions for use on television.

1950 **Ken Murray Show, guest — Mel Tormé** One show from a television series. Mel Tormé appeared as a guest.

1957 **Playhouse 90, Volume 1: The Comedian** (14th February 1957) Mel Tormé plays the part of Mickey Rooney's brother.

1960/1 **The Jo Stafford Show, guest — Mel Tormé** One show each from "The Swingin' Singin' Years" and "The Jo Stafford Show." Mel Tormé appears as a guest on one show.

1963/4 **The Judy Garland Show** See below.

1969 **The Name of the Game: Pineapple Rose** (20th December 1968) Mel Tormé is a member of the cast.

Songs in Films

Mel Tormé is acknowledged as introducing these songs in motion pictures.

1947 **Lucky in Love** (with Peter Lawford and June Allyson) in *Good News*

1948 **Blue Moon** in *Words and Music*

1964 **Sunday in New York** in *Sunday in New York*

The Judy Garland Show

From June 1963 to February 1964, Mel Tormé was a musical associate on *The Judy Garland Show*, made for CBS Television and shown on Sunday nights at 9 P.M. EST from 12th August 1963 to 29th March 1964. His role was that of a writer of special musical material. This involved liaising with Garland and her guests over the material that they would perform in the shows and then writing the musical arrangements and additional lyrics that were needed. In addition, he appeared as a performer on four shows. Tormé was not involved in the last two shows in the series. The list below is a simple listing of the shows with the relevant dates and the names of the guests. Details of the four shows on which Tormé performed as a guest are given in Part 2, where the issues on audio discs will also be found.

The shows are listed in the sequence in which they were recorded.

The orchestra conductor for the series was Mort Lindsey. Jack Elliott was the musical arranger and coordinator for some of the shows. The co-host for the first ten episodes was Jerry Van Dyke who also performed some of his own material.

Extracts from some of the shows were issued on LaserLight video 80515 and video 85701 and on videos issued by Universal/MCA (as *Judy Garland and Friends*) and as one part (*The Best of the Judy Garland Show*) of a 3-cassette package by Century Media (*The Judy Garland Collection*).

Extracts from the soundtracks were issued on Capitol W 2062—*Just for Openers* (LP album), Paragon 1001 (LP album), Broadcast Tributes BTRIB 0002 (LP album) and in 32 Records *The Box* (2 CD set with 100-page book—no catalog number), Wiley Entertainments *Judy Duets / Judy at the Palace* (2 CD set with 24-page booklet & 4-page leaflet—no catalog number), LaserLight 12 467 (this is the whole of the Christmas show apart from some of the non-vocal music and solo songs by Joey Luft and Mel Tormé). Extracts from the soundtracks of other shows also appeared on LaserLight CD set: 12480—*Come Rain or Come Shine*; 12 481—*Over the Rainbow*; 12 482—*The Man That Got Away*; 12 483—*Stormy Weather*; 12 484—*Fly Me to the Moon*. These were issued individually and also collectively in a 5-CD set, LaserLight 15 942—*The Judy Garland Show*.

The material on the individual CDs was also issued as cassettes with the catalog number 72 xxx in place of the 12 xxx e.g., 72 567 for 12 567. The 5-CD set was not issued in cassette format.

Episode number	*Date of recording*	*Date of transmission*	*Show number*
1	24th June 1963 *Guest: Mickey Rooney.* *Issued on a Pioneer* *DVD Video disc*	8th December 1963	10
2	7th July 1963 *Guests: Count Basie* *and his Orchestra,* *Judy Henske, Mel Tormé.*	10th November 1963	7

Episode number	Date of recording	Date of transmission	Show number
3	16th July 1963 *Guests: The Castro Brothers, Liza Minnelli, Soupy Sales. Issued on a Pioneer DVD video disc*	17th November 1963	8
4	23rd July 1963 *Guests: Lena Horne, Terry-Thomas.*	13th October 1963	3
5	30th July 1963 *Guests: Tony Bennett, Dick Shawn.*	15th December 1963	11
6	13th September 1963 *Guests: June Allyson, Steve Lawrence.*	27th October 1963	5
7	20th September 1963 *Guest: Donald O'Connor.*	29th September 1963	1
8	27th September 1963 *Guests: Jack Carter, The Dillards, Leo Durocher, George Maharis.*	20th October 1963	4
9	4th October 1963 *Guests: Ethel Merman, The Smothers Brothers, Barbra Streisand.*	6th October 1963	2
10	11th October 1963 *Guests: Roy Bolger, Jane Powell.*	1st March 1964	22
11	18th October 1963 *Guests: Steve Allen, Jayne Meadows, Mel Tormé.*	5th January 1964	14
12	1st November 1963 *Guests: Zina Bethune, Vic Damone, George Jessel.*	3rd November 1963	6

162 • FILMS AND VIDEOS

Episode number	Date of recording	Date of transmission	Show number
13	8th November 1963 *Guests: Jack Carter, Peggy Lee, Carl Reiner.*	1st December 1963	9
14	30th November 1963 *Guests: Bobby Darin, Bob Newhart.*	29th December 1963	13
15	6th December 1963 *Guests: Tracy Everitt, Jack Jones, Joey Luft, Lorna Luft, Liza Minnelli, Mel Tormé. Issued on LaserLight video 82467 and on Warner Reprise video 38267-3 and in a Sony package that consists of a video and two CDs*	22nd December 1963 (the Christmas show)	12
16	13th December 1963 *Guests: Shelley Berman, Peter Gennaro, Ethel Merman.*	12th January 1964	15
17	20th December 1963 *Guests: Vic Damone, Ken Murray, Nye Louis, Chita Rivera.*	19th January 1964	16
18	14th January 1964 *Guests: Peter Lawford, Rich Little, Ken Murray, Martha Raye.*	26th January 1964	17
19	17th January 1964 *Guests: Louis Jourdan, The Kirby Stone Four, Ken Murray.*	2nd February 1964	18
20	24th January 1964 *Guests: none.*	9th February 1964	19
21	31st January 1964 *Guests: Diahann Carroll, Mel Tormé.*	16th February 1964	20

Episode number	Date of recording	Date of transmission	Show number
22	14th February 1964 Guests: Jack Jones, Ken Murray.	23rd February 1964	21
23*	21st February 1964 Guests: none.	8th March 1964	23
24*	23rd February 1964 Guest: Vic Damone.	15th March 1964	24
25*	6th March 1964 Guest: Robert Cole.	22nd March 1964	25
26*	13th March 1964 Guests: none.	29th March 1964	26

*Mel Tormé was not involved in these four shows.

For those who wish to understand the tribulations of putting together a television series such as this one, there are two books that should be read. They are:

Mel Tormé—*The Other Side of the Rainbow*

Coyne Steven Sanders—*Rainbow's End: The Judy Garland Show*

The Mel-Tones Soundies

The Mel-Tones made four "soundies" for R.C.M. Productions, one of many companies producing short subjects for Soundies Distributing Corporation of America. At the time, these films were used in visual juke boxes but more recently, they have been seen on television. None, to my knowledge, has been issued commercially to the public.

THE MEL-TONES WITH
MEL TORME AND HIS ORCHESTRA

"Dan Koral," Bernie Parke, Les Baxter, Ginny O'Connor, Betty Beveridge, vocals; with instrumental accompaniment by Buddy Cole, piano; Nick Pelico, vibes; Dave Barbour, guitar; Phil Stephens, bass; Nick Fatool, drums.
Soundtracks: Hollywood, 30th July 1945.
Visuals: Los Angeles (?), 14th August 1945.
Dance, Baby, Dance (Tantze Babele) (composer credit is to Tormé)
Back Home in Indiana
Lullaby of Broadway
Juanita.
Mel Tormé maintained that he had nothing to do with the production of these soundies but his name and signature are on the contract as musical director. Musical arrangements are attributed to Tormé and Les Baxter and, according to Ginny

Mancini (née O'Connor), in discussion with Mark Cantor, Tormé was responsible for the vocal arrangements with Baxter handling the instrumental arrangements. In a contemporary magazine, *Band Leaders*, Vol. 3, No. 1, January 1946, there is a photograph showing the Mel-Tones and Mel Tormé with Buddy Cole who is seated at a piano. The caption is "Buddy Cole gives the Mel-tones [sic] the musical business before waxing a recent record date for a Soundie. Cole's becoming one of the ace men in the business."

In conversation with Mark Cantor, Tormé claimed never to have heard of Dan Koral and yet the voice on the soundtrack sounds remarkably like Tormé himself. The additional vocalist seen on the visuals is definitely not Tormé. When Mark Cantor asked Ginny Mancini about the session, she remembered Tormé as definitely being present and this is borne out by his presence in the photograph in *Band Leaders*."

My theory is that as Tormé was under contract to a major film studio at the time, he was able to write the arrangements and permitted to perform vocally but was not able to appear on screen. It was thus necessary for a stand-in to take his place during the filming of the visual element.

PART 5

BOOKS

Tormé as Author

Dollarhide (1955) A novel in the "Western" genre. This was written under the pseudonym Wesley Butler Whyatt.

The Other Side of the Rainbow (1970) The story of a Judy Garland TV series. A slightly revised edition was published in paperback in 1991.

Wynner (1978) A novel.

It Wasn't All Velvet (1988) Autobiography.

Traps, the Drum Wonder (1991) A Biography of Buddy Rich.

My Singing Teachers (1994) An analysis of selected singers, musicians and song writers.

Tormé as Contributor

World of Gene Krupa (Bruce H. Klauber and Eugene D. Wheeler, Pathfinder, 1990) Mel Tormé contributed a Foreword to this book.

Drummin' Man: The Heartbeat of Jazz—The Swing Years (Burt Korall, Simon and Schuster, 1990) Mel Tormé contributed a Foreword to this book. He is also extensively quoted in the book.

Back Beats and Rim Shots—The Johnny Blowers Story (Warren W. Vache, Scarecrow, 1997) Mel Tormé contributed a Foreword to this book.

Tormé as Subject

There is no general biography of Mel Tormé other than the one that he wrote himself. However, he does have a biographical entry in virtually every directory, dictionary and guide to jazz. In addition, there are substantial sections and chapters in a number of books including these three which I regard as among the best.

American Singers—Twenty Seven Portraits in Song (Whitney Balliett, Oxford, 1988)

Jazz Singing (Will Friedwald, Collier/Macmillan, 1992)

Singing Jazz (Bruce Crowther & Mike Pinfold, Blandford/Cassell, 1997)

PART 6

MISCELLANY

The Hit Parade

These recordings by Mel Tormé reached the hit parade in the USA: 1949 **Careless Hands** (Capitol);

1949 **Blue Moon** (Capitol), #2 in the Billboard and Cash Box charts;

1956 **Mountain Greenery** (Coral);

1962 **Comin' Home Baby** (Atlantic) #19

These songs by Mel Tormé were hits for other artists:

1941 **Lament to Love** recorded by Harry James and his Orchestra (Vocal: Dick Haymes);

1946 **The Christmas Song** recorded by Nat King Cole

These recordings by Mel Tormé reached the hit parade in the United Kingdom:

1956 **Mountain Greenery** (Vogue-Coral) This reached number 4.;

1963 **Comin' Home Baby** (London-Atlantic) This reached number 13.

"Desert Island Discs"

"Desert Island Discs" is a long-running BBC Radio program in which celebrities are invited to choose and discuss eight records that they would like to have with them if they were to be marooned on a desert island. Mel Tormé was on the program broadcast on 24th July 1976 and these were his choices.

1. "Westwood Walk," Gerry Mulligan and his Ten-tette
2. Percy Grainger's "My Robin Is to the Greenwood Gone," Eastman-Rochester Pops Orchestra (Fennell)
3. Frederic Chopin's "Prelude No. 7 in A major," Jimmy Lunceford and his Orchestra
4. "The Christmas Song," Nat King Cole
5. Frederick Delius's "On Hearing the First Cuckoo in Spring," Royal Philharmonic Orchestra (Beecham)

6. "The Carioca," Artie Shaw and his Orchestra
7. "Reminiscing in Tempo," Duke Ellington and his Orchestra
8. "Dusk," Light Music Society Orchestra (Dunn)

In addition, the contributor is invited to select a book, other than the works of William Shakespeare and the Bible. Tormé chose *The New York Times' Film Directory*.

Nominations and Awards

Nominations

1957: Nomination, Emmy Awards. Best supporting actor. "The Comedian" (Playhouse 90, TV)

1974: Nomination, Grammy Awards. Best arrangement. The Gershwin Medley in "Mel Tormé: Live at the Maisonette"

1985: Nomination, Grammy Awards. Best Male Vocalist. "An Evening at Charlie's" (with George Shearing) (lost to Joe Williams)

1886: Nomination, Grammy Awards. With George Shearing, "An Elegant Evening"

1888: Nomination, Grammy Awards. With George Shearing, "A Vintage Year"

1891: Nomination, Grammy Awards. With George Shearing, "Mel and George 'Do' World War II"

1994: Nomination, Grammy Awards. "A Tribute to Bing Crosby: Paramount's Greatest Singer"

Awards

1976: Edison Award, The Netherlands. Best Male Vocalist

1977: Edison Award, The Netherlands. Best Male Vocalist

1982: Grammy Award. Best Jazz Male Vocalist. "An Evening with George Shearing and Mel Tormé"

1983: Grammy Award. Best Jazz Male Vocalist. "Top Drawer"

1983: Emmy Award. Best Documentary Profile. The segment with Mel Tormé on the *20/20* TV program

1999: National Academy of Recordings Arts and Sciences. Lifetime Achievement Award.

Appendix 1: Alternative Takes

These pieces of information are intended to assist in the identification of the alternative takes that have been issued for records involving Mel Tormé. I am indebted to Tony Cox for this information.

1. **What Is This Thing Called Love**, Artie Shaw and his Orchestra. Musicraft master 5548, recorded 19th June 1946

    The take issued on Musicraft 78 and reissues. At about 2:12, in Tormé's solo vocal, there is a drum break under Tormé singing ... "and threw it away." At 2:46, the Mel-Tones sing "what is this thing (pause) called love." The pause is silent.

    Alternative take, issued on Everest FS-248. There is no drum break under "and threw it away." In the pause in "what is this thing ... called love," there is a distinct drum beat.

2. **They Can't Convince Me**, Artie Shaw and his Orchestra, Musicraft master 5647, recorded 10th September 1946

    The take issued on Musicraft 78 and LP MVS507 (take -3 shown on the 78). At 2:00, Tormé sings "doesn't she walk and talk, like ordinary people do." The word "and" is clearly enunciated.

    Alternative take, issued on Musicraft LP MVS503. The word "and" is almost lost.

APPENDIX 2: A DISCOGRAPHICAL PROBLEM

In the biography of Johnny Blowers by Warren W. Vaché,* there are two references involving recording sessions with Tormé.

On pages 96–97 there is a quotation from Blowers' journal. The year is not stated but, from the context, it is 1949. The relevant entries are:

Oct. 28 — Played a very nice date for Capitol with Mel Tormé and Pete Rugolo.

Dec. 11 — Date at Decca with Ella Fitzgerald. Sy Oliver has become house leader. We recorded a song called "Smooth Sailing." Ella was backed by the Ray Charles Singers from the Perry Como show with Bill Doggett on organ, bass, guitar, and drums.

Dec. 12 — Decca again, with Gordon Jenkins conducting and Louis Armstrong singing his classic "Blueberry Hill." Only made one side.

Dec. 14 — Decca with Sy Oliver, Ella and Louis.

Dec. 19 — Another Capitol date with Tormé and Rugolo.

I have the Capitol session sheets for all Tormé Capitol sessions in this period that produced an issued master. There is nothing on October 28 in 1949 nor on this date in a subsequent year. This could however be a session that produced no issued material. On December 19, 1949, Tormé did record for Capitol, but not with Rugolo in New York; he recorded with Hal Mooney in Los Angeles. Alvin Stoller was on drums. In case the year was incorrect, I looked also at the Decca sessions. Here is what I found:

Ella's issued master of "Smooth Sailing" did not come until June 26, 1951. Dec 11, 1949 is not a rejected session. Nothing was recorded at Decca on this date.

*Back Beats and Rim Shots, Warren W. Vaché, The Scarecrow Press, Inc., 1997 (ISBN 0-8108-3162-7)

Louis Armstrong had recorded the issued masters of both "Blueberry Hill" and "That Lucky Old Sun" with Gordon Jenkins for Decca on September 6, 1949. Blowers was on drums. Dec 12 was a busy day at Decca with four sessions but none involving Gordon Jenkins. Was this Dec 12 session AT Decca but not FOR Decca?

There is nothing listed in any discography for Louis Armstrong and Ella Fitzgerald at Decca on Dec 14 in 1949 nor for this date in any subsequent year. There were three sessions at Decca on Dec 14; one was by Danny Kaye with Sy Oliver. The drummer is not known for this session.

I am completely at a loss to explain the entries in Blowers' journal even by moving the date to a year other than 1949.

On pages 180–181, Blowers is listed as being present on ten Capitol sides with Tormé under the leadership of Pete Rugolo. Examination leaves doubts about the accuracy of this claim on all but two of the sides.

Capitol 57-591, There Isn't Any Special Reason / actually: Los Angeles, 13 Jan 49 with Sonny Burke

Capitol 57-591, You're Getting to Be a Habit with Me (1) / actually: Los Angeles, 17 Jan 49 with Sonny Burke

Capitol 57-791, There's a Broken Heart.... / actually: Los Angeles, 26 Aug. 49 with Frank De Vol

Capitol 57-791, Oh, You Beautiful / same as last

Capitol 15428, Blue Moon (not Blue Room) / actually: NYC, 21 February 49 with Pete Rugolo

Capitol 15428, Again / same as last

Capitol 880, Cross Your Heart (1) / Los Angeles, 19 Dec 49 with Hal Mooney

Capitol 880, I Hadn't Anyone Till You (1) / same as last

Capitol 1000, The Piccolino (2) / NYC, 3 April 49 with Pete Rugolo

Capitol 1000, Bewitched (2) / same as last.

On the sides marked (1), Alvin Stoller is the designated drummer and on those marked (2) the drummer is quoted as Mel Zelnick.

While it is not unknown for Capitol to label discs with a band leader other than the one actually on the date, it seems unlikely that this happened in any of the cases where the sides were cut in Los Angeles.

This leaves only Capitol 15428 as a probable Blowers recording; with Capitol 1000 as a remote possibility.

The listing of the two sides on Capitol 880 matches the claim by Blowers to have been on a date on 19 Dec 49 but he says in NYC rather than Los Angeles.

Derek Coller kindly put these anomalies to Warren Vaché but Mr. Vaché was unable to shed any light on the matter as he was not responsible for the discographical matter included in the biography.

INDEXES

Songs Recorded by Mel Tormé

To find details of a recording, go to the session in part 2 that is indicated after the song title.

Abraham broadcast 421220
Ac-cent-tchu-ate the Positive Concord 900902
Adios Concord 940512; Verve 590402
After the Waltz Is Over Concord 850501
After You've Gone Concord 910312
Again Atlantic 620325; Capitol 490221
Ah, But It Happens broadcast 4800928
Ah, the Apple Trees *see* When the World Was Young
Air Mail Special Concord 921114
All God's Chillun Got Rhythm Concord 820415; Telarc 921007
All I Need Is the Girl broadcast 630810; Verve 600204
All in Fun World 581208
All in Love Is Fair Gryphon 770601
All Medley Concord 921114
All of Me Concord 921114
All of You broadcast 541201; Concord 921114; Coral 540803
All That Jazz Columbia 660418; film 650003
All the Things You Are Concord 921114
All This and Heaven Too Bethlehem 550828
All You Need Is a Quarter Verve 601109
Alone Together Verve 610702
Along with Me Musicraft 460430
Am I Blue? Decca 450427
…And Mimi Musicraft 470901
And So to Bed Musicraft 460910; Musicraft 461017
And the Angels Sing Concord 921114
Angel Eyes Atlantic 620324; Concord 910312
Angelina Verve 601110
Annie Doesn't Live Here Any More Liberty 680202
Anyone Can Whistle Concord 870800
The Anything Can Happen Mambo Coral 531001
Anything Goes Atlantic 620324; Atlantic 620325
Anywhere I Wander Capitol 520926
April in Paris Macgregor 471001
April Showers film 500824; Macgregor 471001
Aren't You Glad You're You? Concord 900902
Around Midnight *see* 'Round Midnight
Around the Corner Capitol 520215
Around the World Capitol 510105
Astaire Medley Flair 820327
At the Crossroads (Malaguena) Verve 590402
Atlantic City Waltz Bethlehem 570311
Autumn in New York Atlantic 631202; Telarc 921007
Autumn Leaves Bethlehem 570222; Concord 901111; Concord 910312; Flair 820327

Autumn Serenade Concord 950705
Avalon Concord 921114
Away in a Manger Concord 830301

Baby, Don't You Go 'Way Mad see Don't 'Cha Go 'Way Mad
Back in Your Own Back Yard broadcast 480817
Baia Concord 910312; Verve 590402
Ballerina Musicraft 470902
Baubles, Bangles and Beads Verve 590423
Be a Ladies' Man film 470201
Be My Guest television 631018
Because of You broadcast 490001
Bernie's Tune Coral 541215
Bess, Oh, Where's My Bess? Bethlehem 560501
Bess, You Is My Woman Now Bethlehem 560501; broadcast 630513; Finesse 810826
The Best Is Yet to Come Finesse 800612
The Best That You Can Do broadcast 850919
The Best Things in Life Are Free film 470201; Macgregor 471002; Musicraft 470902
Better Use Your Head Columbia 660610
Between the Devil and the Deep Blue Sea Tops 571101
Bewitched Capitol 500331; Capitol 500403
Big City Blues Arista 840101
Birdsong Concord 910312
Birth of the Blues Concord 870800
Bitter Sweet Concord 870800
Black Moonlight Capitol 520515
Bless You (For the Good That's in You) Capitol 491116
The Blossoms on the Bough Capitol 491021
Blue and Sentimental Verve 610202
Blue Moon Atlantic 620324; Capitol 490221; Concord 910312; Coral 541215; film 480202; Verve 600805
Blue Room film 500824
Blue Skies Coral 531001
Blues Atlantic 620324
The Blues Bethlehem 560116; Concord 880800; Macgregor 471003

The Blues in the Night broadcast 480824; Century 780101; Macgregor 471004; Verve 580626; television 640131
Bluesette Century 780101; live 661029
Body and Soul Verve 580628
Born to Be Blue Concord 820415; Musicraft 460604; Verve 610701
Bossa Nova Potpourri Concord 880800; Concord 881200
Boulevard of Memories Musicraft 470601
The Boy Next Door Bethlehem 570222
Brahm's Lullaby broadcast 480817
Brazil Concord 910312
Breezing Along with the Breeze Atlantic 620324
Brigg Fair Concord 850501
Broadway Atlantic 631204
The Brooklyn Bridge Atlantic 631207
Brother, Can You Spare a Dime? Atlantic 620324; Liberty 680201
A Bucket Full of Tears Capitol 690718
A Bunch of Blues Verve 590423
Bundle of Love see I'm Sending You a Bundle of Love
But Beautiful Musicraft 471114
Button Up Your Overcoat Liberty 680202
The Buzzard Song Bethlehem 560501
By Myself Verve 610718
Bye Bye Blackbird Atlantic 620324; Gryphon 770601

Cab Driver Liberty 680202
The California Suite Bethlehem 570311; Capitol 491101; Reprise 631120
Careless Hands Capitol 490117
The Carioca Bethlehem 560116; Capitol 500831; Concord 881200
Cast Your Fate to the Wind Atlantic 630208
Casually Capitol 520926
Catch a Robber by the Toe Capitol 691211
Caught in the Middle of My Years Concord 831001
Cement Mixer Coral 540803
Changing My Tune Musicraft 460816
Charade Gryphon 770601

Chase Me Charlie Concord 831001; Finesse 800612
Chattanooga Choo Choo GRP 830120
Cheek to Cheek Bethlehem 561101
Cheer for Old Hyde Park television 631018
Chestnuts Roasting on an Open Fire see The Christmas Song
The Christmas Feeling Telarc 920619
Christmas Medley Telarc 920405
The Christmas Song Columbia 661001; Concord 881200; Concord 901111; Coral 541215; Telarc 920619; Verve 610702; World 581208; television 631206
The Christmas Waltz Telarc 920619
Christmas Was Made for Children Telarc 920619
Christmastime Is Here Telarc 920405
Ciao Baby Columbia 670427
The City Concord 881200
Come Out Singing Capitol 510201
Come to Baby Do Concord 901111
Comin' Home Baby Atlantic 620913; broadcast 630901; television 631018; Columbia 660611
Coney Island Capitol 491101
Coney Island Theme Bethlehem 570311
Coronado Cruise broadcast 541201
A Cottage for Sale Finesse 810826; Macgregor 471003; Musicraft 471114
Cotton Tail Concord 881200; Concord 900902
Country Boy Macgregor 471002
County Fair Coral 541215; Macgregor 471001; Musicraft 471116; Verve 610702
Cow Cow Boogie Concord 860500
Cross My Heart broadcast 580505
Cross Your Heart Capitol 491219
Cry Like the Wind Verve 601110
Cuban Love Song Verve 590402
The Cuckoo in the Clock Decca 560921

Dancing in the Dark Verve 610701
Danny Boy Philips 570701
Darn That Dream Concord 850501; GRP 920129
Dat Dere Atlantic 620711; broadcast 630901
Day by Day Decca 450913
Day Dreaming World 590101
Day In, Day Out Concord 900801; Flair 820327; World 581208
A Day in the Life of Bonny and Clyde Liberty 680201
The Day You Came Along Concord 940512; Musicraft 470902
Dear Old Fairmont broadcast 480824
Deck the Halls television 631206
Deep in a Dream Concord 900801
Desert Serenade broadcast 541201
Didn't We? Liberty 680301
Disgustingly Rich film 430001
The Divorce Scene Bethlehem 560501
Do-Do-Do Atlantic 740901; Capitol 490113
Do I Love You Because You're Beautiful? Columbia 641216
Do It Again Musicraft 471116
Do Nothing Till You Hear From Me Concord 860500
Dominique's Discotheque Columbia 660128
Don't Be That Way Concord 921114
Don't 'Cha Go 'Way Mad Concord 860500; Concord 901111; broadcast 550301
Don't Do Something to Someone Else Capitol 491021
Don't Dream of Anybody But Me (Li'l Darlin') television 630707; Verve 590423
Don't Fan the Flame Capitol 510710
Don't Get Around Much Anymore Atlantic 620324; broadcast 561202; Concord 900902; Telarc 921007; Verve 601212
Don't Leave Me Capitol 520515
Don't Let That Moon Get Away broadcast 630810; Concord 940512; Verve 600804
Don't Take Your Love from Me Atlantic 620325; Macgregor 471004

Don't Worry 'Bout Me Tops 571102
Don't You Believe It, Dear Musicraft 461017
Down for Double Concord 900802; Verve 610202
Dream Awhile Musicraft 461018
Dream Dancing Concord 831001
Dream Medley Concord 850501
Duke Ellington Medley Concord 860500; Concord 900902

Early Autumn Atlantic 620324; Concord 900801
East Coast see Atlantic City Waltz; Coney Island Theme
East Side, West Side broadcast 460001
Ellington Medley see Duke Ellington Medley
Embraceable You Atlantic 740901
Evenin' Ladies, Hello Boys see Porgy's Return from Begging
Everything Happens to Me broadcast 480921
Ev'ry Day's a Holiday Columbia 641005
Ev'ry Time We Say Goodbye Concord 910312; Concord 921114; Concord 970723
Ev'ry Which Way Philips 570701
Exactly Like You Concord 910312

Fairmont College see Dear Old Fairmont
Far Away from Home Verve 601110
Fascinating Rhythm television 630707; Bethlehem 560116
Feelin' Groovy (The 59th Street Bridge Song) Concord 910312
The 59th Bridge Song see Feelin' Groovy
Fine and Dandy broadcast 480713; Musicraft 470902
A Fine Romance Bethlehem 561101; broadcast 480948
Fireworks Verve 601109
The First Time Ever I Saw Your Face Gryphon 770601
Five-Four Liberty 680301
The Five O'clock Whistle Concord 900902
The Flat Foot Floogie Coral 540803
Fly Me to the Moon Atlantic

620324; Concord 910312; Finesse 800612
A Foggy Day Atlantic 620324; Atlantic 740901; Bethlehem 561101; broadcast 630513; Musicraft 471116
The Folks Who Live on the Hill Columbia 641219; Concord 870800; Finesse 800612; Flair 820327
Foolish Little Rumors Capitol 511015
For Whom the Bell Tolls Concord 880800
For You, for Me, for Evermore Musicraft 460816
Forty-Second Street Atlantic 631202
Four Brothers live 661029
The Four Winds and the Seven Seas Capitol 490521
The French Lesson broadcast 480713
Frenesi Verve 590321
Friendship broadcast 480810
From a Prison Cell Verve 601110
From This Moment On Coral 541215
Fugue for Tinhorns Concord 900801

Games People Play Capitol 690602
Geometric Blues see Pythagoras, How You Stagger Us
Geordie Capitol 491219
Georgie Philips 570701
Gershwin Medley Atlantic 740901
Get Happy Concord 921114; Coral 541215
Get Me to the Church on Time Concord 880800
Get Out and Get Under broadcast 480907
Get Out of Town Coral 541215; Musicraft 460606; Musicraft 460625
Get Your Kicks on Route 66 see Route 66
The Gift Atlantic 630208; Concord 880800; Concord 881200
The Girl Friend television 631018
Girl Talk Concord 910312
Give Me the Simple Life Concord 820415
The Glory of Love television 631018; World 590101
Gloomy Sunday Verve 580626
Glow Worm Telarc 920619

Goin' Out of My Head Concord 900801
The Golden West Bethlehem 570311; Capitol 491101
Gone with the Wind broadcast 610909; Macgregor 471003; Musicraft 471115
Good King Wenceslas Telarc 920405
Goodbye Capitol 490113
The Goodbye Look Concord 880800
Goodman Medley Concord 921114
Goody Goody Coral 541215
Got the Gate on the Golden Gate Capitol 491101
Gotta Be This or That Concord 921114
Gravy Waltz Atlantic 630208
Green Dolphin Street see On Green Dolphin Street
Greensleeves Philips 570701
Guess I'll Hang My Tears Out to Dry Concord 921114
Guilty Concord 910312; Musicraft 460910; Musicraft 460919; World 440901
Guys and Dolls Concord 900801
Guys and Dolls Medley Concord 900801
The Gypsy Song see Love Is Such a Cheat

A Handful of Stars Concord 860500
Hang on to Me Columbia 660225
Happy Holiday Telarc 920619
Happy Together Capitol 690602
Hark! The Herald Angels Sing television 631206
Harlem Nocturne Atlantic 631202
Have You Met Miss Jones? Concord 950705; Coral 541215
Have Yourself a Merry Little Christmas Telarc 920619
Haven't We Met? Columbia 650309
Heart and Soul Capitol 511004; Concord 910312
Hello, Suzanne Capitol 440621A
Hello Young Lovers broadcast 630513; Verve 600121
Her Face Verve 610309

Here I Go Again see Taking a Chance On Love
Here I'll Stay broadcast 481005
Here We Come A-Carolling television 631206
Here's That Rainy Day Century 780101
Here's to My Lady Concord 830301
He's a Ladies Man see Be a Ladies' Man
He's Got the Whole World in His Hands Verve 610309
Hey, Look Me Over Atlantic 620324; broadcast 630513; Verve 601109
Hi-Fly Concord 830301; Concord 950705
Hit the Road to Dreamland Verve 590423
Ho-ba-la-la Columbia 650309
Hold Tight Coral 540802
Hollywood see Prelude to "Poor Little Extra Girl"
Home by the Sea Bethlehem 570222
Homeward Bound Columbia 660418
Honeysuckle Rose broadcast 470531; Concord 910312
Hooray for Love broadcast 480706; Decca 560922
House Is Haunted by the Echo of Your Last Goodbye Verve 580626
A House Is Not a Home Concord 860500
How? Coral 550112
How About Me? Atlantic 620324
How Are Things in Glocca Morra? Atlantic 620324; Macgregor 471001
How Did She Look? Verve 580628
How Do You Say Auf Wiedersehen? Concord 830301
How High the Moon broadcast 470531; broadcast 481005; Concord 870800; Macgregor 471002; Verve 600805
How Insensitive Concord 880800; Concord 881200
How Long Has This Been Going On? Atlantic 740901; Bethlehem 550828; Macgregor 471002; Musicraft 470601
Hung Up Being Free Capitol 691211
Hurry On Down (In My House, Honey) Capitol 690718

The Hut-Sut Song Coral 540803

I Believe Musicraft 461017; Musicraft 461108
I Can't Believe That You're in Love with Me Tops 571101
I Can't Escape from You Concord 940512
I Can't Get Started with You Macgregor 471002
I Can't Give You Anything But Love Musicraft 470901; Tops 571101
I Can't Puzzle This Thing Out Bethlehem 560501
I Concentrate on You Liberty 680202; Telarc 921007; World 581208
I Could Have Told You Concord 900801; World 581208
I Could Write a Book Concord 900902
I Cover the Waterfront Macgregor 471003; Musicraft 471116; broadcast 541201
I Cried for You London 710101
I Didn't Know About You Concord 900902; Telarc 921007
I Don't Stand a Ghost of a Chance with You Tops 571102
I Don't Think I'll Fall in Love Today Concord 910312
I Don't Want to Cry Anymore Verve 580626
I Don't Want to Walk Without You Concord 900902; Decca 560924
I Fall in Love Too Easily Decca 450427
I Found a Million Dollar Baby Bethlehem 550828; Concord 910312; Liberty 680202
I Get a Kick Out of You Concord 950705
I Get Along Without You Very Well broadcast 481005
I Got It Bad and That Ain't Good Bethlehem 550828
I Got Plenty o' Nuttin' see I Got Plenty of Nothing
I Got Plenty of Nothing Bethlehem 560501; Finesse 810826
I Got Rhythm Atlantic 740901
I Got the Sun in the Morning Musicraft 460430
I Gotta Right to Sing the Blues broadcast 480914
I Guess I'll Have to Change My Plan Finesse 810826; Verve 610702

I Had the Craziest Dream Concord 850501
I Hadn't Anyone Till You broadcast 550301; Capitol 491219; Verve 590423
I Hear Music Atlantic 620324
I Know Why (And So Do You) Bethlehem 550828; Concord 900902
I Know Your Heart Columbia 640310A
I Let a Song Go Out of My Heart Telarc 921007; Tops 571101
I Like the Sunrise Verve 601212
I Like to Recognize the Tune Bethlehem 560116; Capitol 500831; Flair 820327
I Love Each Move You Make Capitol 511015
I Love to Watch the Moonlight Bethlehem 560116
I Love You, Porgy Bethlehem 560501
I Loved You Once in Silence Verve 601110
I May Be Wrong (But I Think You're Wonderful) Concord 910312
I Met My Love at the Golden Gate Bethlehem 570311
I Never Had a Chance World 590101
I Owe a Kiss to a Girl in Iowa Capitol 500811B
I Remember Suzanne Columbia 660225
I Remember You Concord 970723
I See It Now Columbia 640310B
I Should Care Verve 580628
I Surrender Dear Tops 571102
I Thought About You Concord 910312
I Understand World 581208
I Want to Stay Here Bethlehem 560501
I Wish I Were in Love Again Bethlehem 570222; Concord 910312; Coral 541215; World 590101
I Wished on the Moon Verve 600805
I Won't Last a Day Without You Century 780101
If Capitol 690718
If I Had a Girl Like You Musicraft 470902
If I Had a Hammer Columbia 660611
If I Were a Bell Concord 900801

If You Could See Me Now Concord 950705
I'll Always Be in Love with You Musicraft 470901
I'll Be Around Concord 950705
I'll Be Home for Christmas Aero Space 950001
I'll Be Seeing You broadcast 630810; Concord 850501
I'll Build a Stairway to Paradise Atlantic 740901
I'll Remember April Telarc 921007
I'll Walk Alone Concord 900902
I'm a Debutant film 430001
I'm Beginning to See the Light Atlantic 620324; Bethlehem 570222; Concord 900902
I'm Down to My Last Dream World 440901
I'm Getting Sentimental Over You Tops 571101
I'm Glad There Is You Concord 950705
I'm Gonna Go Fishin' Telarc 921007; Verve 601212
I'm Gonna Laugh You Out of My Life Verve 580628
I'm Gonna Miss You broadcast 630810; Flair 820327
I'm Gonna Move to the Outskirts of Town Verve 610202
I'm Hip Concord 831001
I'm Nothing Without You, You're Nothing Without Me Concord 910312
I'm Sending You a Bundle of Love Capitol 510409A
I'm Shooting High Telarc 921007; Verve 601001
I'm Wishing Concord 880800
I'm Yours Musicraft 461129
Imagination Coral 541215
In Love in Vain World 581208
In Other Words see Fly Me to the Moon
In the Evening When the Sun Goes Down Verve 610202
In the Still of the Night Concord 950705
Into Something Capitol 691211
Introduction to Maisonette set Atlantic 740901
I'se a Muggin' Coral 540802
Isn't It a Lovely Day? broadcast 550301
Isn't It a Pity? Columbia 641216; Concord 910312; Finesse 800612
Isn't It Romantic? Bethlehem 550828; broadcast 480914; Fi-

nesse 810826; World 581208
Isn't This a Lovely Day? Macgregor 471001
It Ain't Necessarily So broadcast 630513; Finesse 810826
It Don't Mean a Thing If It Ain't Got That Swing Coral 540802; Concord 860500; Telarc 921007
It Happened in Monterey Musicraft 460604; Verve 590423
It Happened in Sun Valley Telarc 920619
It Made You Happy When You Made Me Cry Capitol 520515
It Might As Well Be Spring Concord 820415
It Must Be True Concord 940512
It Never Entered My Mind Atlantic 620324; World 590101
It Seems to Me, I've Heard That Song Before Concord 900902
It Takes a Long Pull to Get There Finesse 810826
It Takes Too Long to Learn to Live Alone Atlantic 740901
It's a Blue World broadcast 551129; Bethlehem 550828
It's a Most Important Affair film 430001
It's a Most Unusual Day broadcast 480914
It's All Right with Me Atlantic 620324; Bethlehem 570222; Concord 921114
It's Dark On Observatory Hill broadcast 480706
It's Delovely Atlantic 620325; Bethlehem 570222
It's Dreamtime Musicraft 461129
It's Easy to Remember Concord 940512; Concord 970723; Macgregor 471003; Musicraft 470601; World 581208
It's Magic broadcast 480713
It's Only a Paper Moon Bethlehem 570222
It's the Same Old Dream Musicraft 461017; Musicraft 461108
It's the Sentimental Thing to Do broadcast 480817
It's Too Late Gryphon 770601
It's Too Late Now Capitol 490521
I've Got a Feeling I'm Falling Capitol 500831
I've Got a Gal in Kalamazoo GRP 830120

I've Got a Lovely Bunch of Coconuts Philips 570701
I've Got a World That Swings broadcast 630901
I've Got Rhythm see I Got Rhythm
I've Got the Sun in the Morning broadcast 480907
I've Got the World On a String Tops 571101
I've Got You Under My Skin Columbia 641219; Musicraft 460606
I've Heard That Song Before see It Seems to Me...
I've Never Been in Love Before Concord 900801; Verve 590423

Jeepers Creepers Coral 541215
Jersey Bounce Concord 921114
Jet Set Atlantic 740901
Jingle Bells Telarc 920405
Johnny One Note broadcast 490001
Juanita broadcast 450503
Just a Sittin' and a Rockin' Verve 601212
Just Friends Concord 860500
Just Imagine film 470201
Just in Case We Have to Say Goodbye Capitol 500811A
Just in Time Concord 881200; Verve 600211
Just Look Around Telarc 920619
Just One More Chance Coral 531001
Just One of Those Things Bethlehem 570222; Concord 831001; Concord 970723; Telarc 921007

Keeping Myself for You Bethlehem 560116
Keester Parade see A Bunch of Blues
The King Columbia 670427
Kokomo, Indiana Musicraft 470601

Lady Be Good see Oh Lady Be Good
The Lady Is a Tramp Bethlehem 560116; broadcast 561201
The Lady's in Love with You Atlantic 620716; broadcast 630513
Last Night, When We Were Young Concord 850501

Learn to Croon Concord 940512
Lemon Tree television 630707
Let Me Off Uptown Atlantic 631204
Let There Be Love Philips 570701
Let's Call the Whole Thing Off Bethlehem 561101
Let's Do It television 631018
Let's Face the Music and Dance Bethlehem 561101
Let's Fall in Love broadcast 480921
Let's Start the New Year Right Telarc 920619
Let's Take a Walk Around the Block Finesse 800612
Li'l Darling see Don't Dream of Anybody but Me
Like a Lover Gryphon 770601
Lili Marlene Concord 900902
Lima Lady Columbia 671117
Limehouse Blues Philips 570701
Line for Lyons Finesse 810826
A Little Kiss Each Morning Musicraft 461018
Little Man You've Had a Busy Day Concord 870800
Little White Lies Liberty 680202; Musicraft 471116
Live Alone and Like It television 890000
Liza (All the Clouds'll Roll Away) Concord 950705
London Pride Atlantic 620324; Philips 570701
Londonderry Air see Danny Boy
Lonely Girl live 661029
Lonely Town Verve 600204
A Lonesome Cup of Coffee Capitol 510105
Long Ago and Far Away Intersound 940600; World 581208
Look at That Face broadcast 680401; Concord 901111
Looking at You Bethlehem 570222; broadcast 580505; Concord 901111; Flair 820327
Losing My Mind Concord 900801
Love Concord 820415; Concord 900902; Concord 921114
Love and the Moon Concord 850501
Love for Sale Atlantic 620324; Concord 970723; Finesse 810826
Love in Bloom Concord 940512

Love Is Here to Stay see Our Love Is Here to Stay
Love Is Just a Bug Bethlehem 570222
Love Is Just Around the Corner Atlantic 620324; Concord 831001
Love Is Such a Cheat (The Gypsy Song) Capitol 510626
Love Is Sweeping the Country Atlantic 740901
Love Is the Sweetest Thing Musicraft 471115
Love Is the Tender Trap see The Tender Trap
Love Me or Leave Me Atlantic 620324; Concord 870800; Macgregor 471004
Love Walked In broadcast 551129; Atlantic 740901; Concord 950705
Love, You Funny Thing Musicraft 470901
Love You Madly Concord 910312
A Lovely Way to Spend An Evening Telarc 921007
Lover Come Back to Me Bethlehem 570222; Concord 921114; Concord 970723
Lover's Delight see Malt Shop Special
Lover's Roulette Columbia 670427
Luck Be a Lady broadcast 490001; Concord 900801
Lucky in Love film 470201
Lullaby of Birdland Atlantic 631207; Bethlehem 560116; Concord 820415
Lullaby of Broadway Atlantic 620324
Lullaby of the Leaves Capitol 500331; Capitol 500403
Lulu's Back in Town Bethlehem 560116; broadcast 561201; broadcast 630513; Concord 921114; Flair 820327

Mack the Knife Concord 870800
Magic Town Musicraft 470902
Makin' Whoopee Macgregor 471001; Musicraft 471116; Verve 590423; television 631018
Malaguena see At the Crossroads
Malt Shop Special broadcast 480831
A Man and His Dreams Concord 940512

Manhattan Atlantic 631202; Bethlehem 570222
Manhattan, Manhattan Bethlehem 570311
May I? Concord 940512
Maybe You'll Be There broadcast 480817
Me and My Girl Concord 870800
The Meadows of Heaven Capitol 490826
Medley see subject of medley e.g. Gershwin, Astaire, etc.
Medley of Porgy and Bess tunes see Porgy and Bess medley
Memories of You Concord 921114
The Miami Waltz Capitol 491101
The Midnight Sun Concord 870800
Midnight Swinger Capitol 690602
Mine Atlantic 740901
Minuet in Boogie film 430001
Misty Atlantic 620324
Moanin' Atlantic 620711
Molly Marlene Columbia 670427
The Money Song broadcast 480928
Monsters Lead Such Interesting Lives television 870100
Mood Indigo Concord 860500
Moon Medley Concord 850501
Moon Song Verve 600803
The Moon Was Yellow broadcast 630810; Verve 600804
Moonlight Becomes You Concord 940512
Moonlight Cocktail Verve 600803
Moonlight in Vermont Coral 541215; Verve 600803
More Than You Know Concord 880800; Concord 881200
Mornin', Lawyer, Looking for Somebody? see The Divorce Scene
Morning Star London 710101
Moten Swing Concord 901112
Mountain Desert Theme Bethlehem 570311; Capitol 491101
Mountain Greenery Atlantic 620324; Atlantic 740901; broadcast 480831; Coral 541215; Finesse 800612
Mrs. Whiffen film 430001
The Music Goes Round and Round Liberty 680202

My Baby Just Cares for Me Musicraft 470901
My Buddy Capitol 510626
My Christmas Dream Aero Space 950001
My Foolish Heart Concord 850501
My Funny Valentine Macgregor 471002
My Gal's Back in Town Atlantic 630208
My Little Red Book Columbia 660611
My One and Only Highland Fling Philips 570701
My Romance Columbia 641216
My Rosemarie Coral 550112
My Shining Hour Coral 541215
My Sweetie Went Away Concord 950705
My Time of Day Atlantic 631202 Concord 900801

The Nearness of You Columbia 641216; Concord 910312
Never Look Back Gryphon 770601
Nevertheless Atlantic 620325
New York, New York Atlantic 631207; Concord 870800
New York, New York Medley Concord 870800
New York State of Mind Concord 901112; Finesse 800612; Gryphon 770601
Nice Work If You Can Get It Bethlehem 561101
Night and Day Musicraft 471116
Night Must Fall World 440901
The Night We Called It a Day World 581208
A Nightingale Sang in Berkeley Square Atlantic 620324; Bethlehem 570222; Concord 820415; Concord 901111; Concord 970723; Philips 570701
Nina Verve 590321; World 590101
No Moon at All Concord 850501; Verve 600804
No, No, Brother, Porgy Ain't Soft on No Woman see Porgy's Return from Begging
Nobody Else But Me Concord 950705
Nobody's Heart Bethlehem 570222; Verve 580628

Of Thee I Sing Atlantic 740901
Oh Bess, Oh Where's My Bess? Atlantic 740901; Finesse 810826
Oh, Lady Be Good Atlantic 740901; Century 780101; Concord 970723
Oh Lawd, I'm on My Way Bethlehem 560501
Oh Lawd, What Am I Gonna Do? Bethlehem 560501
Oh What a Night for Love Verve 610202
Oh You Crazy Moon Verve 600805
Oh, You Beautiful Doll Capitol 490826
Oh, You Crazy Moon Concord 850501
Old Devil Moon Verve 600211
Old Folks World 581208
Old Man River broadcast 460501
The Old Master Painter Capitol 491116
The Oldest Established Concord 900801
Oleo Concord 830301
On a Little Street in Singapore Capitol 500831
On a Slow Boat to China broadcast 481012
On Green Dolphin Street Atlantic 620711; Concord 831001; Concord 970723; Telarc 921007
On the Alamo Concord 910312
On the Atchison, Topeka and the Sante Fe broadcast 460001
On the Street Where You Live Concord 881200; Verve 600211
On the Swing Shift Concord 900902; Concord 950705
Once in a Lifetime Columbia 640310B
Once in Love with Amy Verve 600121
The One for Me Capitol 510626
One for My Baby Bethlehem 570222; Musicraft 461018
One Little Snowflake Columbia 641005
One Morning in May Tops 571102
One Note Samba Concord 880800; Concord 881200
The One That Got Away Atlantic 620325
Only the Very Young Columbia 660225

Only When I'm Lonely Columbia 671117
Oo-Ya-Ya Coral 531001
Ordinary Fool Gryphon 770601
Our Language of Love Verve 601110
Our Love Is Here to Stay Atlantic 740901; Coral 541215
Out of This World Concord 870800
Overflow Bethlehem 560501
Overture to the California Suite see The California Suite

Paris Smiles Columbia 6610001
The Party's Over television 631018; Atlantic 740901; Telarc 921007
The Patty Cake Man Capitol 440621A
Pennies from Heaven Concord 940512
Pennsylvania 6-5000 GRP 830120
Perfidia Verve 590402
A Phone Call to the Past London 710101
The Piccolino Bethlehem 561101; Capitol 500331; Capitol 500403
Pick Yourself Up Concord 970723; Finesse 810826
Pieces of Dreams Flair 820327
Please Concord 940512
Please Do It Again see Do It Again
Polka Dots and Moonbeams Atlantic 620324; Bethlehem 550828
Poor Little Extra Girl Bethlehem 570311; Capitol 491101
Poor Wayfaring Stranger Verve 600329
Porgy and Bess Bethlehem 560501
Porgy and Bess Medley Atlantic 620324; broadcast 630513; Finesse 810826
Porgy, I Hates to Go see I Want to Stay Here
Porgy's Return from Begging Bethlehem 560501
Portia Brown broadcast 630810
The Power of Love Columbia 660128
Prelude to "Poor Little Extra Girl" Bethlehem 570311; Capitol 491101
Prelude to a Kiss Tops 571102
Pretty Flamingo Columbia 660611

Prove It by the Things You Do Decca 450913
P.S. I Love You Columbia 650309
Puttin' on the Ritz Atlantic 620716
Pythagoras, How You Stagger Us broadcast 480706

The Queen of Hearts Is Missing Capitol 491219
Quiet Night of Quiet Stars broadcast 630901

Rachel's Dream Concord 970723
Raindrops Keep Fallin' on My Head Capitol 691223
Real Thing Finesse 810826
Recipe for Romance Capitol 500811A
Red Rubber Ball Columbia 660611
Reminiscing in Tempo Verve 601212
Requiem: 820 Latham Capitol 691201
The Rhumba Jumps Verve 590402
Ridin' High Telarc 921007
Right Now Atlantic 620913
The Right to Love Capitol 690603
Rockin' in Rhythm Telarc 921007
Rose O'Day Coral 540802
Rosita Verve 590402
'Round Midnight broadcast 630513; broadcast 630810

'S Wonderful Atlantic 740901
Sailin' Away on the Henry Clay Capitol 510105
Saint Louis Blues broadcast 460001
Sam's Got Him Capitol 440621B
San Francisco see I Met My Love at the Golden Gate
Santa Claus Is Coming to Town Telarc 920405
Satin Doll Concord 860500
Say No More Capitol 500811B
The Second Time Around Columbia 650309
Secret Agent Man Columbia 660611
Send a Little Love My Way Concord 870800
Send in the Clowns Gryphon 770601
Sent for You Yesterday and Here

You Come Today Concord 900802; Concord 901112; Verve 610202
September Song Concord 860500; Coral 541215; Macgregor 471001
Seventeen Columbia 660225
Shaking the Blues Away Atlantic 620324; Finesse 800612
Shenandoah Valley Capitol 520926; Decca 560922
She's a Home Girl Capitol 490113
She's Leaving Home Capitol 690603
A Shine on Your Shoes Concord 830301; Concord 901111; Verve 610718
Shooting High Atlantic 620325
The Sidewalk Shufflers Capitol 510105
Sidewalks of New York Atlantic 631204
Sidney's Soliloquy Atlantic 620713; broadcast 630901
Silly Habits Finesse 800612
Silver Bells Telarc 920619
Since I Fell for You Concord 870800; Concord 970723
Sing (Sing a Song) Concord 910312; Concord 900801
Sing for Your Supper Bethlehem 560116; Concord 900801
Sing, Sing, Sing Concord 900801; Concord 921114
Sing, You Sinners Atlantic 620716
Sit Down, You're Rocking the Boat Concord 900801
Six Lessons from Madame La Zonga Verve 590321
Skylark Capitol 500331; Capitol 500403
A Sleepin' Bee Verve 600204
Sleigh Ride Telarc 920619
Slipped Disc Concord 970723
Smoke Gets in Your Eyes Concord 830301
A Smooth One Concord 970723 Verve 590423
Softly with Feeling see Oh What a Night for Love
Some Like It Hot Verve 590423
Someday I'll Find You Concord 870800
Something Capitol 691201
Something to Live For Tops 571102
Something's Gotta Give Bethlehem 561101; broadcast 490001

The Song Is You Concord 860500
Sonny Boy Capitol 490826
Soon Concord 940512
Sophisticated Lady Concord 860500; Flair 820327; Telarc 921007
South America, Take It Away Musicraft 460604
South of the Border Verve 590321
Spain (I Can Recall) Concord 880800
Spellbound Coral 540803
Spinning Wheel Capitol 691223
Spring Can Really Hang You Up the Most Atlantic 620324
Stairway to the Stars Concord 970723
Star Eyes World 581208
Stardust Concord 901111; Concord 830301; Concord 970723; Telarc 921007
Stars Gryphon 770601
Stars Fell on Alabama Concord 860500
Stay as Sweet as You Are Bethlehem 550828
Stomping at the Savoy Capitol 490117; Concord 921114
Stormy Weather Flair 820327
Straighten Up and Fly Right broadcast 450503
A Stranger in Town Capitol 520515; Coral 541215;; Macgregor 471002; Verve 610701; World 440901
Strangers in the Night Columbia 660610
Strawberry Woman Finesse 810826
Strike Up the Band Atlantic 740901
Summertime broadcast 630513; Finesse 810826
Sunday in New York film 631115; Atlantic 631204
Sunday Night in San Fernando Bethlehem 570311; Capitol 491101
Sunshine Superman Capitol 691223
Superstition Atlantic 740901
Sure Thing World 590101
The Surrey with the Fringe on Top broadcast 630513; Verve 600211
Swanee Atlantic 740901
Sweet Georgia Brown Concord 880800; Concord 881200

Sweet Sue Concord 910312
Swingin' the Blues Concord 901112
Swinging on the Moon broadcast 630810; Verve 600804

Take a Letter Maria Capitol 691201
Take a Letter Miss Jones Finesse 810826
Take Care of You for Me Capitol 440621A
Take My Heart Capitol 510626
Take the "A" Train Concord 860500; Concord 910312; Verve 601212
Taking a Chance On Love Bethlehem 570222
Tall Hopes Verve 601109
Telling Me Yes, Telling Me No Capitol 510710
The Tender Trap Bethlehem 570222
Tenderly Bethlehem 570222
Thanks Concord 940512
That Face broadcast 680401; Flair 820327
That Old Black Magic broadcast 480810; Coral 541215
That Old Devil Moon Coral 541215
That Old Feeling broadcast 610909; Verve 580626
That's All Columbia 641219
That's Where I Came In broadcast 460501; Musicraft 460319
Theme from Arthur broadcast 850919
Then I'll Be Tired of You Concord 831001
There Isn't Any Special Reason Capitol 490113
There's a Broken Heart for Every Light on Broadway Atlantic 631207; Capitol 490826
There's an "X" in the Middle of Texas Capitol 491219
There's No Business Like Show Business Musicraft 461018
There's No One But You Musicraft 460319
There's No You Concord 910312
These Desperate Hours film 550302; Verve 601001
These Foolish Things Concord 921114; Philips 570701
They All Laughed Bethlehem 561101
They Can't Convince Me Musicraft 460430; Musicraft 460910

They Can't Take That Away from Me Bethlehem 561101; Macgregor 471002
They Didn't Believe Me Macgregor 471002
They Go to San Diego Bethlehem 570311; Capitol 491101
They Pass by Singing Finesse 810826; Bethlehem 560501
This Can't Be Love Macgregor 471001
This Is a Lovely Way to Spend An Evening Concord 900902; Telarc 921007
This Is My Night to Dream Concord 940512
This Is the Army, Mister Jones Concord 900902
This Is the Moment broadcast 480907
This Time the Dream's On Me Concord 850501
Three Little Words Concord 921114; Concord 970723; Macgregor 471004; Musicraft 470901
'Till the Clouds Roll By Bethlehem 550828
Time Columbia 660418
A Time for Us Capitol 690603
Time Was Philips 570701; World 590101
Tiny's Blues see A Bunch of Blues
TNT see A Bunch of Blues
Too Close for Comfort Concord 881200; Flair 820327; Verve 600121
Too Darn Hot Concord 900801; Verve 600204; World 590101
Too Late Now World 581208
Top Hat, White Tie and Tails Bethlehem 561101
Traces Capitol 691223
Tribute to Benny Goodman (Medley) see Goodman medley
Tribute to Fred Astaire see Astaire medley
The Trolley Song Concord 880800; television 640131
Trouble Is a Girl film 500824
Truckin' Verve 590423; television 631018
Try a Little Tenderness Musicraft 460604; Philips 570701
A Tune for Humming Concord 870800

Tutti Frutti Coral 540802
Two Tune Medley Concord 910312
Two Tune Verse Concord 910312

Until the Real Thing Comes Along Musicraft 471114

Vaya Con Dios Verve 590321
A Velvet Affair Verve 600805
Velvet Moon Verve 600803
Venus de Milo Finesse 810826

Wait Until Dark Columbia 671117
Walk Between Raindrops Concord 880800
Walk Like a Dragon film 600301; Verve 600329
Walk Medley Concord 900902
Walk on By Columbia 660418
Walkin' Atlantic 620713
Walkin' Shoes Atlantic 620713; Decca 560921; Finesse 810826
Walking My Baby Back Home broadcast 551129
Waltz for Young Lovers Decca 560924
Wanderin' Star Capitol 691201
Warm Hands, Cold Heart film 491024
Watch What Happens Concord 910312; Finesse 800612
Wave Concord 901111; Finesse 810826
The Way You Look Tonight Bethlehem 561101; Concord 870800
We Mustn't Say Goodbye Concord 900902
We Think the West Coast Is the Best Coast Bethlehem 570311; Capitol 491101
Welcome to the Club Verve 610702
We're in the Money Liberty 680202
What Are You Doing New Year's Eve? Musicraft 470902; Telarc 920619
What Are You Doing the Rest of Your Life? Atlantic 740901; Flair 820327
What Is There to Say Columbia 641219
What Is This Thing Called Love? Bethlehem 570222; broadcast 480921; Musicraft 460606; Musicraft 460619; Verve 590423
Whatever Lola Wants Verve 600121
What's New at the Zoo? Verve 601110
What's This? Concord 830301; Gryphon 770601
When April Comes Again Bethlehem 560116
When I Found You Century 780101
When Is Sometime? Musicraft 471115
When It's Sleepy Time Down South Macgregor 471003
When Sunny Gets Blue Concord 870800
When the Red Red Robin Comes Bob Bob Bobbing Along broadcast 480810
When the Sun Comes Out Bethlehem 560116; broadcast 561201; Concord 881200; Flair 820327
When the World Was Young Atlantic 620324; Finesse 810826; Gryphon 770601
When You Wish Upon a Star Concord 880800
Where Are You? World 581208
Where Can I Go Without You? Verve 580628
Where or When? Concord 910312; Jewel 440001
Whisper Not Atlantic 620713; Concord 870800
White Christmas Jewel 440001; Telarc 920619
The White Cliffs of Dover Philips 570701
Who Cares? Atlantic 740901
Who Cares What People Say? Musicraft 461129
Who Sends You Orchids? Capitol 510409A
Who'll Be the Fool? Jewel 440002
Whose Garden Was This? London 710101
Why Don't You Do Right? Concord 921114
Willie & Laura Mae Jones Capitol 690718
Willow Road Musicraft 460319
Windmills of Your Mind Capitol 690602
Winter Weather Telarc 920405
Winter Wonderland Telarc 920405
Wish I May, Wish I Might broadcast 480831
With Every Breath I Take Concord 940512
With Plenty of Money and You Liberty 680202
With You Musicraft 471115
Without a Word of Warning Concord 940512
Wonderful One Bethlehem 550828
The World Is Your Balloon Capitol 510409B
Wrap Your Troubles in Dreams broadcast 480817; television 631018

Yes Indeed Coral 531231; Verve 610309
Yesterday When I Was Young Concord 910312; Gryphon 770601; Capitol 690603
You and the Night and the Music Concord 910312; Finesse 800612; Verve 610718
You Are the Sunshine of My Life Century 780101
You Belong to Me Atlantic 620716
You Can't Love 'Em All Atlantic 630605
You Changed My Life Concord 850501
You Don't Have to Say You Love Me Columbia 660610
You Gotta Try Telarc 921007
You Leave Me Breathless Bethlehem 550828
You Locked My Heart Capitol 510409B
You Make Me Feel So Young Concord 900801; Concord 970723; World 590101
You Ought to Be in Pictures broadcast 550301; film 500824; Macgregor 471002; broadcast 541201
You Took Advantage of Me World 581208
You'd Be So Nice to Come Home To Concord 820415
You'd Better Love Me Columbia 640310A
You're a Heavenly Thing Capitol 511004
You're Driving Me Crazy Atlantic 620325; broadcast 480706; Concord 850501;

Concord 900802; Concord 901112; Coral 541215; film 500824; Musicraft 461129
You're Getting to Be a Habit with Me Capitol 490117

You're on Your Own film 430001
You're the Cream in My Coffee broadcast 480713 broadcast 550301 Liberty 680202; Macgregor 471001

You're the Top broadcast 481012
You've Laughed at Me for the Last Time World 440901
You've Made Me So Very Happy Capitol 691211

Zaz Turned Blue Geffen 820401

Musicians

To find details of a recording, go to the session in part 2 that is indicated after the musician's name.

Aarons, Al 630702
Adlam, Buzz 550301
Adler, Murray 940512
Adrian, Louis 631219
Alberti, Bob 921007
Alden, Howard 940512
Allen, Steve 631018
Allen, Sue 590423
Allyson, June 470202
Almeida, Laurindo 630208
Alonje, Tom 500331, 500403
Alsop, Marin 820401
Amaro, Eugene 860500
Anastos, Tom 661029
Anderson, Carol 950801
Anderson, Dale 631219
Anderson, John 610202
Andre, Wayne 830120
Anthony, Leo 950801
Appleyard, Peter 921114
Armstrong, Bill 950801
Arno, Victor 630208
Artin, Tom 921007
Atkins, Leonard 631219
Atkinson, William 440621A, 440621B, 460319
Audino, John 580505, 680201
Aue, Margaret 631202
Auld, George 540802, 540803, 680201

Babasin, Harry 460530, 491101, 490521, 580505
Babitz, Sol 631219
Bagley, Don 601109, 601110
Bain, Bob 690603
Baird, Eugenie 450427
Bakaleinikoff, Constantin 430001
Baker, Israel 550828, 560501, 601109, 601110, 631202, 940512
Baker, Marilyn 940512
Baptist, Rick 950801

Barber, Bill 920129
Barbour, Dave 450913, 460606, 460619, 460625, 461108, 461129, 471003, 471004, 491116, 631202
Barene, Robert 650610
Bargeron, Dave 920129
Barker, Guy 910312
Barnet, Charlie 580505
Baron, Art 901111B
Barres, George 460606
Barrett, Dan 881200
Barrett, Michael 940600
Barth, Benny 630901
Basie, Count 630707
Basso, Guido 860500, 950505
Baxter, Les 440001, 440002, 440901, 450427, 450913, 460530, 460319, 460430, 460604, 460606, 460619, 460816, 460910, 460919, 461017, 461018, 480706, 480713, 480810, 480817, 480824, 480907, 480914, 480921, 480928, 491101, 491219
Beach, Frank 460530, 461017, 461108, 550828, 560501, 580626, 580628, 590321, 590402, 631204
Beau, Heine 460430
Beck, Ed 510409A, 510409B
Beck, Gordon 700601
Bell, Aaron 650003
Belnick, Arnold 630208, 650610
Bennett, Max 560501, 561101, 570222, 570311
Benson, Walter 490117
Berghofer, Chuck 880800, 881200
Bergman, Edward 461129
Bergstrom, Paul 630208
Berman, Edgar 461017
Bernard, Cy 460619, 460625, 460910, 460919, 461017, 461108, 471116
Bernardinelli, Herman 460606, 460625
Bernhart, Milt 620711, 620713
Berry, Bill 921007
Best, Johnny 541201, 540802, 540803
The Bethlehem Chorus 560501, 570311
The Bethlehem Orchestra 560501, 570311
Betts, Harry 620711, ?620713
Beveridge, Betty 440001, 440002, 440901, 450427, 450913, 460530, 460319, 460430, 460604, 460606, 460619, 460816, 460910, 460919, 461017, 461018
Bickert, Ed 860500
Biviano, Lyn 661029
Bivona, Gus 491219
Blair, Eddie 560921
Bloom, William 460430
Bluestone, Harry 460619, 460625, 460816, 460910, 460919, 461017, 461108, 461129, 471116, 631202, 650610
Bodner, Phil 830120
Bohannon, Hoyt 460430
The Boss Brass *see* McConnell, Rob
Boyle, Dave 780101
Brandt, Carl 610909
Breen, Larry 490117
Brenner, Adam 921007
Brewster, Ralph 480706, 480713, 480810, 480817, 480824, 480907, 480914, 480921, 480928
Broadbent, Alan 940512
Brosseau, Robert 940512
Brown, Eddie 500331, 500403

Brown, Maurice 500331, 500403
Brown, Ray 900801B
Bruce, Bobby 940512
Budwig, Monty 550828, 630513
Bundock, Rollie 631219
Bunker, Larry 570222, 590321, 620711, 620713, 630513
Burdick, Huntington 490521, 491101
Burke, Sonny 460319, 460604, 460606, 460619, 460816, 460910, 460919, 461017, 461108, 461129, 471116, 490113, 490117, 540803
Burnett, Jodi 940512
Burnett, Joe 620711, 620713
Burns, Bob 450503
Busch, Lou 491116
Butterman, Cheryll 550828
Byrne, Bill 661029

Callendar, Red 590321, 590402, 600121, 600204, 600211, 600804
Campbell, Duncan 560921
Campbell, John 900801A, 900801B, 901111A, 901111B
Candoli, Pete 560116, 561101, 561201, 570311, 590321, 590402
Cantor, Ross 940512
Caplan, Alan 950801
Capriano, Gene 631219, 631204
Carls, Emmett 421220
Cartcart, James 460606
Carter, Benny 540802, 540803, 650003
Casey, Al 470531
Castellucci, Stella 570311, 571101, 571102
Cates, George 540802, 540803, 550112
Catlett, Buddy 630702
Cavanaugh, Page 470901, 470902, 471001, 471002
Cave, John 550828, 560116, 560501, 561201
Chamberlain, Ronnie 560921
Chase, Bill 661029
Chassman, Joseph 460606
Cheever, Russell 440621A, 440621B
Childers, Buddy 560501, 680201
Childers, Marion 580626, 580628
Chycoski, Arnie 860500, 950505
Cincinnati Symphonietta 920405
Cipriano, Gene 590321, 590402
Clark, Bobby 421220
Clark, Buddy 590402

Clark, John 920129
Clark, Mahlon 460319
Clarke, Arthur 901111B
Clarkson, Geoff 601109, 601110
Clayton, Buck 510710
Clow, Irma Louise 500824
Cohn, Sonny 630702
Coker, Henry 630702
Cole, Buddy 450913, 471003, 471004
Coleman, Cy 800612
Coleman, Gary 650610
Colianni, John 920405, 921007, 921114, 940512
Colianni, Ray 910312
Collette, Buddy 620711, ?620713, 630513, 631204
Collins, Jerry 661029
Collins, Richard 580626, 580628
Coluccio, Mike 470531
Comfort, Joe 540802, 540803
Conlon, Jud 491101 *see also* Jud Conlon (*under J*)
Conniff, Ray 461018
The Cookies 620913
Cooper, Bob 560116, 561201, 620711, 620713
Cooper, Sid 500331, 500403
Copeland, Allen 460319
Cornell, Richard 570311
Cottler, Irv 491101, 550828
Courage, Sandy 550828
Covington, Warren 510710
Crosby, Bing 450913
Cyr, John 581208, 680201
Cytron, Sam 460430, 460625, 460816, 460910, 461017, 461108

Dale, Jim 860500
Dankworth, John 910312
The Dave Lambert Octet 500331, 500403
David, Dean 910312
David, Martyn 910312
Davis, Sammy, Jr. 631120
Dawes, Bob 580505
Dean, Alex 950505
Deasy, Michael 680201
Decker, Bob 460319
Decker, Ellis 460319
Decker, James 460606, 631219
De Rosa, Vince 460625, 560116, 560501, 561101, 561201, 570311, 571101, 571102, 580626, 580628, 600121, 600204, 600211, 600804, 601109, 601110
De Vol, Frank 490521 490826, 491021, 491101

Dicterow, Maurice 940512
Dietterman, Howard 421220
DiFiore, Joseph 650610, 630208
Dinkin, Allan 630208
Dinkin, Alvin 460606, 560501, 570311, 631202, 631219
Dinovi, Eugene 680201
Disruhd, Sheldon "Diz" 480706, 480713, 480810, 480817, 480824, 480907, 480914, 480921, 480928
Dixon, Eric 630702
Doling, John 560501
Douglas, Bonnie 940512
Du Long, Jack 541201, 560116, 561101, 561201
Dumont, Jack 460319, 471116
Dunbar, Ted 900801B, 901111B
Dunn, Deacon 460319, 460430
Dupre, James 541215
Duvivier, George 840101

Edelstein, Walter 460430, 460919, 461017, 461129
Edgar, Leon 440002
Edison, Harry 900801B
Edwards, Teddy 601212, 610202
Efford, Bob 880800, 881200, 950801
Ehrlich, Jesse 631219
Eiler, Barbara 480706, 480713
Eldridge, Roy 470531
Elias, Lewis 461017
Elliott, Dean 480706, 480713, 480810, 480817, 480824, 480907, 480914, 480921, 480928, 481005, 481012
Ellis, Herb 680201
Ellis, Peter 460430, 460625, 460910, 460919, 461108
Elman, Ziggy 490117
Enevoldsen, Bob 560116, 560501, 561101, 561201, 570311, 571101, 571102, 630810, 880800, 881200
Errol, Leon 430001
Ershoff, Elizabeth 631219
Estes, Gene 620711, 620713
Estren, Joe 541201
Exiner, Billy 510710
Ezzard, Bert 560921

Fagerquist, Don 560116, 560501, 561101, 561201, 570222, 570311, 571101, 571102, 600805, 610202
Farlow, Tal 500831
Farnham, Allen 881200
Faso, Tony 500331, 500403
Fatool, Nick 450913, 460319, 460430, 460604, 460619,

460910, 460919, 461017,
  461108, 461129, 471116,
  540802, 540803
Faulise, Paul 830120
Faye, Frances 560501
Feldman, Vic 590423
Feller, Sid 510409B, 510710
Ferguson, Maynard 560501
Ferrier, Jack 541201
Field, Gregg 950801
Fitzpatrick, Bob 541201
Fletcher, Stan 440621A, 440621B
Flory, Med 580626, 580628
Fontana, Carl 661029
Foster, Frank 630702
Foster, Gary 880800, 881200
Fowlkes, Charlie 630702
Fox, Fred 460606
Franklyn, Robert 470201
Freed, Sam 460430, 460619,
  460625, 460816, 461017,
  461108
Freeman, Ernie 660427
Friedman, Morton 460910,
  460919, 491219
Frigo, Johnny 421220
Frisina, David 460430, 460625,
  460816, 471116, 600805
Frosk, John 830120
Fuller, Jerry 860500

Galbraith, Barry 500331,
  500403, 510710
Galinas, Gabe 421220
Gangursky, Nat 460606, 460625
Garcia, Russell 550828, 560501,
  600329, 600803, 600804,
  600805, 601109, 601110
Garland, Judy 630707, 631018,
  631206, 640131
Garson, Mort 641005, 650002,
  650610, 660225, 660611
Gasselin, Jacques 461129,
  631219
Gates, Charles 460430
Geil, Paul 440621A, 440621B,
  490117
Geller, Herb 561101
Gentry, Chuck 460319, 460430,
  460604, 460606, 460619,
  460625, 460816, 491101,
  550828, 590321, 590402,
  610202
Gershunoff, Alex 491219
Getzoff, James 460606, 630208,
  631202, 650610, 940512
Gibbons, Bob 590321, 590402
Gibbons, Joe 590423
Gibson, Bob 551129
Gifford, Charles see Griffard,
  Charles

Gilbert, Les 560921
Gill, Benny 631219
Goerner, Fred 460430, 460606,
  460619, 460625, 460816,
  460910, 460919, 461017, 461108
Goland, Arnold 671117
Goodman, Irving 421220
Gordon, Jim 650610
Gordon, Justin 590321, 590402
Gozzo, Conrad 491101, 540802,
  540803, 590321, 590402
Graham, George 950801
Granat, Endre 940512
Graver, Charles 460606, 460625
Graves, Joe 610909
Gray, Jerry 541201
Gray, John 631219
Great American Songbook Orchestra 921007
Green, Bill 680201
Green, Freddie 630702
Green, Urbie 630702
Grey, Al 900801B
Griffard, Charles 440621A,
  440621B, 460319
Griffin, Chris 510409A,
  510409B
Gross, Walter 470601
Grusin, Dave 631219, 650001
Guion, King 440621A, 440621B
Gunkler, Hynie 571101, 571102
Gunning, Chris 700601

Haggart, Bob 510409A, 510409B
Halbert, Howard 460606,
  460619, 460625, 460816,
  460910, 460919, 461108
Hale, Corky 550828
Halliburton, John 541201
Halopoff, Gary 950801
Hamilton, Jeff 880800
Hansell, Ralph 491101, 601109,
  601110, 610909
Harper, Herbie 560501
Harshman, Allan 600805,
  601109, 601110, 631202,
  631219
Hartman, Grace 430001
Hawksworth, Johnny 560921
Haymer, Herbie 461108
Hayton, Lennie 460606, 470201,
  480202
Hazard, Dick 631202, 640310
Heath, Ted 560921
Hefti, Neal 491101, 531001
Heglin, Wally 491024
Hendrickson, Al 460319,
  460430, 460604, 460816,
  471116, 550828, 590423,
  601212, 610202, 630208
Henske, Judy 630707

Herfurt, Skeets 460604,
  460606, 460619, 460625,
  460910, 460919, 461017,
  461108, 461129, 471116,
  490117, 490521, 491101,
  610909
Herman, Woody 661029
Hill, Jay 690602
Hochhalter, Paula 940512
Hodges, Brian 700601
Hohman, Jack 580505
Holland, Milt 490521, 491101,
  630208
Holman 560501
Hood, Bill 600121, 600204,
  600211, 620711, ?620713,
  630513
Horn, Paul 630513, 631204
Horrox, Frank 560921
Howard, Francis 460319,
  460604, 490117, 490521,
  491101
Howard, Joe 460619, 460910,
  460919, 461017, 461108,
  560501, 610202
Hughes, Ron 860500
Hurley, Clyde 460319, 460430,
  460604, 460619, 460816,
  460910, 460919
Hylton, Clyde 440621A,
  440621B

Ian, Janis 800612

Jacob, Jules (Julie) 460530,
  491101
Jaffe, Jill B. 820401
Jenkins, Les 460319
Johnson, Burton 440621A,
  440621B
Johnson, Dean 920129
Johnson, Jerry 950505
Johnson, John 950505
Johnson, Plas 631219
Johnstone, Marcia 600805,
  601109, 601110
Jolly, Pete 600805, 880800
Jones, Dick 460606, 460619,
  491101
Jones, Hank 780101
Jones, Jimmy 690602, 690603,
  690718, 601201, 691211,
  691223
The Jud Conlon Rhythmaires
  491101
The Jud Conlon Singers 520801
Jung, Bob 580505
Juris, Vic 700601

Kafton, Arthur 460816, 460910
Kaminsky, Anatol 550828

Kaproff, Armand 631219, 650610, 630208
Karpenia, Stank 500331, 500403
Kasper, Jerome 490521, 491101
Kast, George 460430, 460619, 460625, 460816, 460910, 460919, 461017, 461108
Kaufman, Bernie 510409A, 510409B
Kay, Alastair 950505
Kelly, Bev 560501
Kennedy, Charlie 610202
Kennedy, Dave 780101
Kennedy, Ric 560921
Kenny, Tom 590423
Kernan, Jack 580505
Kessel, Barney 421220, 471114, 440621A, 440621B, 490117, 490521, 490826, 491101, 570311, 590423, 631219, 680201
Kiddier, Ken 560921
Kievman, Louis 631219
Kimberly, Kim 421220
King, Morris 460606, 460625, 461017, 461108
Kinsler, Jules 490521, 491101
Kirby, George 560501
Kirkland, Dale 780101
Kirksmith, Jack 460606, 460625
Kitzmiller, John 580626, 580628, 620711, 620713, 631204
Klee, Harry 460530, 460604, 460816, 460910, 460919, 461017, 461108, 461129, 471116, 490117, 550828
Klein, Mannie 460319, 460430, 460619, 460816, 460910, 460919, 461017, 461108, 471116, 540802, 540803, 590321, 590402
Kluger, Irv 560501
Koblentz, Arnold 631202
Koffman, Moe 860500, 950505
Konikoff, Ross 921007
Koonse, Larry 910312
Krafton, Arthur 460919
Kramer, Ray 940512
Krechler, Joe 460606, 460619
Kreindler, Sarah 601109, 601110, 631219
Kronstadt, Bob 940512
Kronstadt, Gina 940512
Kruczek, Leo 500331, 500403
Kundell, Bernard 630208
Kusby, Ed 460604, 460816, 460910, 460919, 461017, 461108, 471116, 490117, 491101, 540802, 540803, 590321, 590402, 610909

Laine, Cleo 910312
LaMagna, Carl 600803, 631219
Lamas, Eugene 460606, 460619, 460625, 460910, 460919
Lambert, Dave 500331, 500403
Lane, Frank 580505
Lang, Ronnie 570311, 571101, 571102, 631204
Lapolla, Ralph 950801
LaRosa, Christopher 830120
LaRosa, Julius 830120
LaRue, Eddie 440901
Laughton, Gail 460604, 460606, 461129, 471116
Lauidsen, Beverley 820401
Law, Alex 461017
Lawford, Peter 470201
Lawson, Bob 461017, 461108, 461129, 471116, 490117, 491101
Lawson, Harold 460606, 460619, 460625, 461017
Leaf, Karl 440621A, 440621B
Lee, Peggy 491101, 491116, 510710
Lee, Ralph 460530
Lefkowitz, Morris 500331, 500403
Leighton, Bernie 830120
Leitham, John 860800, 910312, 920405, 921007, 921114, 940512, 960723
Leonard, Brian 860500, 950505
Leonard, Robert 860500, 950505
Leonardi, Tony 661029
Leonhart, Jay 810826, 820327, 820401, 830120, 850919
Levent, Mark 460430, 460606
Levey, Stan 560501
Levin, Dave 620324, 620325
Levinsky, Walt 830120
Levy, Lou 630513
Lewis, Harold 460606, 460625
Lewis, Joe 510710
Lewis, John 920129
Lewis, Mel 560116, 561201, 570222, 570311, 571101, 571102, 600121, 600204, 600211, 600803, 600804, 600805
Lewis, Morty 830120
Limonick, Marvin 460606, 550828, 560501, 570311, 631202
Lincoln, Abe 440621A, 440621B
Lind, Perry 630901
Lindsey, Mort 630707, 631018, 631206, 640131
Linn, Ray 460530, 460319, 460430, 460604, 460619, 460816, 460910, 460919,

461017, 461018, 461108, 461129, 490117, 490521, 560501
Lipman, Joe 510409A
Livingston, Bob 860500, 950505
Lockhart, Keith 920405
Loeffler, Carl 471116
Loeffler Karl 491219
Lombardi, Clyde 511004, 511015
London, Frank 921007
Long, Gary 630901
Love, Geoff 610703
Lovelle, Herbie 650003
Lowe, John 631204
Lowe, Mundell 840101
Lozano, Sal 950801
Lube, Dan 460619, 600803, 600805
Luening, Warren 880800, 881200
Lusher, Don 560921
Lustgarten, Alfred 630208
Lustgarten, Edgar 460606, 460619, 460625, 570311, 631202

McBeath, Carlton 541201
McConnell, Rob 860500, 950505
McCracken, Joan 470201
McCreary, Lew 580505, 631204
McDade, Steve 950505
MacDonald, Doug 950801
MacDonald, James 860500, 950505
McDougall, Ian 860500
McGarity, Lou 510409A, 510409B, 510710, 880800
McGhee, Howard 560501
McGuire, Narcy 430001
McIntyre, Mark 460606, 460625
Mackenzie, Henry 560921
McKibbon, Al 650610
MacLeod, John 860500, 950505
McMickle, Dale 510409A, 510409B
McMurdo, Dave 860500
McReynolds, Gus 460530
Madden, Dave 580505
Mahzline, Walt 580505
Maini, Joe 601212, 610202
Maize, Bob 900801A, 900801B, 901111A, 901111B
Majewski, Virginia 550828, 630208
Mance, Junior 650003
Mandel, Hy 460530
Mandel, Johnny 601212, 610202, 921007

Manilow, Barry 840101
Manne, Shelly 580626, 580628, 601212, 610202, 630513, 631202, 840101
Marcus, Steve 780101
Marino, Amerigo 601109, 601110
Marino, Rickey 600805
Mark, Michael 830120
Markowitz, Markie 830120
Marlowe, Charles 471116
Marmarosa, Dodo 460530, 460816, 461017, 461108, 461129
Marsala, Marty 421220
Marshall, John 780101
Marshall, Patricia 470201
Martin, Andy 950801
Martin, Lloyd 471116
Marx, Chico 421220
Mason, Ann 460319
Masson, George 830120
Matlock, Matty 540802, 540803
Maxey, Virginia 480706, 480713, 480810, 480817, 480824, 480907, 480914, 480921, 480928
Maxon, Chuck 421220
Maxwell, Jimmy 830120
May, Billy 440621A, 440621B, 491101, 540803, 590321, 590402
Mayhew, Jack 460625
Mayorga, Lincoln 680201, 680202
Mays, Bill 840101
The Mellomen or The Mellowmen 491116
Melton, Susan see Lee, Peggy
The Mel-Tones 440001, 440002, 440901, 450427, 450913, 460530, 460319, 460430, 460604, 460606, 460619, 460816, 460910, 460919, 461017, 461018, 480706, 480713, 480810, 480817, 480824, 480907, 480914, 480921, 480928, 491021, 491101, 491219, 500811A, 550113, 590423
Melvoin, Michael 650610
Mercer, Johnny 440621B
Mersey, Robert 641005, 641216, 641219, 650309, 650310
MGM Studio Chorus 470201
MGM Studio Orchestra 470201, 480202, 491024
Miles, Barry 700601
Milikan, Bob 921007
Miller, Bill 581208
Miller, Sydney 480706, 480810

Miller, William 600805
Mills, Jackie 460530
Mills, Verlye 590321, 590402, 610909
Minger, Pete 900801B, 901111B
Mingus, Charlie 500831
Mitchell, Billy 900801B, 901111B
Mitchell, Grover 630702, 901111B
Mitchell, Keith 590423
Mitchell, Oliver 620711, ?620713
Mitchell, Red 550828, 560116, 561201
Mondello, Toots 510409A, 510409B
Mondragon, Joe 571101, 571102, 580626, 580628, 600121, 600204, 600211, 601212, 610202, 620711, 620713, 630208, 631202, 631204
Montrose, Jack 541201, 560116, 561101, 561201
Mooney, Harold (Hal) 461018, 461129, 471114, 471115, 471116, 491101, 491219, 520513, 550828
Moraga, Jorge 940512
Moran, Pat 560501
Morgan, Lanny 580505
Morley, Angela 940512
Morrow, Buddy 510409A, 510409B, 510710
Morse, Ella Mae 440621A
Mosca, John 780101
Mosher, John 541201
Most, Sam 560501
Motsinger, Buddy 580505
Mottola, Tony 470601
Mucci, Louis 500331, 500403, 510409A, 510409B
Mukogawa, Carole 940512
Mulligan, Gerry 800826, 920129

Napoleon, Marty 421220
Napoleon, Teddy 500331, 500403
Nash, Dick 600804, 610202, 631204
Nash, Ted 570311, 590321, 590402
Neal, Buddy 491101
Neikrug, George 600805, 601109, 601110
Neiman, Al 600803, 600805
Nelson, Marty 830120
Nelson, Skip 421220
Nero, Peter 631115, 940600
Nestico, Sam 921007
Neufeld, Erno 471116, 560501, 570311
Neumann, Irma 560501, 570311

Neumann, Robert 950801
Newman, Joe 630702, 900801B, 901111B
Newman, Timothy 921007
Nicholls, Dale 440621A, 440621B
Nistico, Sal 661029
Noel, Richard 610202
Norman, Loulie-Jean 491101, 491219, 560501
Norvo, Red 500831

O'Brien, Larry 830120
Ochi-Albi, Nicolas 460430, 460625, 460816
O'Connor, Ginny 440001, 440002, 440901, 450427, 450913, 460530, 460319, 460430, 460604, 460606, 460619, 460816, 460910, 460919, 461017, 461018, 491101, 491219, 590423
Ogermann, Claus 620913
Oliver, Sy 531231, 610309
Olson, Anthony 461129
Orenstein, Louis 661029
Osborne, Donny 800612, 810826, 820327, 831001, 850919, 860800, 900801A, 900801B, 900902, 901111A, 901111B, 910312, 920405, 921007, 921114, 940512, 960723
Osborne, Mary 511015
Osborne, Tony 610701
Otto, Lloyd 460530

Paich, Marty 541201, 550302, 550828, 560116, 561101, 561201, 561202, 570222, 570311, 571101, 571102, 580626, 580628, 590423, 600121, 600204, 600211, 630208, 630707, 631120, 880800, 881200
Parke, Bernie 440001, 440002, 440901, 450427, 450913, 460530, 460319, 460430, 460604, 460606, 460619, 460816, 460910, 460919, 461017, 461018, 480706, 480713, 480810, 480817, 480824, 480907, 480914, 480921, 480928, 491101, 491219, 590423
Parker, Bob 460319
Parshal, Harry 460606
Pattison, Ernie 950505
Pattison, Gary 950505
Paul, Les 450913
Payne, Sonny 630702

Peagler, Curtis 900801B, 901111B
Pederson, Pullman (Tommy), 490521, 560501, 590321, 590402, 600804
Pell, Dave 570311, 580626, 580628, 680201
Pellegrini, Al 500824, 510409A, 510409B, 520801, 540802, 540803, 541215, 550828, 551129, 590402
Pemberton, Steve 940600
Pena, Ralph 590321, 600803, 600804, 600805
Peplowski, Ken 880800, 881200, 921114, 940512
Pepper, Art 590423, 600121, 600204, 600211
Perissi, Richard 460625, 580626, 580628, 631219
Perkins, Bill 580626, 580628, 600121, 600204, 600211, 601212, 610202
Perlmutter, Maurice 460625, 461017, 461108
Perrer, Jack 601109, 601110
Perrissi, Richard *see* Perissi, Richard
Perry, Ronny 541201
Phillips, Flip 470531
Pierce, Dale 460530
Pierce, Nat 661029
Pierson, Bob 661029
Pirozzi, Roland 490521, 491101
Pisani, Nick 460430, 460619, 460625, 460910, 460919, 461017, 461108, 461129, 460816
Pitman, Bill 571101, 571102, 590423
Pizzarelli, Bucky 830120
Pohlman, Ray 680201
Pollan, Albert 560116, 560501, 561101, 561201, 570311
Pometti, Vincenzo 460606
Poole-Cross, Carol 820401
Pope, Gordon 460606, 460625
Popp, Lewis 461129
Porcaro, Joe 880800
Porcino, Al 580505, 600121, 600204, 600211, 620711, ?620713, 631204, 740901
Powell, Benny 630702, 900801B
Powell, Specs 470531
Pratt, Bobby 560921
Pratt, Dean 780101
Pratt, Jimmy 541201
Pratt, Lloyd 470901, 470902, 471001, 471002
Previn, Andre 550828
Pribeck, Gary 780101

Price, Red 560921
Price, Tony 780101
Priddy, Jimmy 541201
Privin, Bernie 510710
Purviance, Doug 901111B

Rader, Don 630702
Raderman, Lou 600805, 630208, 631202, 631219
Raeburn, Boyd 460530
Raffell, Don 460319, 460430, 460604, 460619, 460816, 460910, 460919, 461129, 471116, 490117
Ramsey, Bill 900801B, 901111B
Rasey, Uan 490521, 491101, 491219, 560501
Raskin, Milt 460319, 460604, 460619, 460910, 460919, 471116, 491219
Rauch, Billy 510409A, 510409B
Reher, Kurt 460606, 550828, 600803, 600805
Reid, Rufus 800612
Remsen, Dorothy 631202
Renzi, Mike 800612, 810826, 820327, 850919, 870100, 960723
Repass, Morris 950801
Repay, Ted 440621A, 440621B
Restivo, David 950505
Resto, Luis 820401
Reuss, Allan 460910, 460919, 461017, 491101, 540802, 540803, 581208, 610909
Ricard, Fip 630702
Rice, Samuel 440621A, 440621B
Rich, Buddy 780101
Richman, Al 500331, 500403
Ricord, Chester 610909
Riddle, Nelson 510626
Rizzi, Tony 460530, 590423
Roberts, George 580626, 580628, 600804, 630513
Roberts, Howard 511004, 600803, 600804, 600805, 601109, 601110, 650610
Robinson, Les 460430, 460816, 440621A, 440621B
Robyn, Paul 460619, 460625, 460816, 460910, 460919, 471116, 560501, 570311
Rogers, Clyde 440621A, 440621B
Rogers, Shorty 620711, 620713, 630513, 631207, 650001, 680301
Romersa, Ernest 490521, 491101
Roney, Wallace 920129
Rosa, Eddie 550828
Rose, Gene 430001

Rosolino, Frank 560501, 580626, 580628, 600121, 600204, 600211, 601212, 680201
Ross, Arnold 490521, 490826, 491101
Ross, Nathan 560501, 650610
Rosso, Sonny 830120
Roten, Ethmer 550828
Roth, Henry 631202, 650610
Rowles, Jimmy 581208, 590321, 601212, 610202, 631202, 631204
Royal, Marshal 630702, 900801B
Rugolo, Pete 490221, 500331, 500403, 500811A, 500811B, 510105
Ruick, Barbara 571101, 571102
Rumpler, Harry 460606
Rupert, Jeff 921007
Russell, Jan 460619
Russell, Mischa 460430, 460619, 460625, 460816, 460910, 460919, 461017, 461108, 471116, 631219
Russin, Babe 460604, 460816, 460919, 461017, 461108, 461129, 471116, 490117, 540802, 540803
Ryan, John 491219

Sabinsky, Ray 500331, 500403
Sadler, Myron 650610
Safranski, Eddie 470531, 500331, 500403
Salinger, Conrad 470201
Sandke, Rande 940512
Sandler, Myron 600805, 601109, 601110; *see also* Myron Sadler (probably the same)
Saplin, Bill 830120
Satterwhite, Collen 490521, 491101
Schaefer, Bill 461017, 461108, 491219
Schlinger, Sol 830120
Schmacher, Dave 921007
Schmidt, Chuck 780101
Schneider, Elmer 421220
Schrager, Gertrude 631219
Schuchman, Harry 491219
Schwager, Reg 950505
Schwartz, Jonathan 800826
Schwartz, Wilbur 460530, 550828, 590402
Seaberg, George 471116, 490117, 491101
Seder, Jules 460606, 460625
Self, Jim 880800, 881200
Sewell, Jack 461017, 461108

Seykora, Fred 650610, 940512
Shanahan, Richard 541215
Shank, Bud 560116, 561201, 580626, 580628, 590321, 600803, 600804, 620711, 620713
Shapiro, Artie 460606, 460619, 460625, 460910, 460919, 461108, 471116
Shapiro, Eudice 550828, 560501
Sharon, Ralph 560501
Sharp, Sidney 650610
Shaw, Artie 460430, 460606, 460619, 460625, 460816, 460910, 460919, 461017, 461108
Shaw, Roland 560924
Shawker, Bunny 510409A, 510409B, 511004, 511015
Shearing, George 820415, 830301, 831001, 850501, 860800, 900902
Sheldon, Jack 580626, 580628, 590423, 601212, 610202, 880800, 881200
Shelladay, Nelson 460530
Shepard, Tommy 600804
Sherock, Shorty 540802, 540803
Shroyer, Ken 620711, ?620713, 630513
Shubring, Clarence 600805
Shulman, Joe 510710
Shure, Paul 550828, 560501, 570311, 630208, 631202, 631219, 940512
Silva, John 440621A, 440621B
Silverlight, Terry 700601
Simpson, Don 950801
Singer, Lou 460606, 460625, 460816, 590402
Skiles, James 440621A, 440621B
Slatkin, Eleanor 471116, 550828, 570311, 560501
Slatkin, Felix 461108, 461129, 471116, 550828, 560501, 570311
Smith, Chris 910312
Smith, Greg 780101
Smith, Hal 460530
Smith, Kirk 950801
Smith, Wally 560921
Smithers, Elmer 460430, 460604, 460619, 460816, 461017
Soloman, Phil 500331, 500403
Sopp, Harry 421220
Sosnik, Harry 490001
Sosson, Marshall 460606, 460619, 460625, 460816, 460910, 460919, 461108,
471116, 560501, 570311, 601109, 601110, 630208, 650610
Southall, Henry 661029
Sperling, Jack 580505
Spiegelman, Stanley 460430, 460606, 460619, 460816, 460910, 460919, 461108
Spurling, Jack 631219
Stagliano, James 460625
Stamm, Marvin 661029, 830120
Stapleton, Cyril 560922
The Starlighters 491101
Stein, Manny 460606, 460625
Stepansky, Joseph 630208
Stephens, Phil 450913, 460319, 460604, 460816, 461017, 471116, 460430, 491101, 500824, 581208
Sterkin, David 460606, 460625, 460816, 460910, 460919, 461017, 461108, 471116
Stevens, Phil see Stephens, Phil
Stimpson, George 860500
Stoll, Georgie 491024
Stoller, Alvin 490117, 491219, 540802, 540803, 560501, 561101, 570311, 580626, 580628, 590321, 590402, 590423, 601109, 601110, 630208, 631204
Stone, Lew 500331, 500403
Stott, Wally 570701, 610702
Stuckley, Jack 921007
Stulce, Fred 440621A, 440621B
Swainson, Neil 900902
Swinfield, Ray 910312
Szabo, Frank 950801
Szatmert, Sandor 500331, 500403

Talbot, Jamie 910312
Tannenbaum, Julius 460606
Tanner, Paul 541201
Terri, Vincent 500824, 581208
Tesone, Ace 620324, 620325
Thaler, Mannie 500331, 500403
Thomas, Whitney 541201
Thompson, Don 830301, 831001
Thompson, Kathryn 460625
Tizol, Juan 580505
Todd, Tommy 460430
Tole, Bill 950801
Tooley, Ron 901111B
Torff, Brian 820415
Toro, Efrain 880800
Toth, Jerry 860500
Traugott, Erich 860500
Trenner, Donn 630810
Triscari, Joe 490521, 491101, 491219, 580505
Triscari, Ray 580505, 610202, 620711, ?620713, 631204
Trotter, John Scott 460001
Turcott, Kevin 950505

Ulyate, Bill 550828
Ulyate, Lloyd 540802, 540803, 560501, 631204, 950801

Vail, Evan 460530
Vail, Olcott 460619, 460625, 460910, 460919, 461017, 461108, 461129, 471116
Van Dyke, Jerry 630707
Van Eps, George 491219
Ver Planck, Marlene 830120
Verrell, Ronnie 560921
Vesely, Ted 540802, 540803
Villepique, Paul 491101
Vincent, Ron 920129
Vinci, Gerald 560501, 600805, 630208, 631202, 631219
Viola, Al 470901, 470902, 471001, 471002
Vivian, Jim 950505
Von Ohlen, John 881200
Vu Gauvin, Alan 780101

Waldo, Janet 480706, 480831, 480914, 480928, 491012
Wallace, Steve 860500
Wallington, Jimmy 541201
Walsh, John 921007
Warren, Ted 950505
Warrington, Tom 780101
Was, Don 820401
Wasserberger, Oscar 460606
Webb, Stan 510409A 510409B
Weiland, June 490521, 491101
Weinstine, Heimann 601109, 601110
Weiss, Harry 461017
Weldon, Jerry 921007
Wells, Dave 590321, 590402
Wendt, George 460604
Weschler, Walter 490117
Wess, Frank 630702, 900801B, 901111A, 901111B
Westley, Ira 610909
Weston, Riley 541201
Wettling, George 421220
Whited, John 560501
Whiting, Margaret 601109, 601110
Wickes, Mary 430001
Wilkins, Rick 860500, 950505
Willey, Rich 921007
The Williams Brothers 470201
Williams, Johnny 600301, 631204
Williams, Pat 660001, 661001

Williamson, Claude 560501
Williamson, Stu 600121, 600204, 600211, 601212, 610202, 631204
Wilson, Chick 780101
Wilson, Dennis 901111B
Wilson, Dooley 430001
Wilson, Ollie 460530, 460430, 460816
Winding, Kai 500331, 500403
Wisner, Jimmy 620324, 620325, 630208
Wittenberg, Helaine 940512
Wittenberg, John 940512

Wofford, Mike 620711, 620713
Woods, Dave 860500
Woods, Phil 700601, 920129

Yaner, Milt 500331, 500403
Yokum, Vernon 421220
Young, Graham 541201
Young, Snooky 901111B

Zarchey, Zeke 460430, 460604, 460619, 460816, 460910, 460919, 461017, 461108, 471116, 491219

Zelig, Tibor 601109, 601110, 940512
Zelnick, Mel 500331, 500403
Zentner, Si 460319, 460604, 460619, 460910, 460919, 461108, 461129, 471114, 471115, 471116, 490117, 491101, 491219, 590321, 590402
Ziebel, Sigmund 601109, 601110
Zito, Freddy 460530
Zito, Ronnie 661029, 830120
Zornig, George 500331, 500403
Zundel, Olgar 601109, 601110

www.ingramcontent.com/pod-product-compliance
Lightning Source LLC
Chambersburg PA
CBHW081559300426
44116CB00015B/2935